Keirn Chronicles Volume One: The Fabulous Wrestling Life of Steve Keirn

Keirn Chronicles Volume One: The Fabulous Wrestling Life of Steve Keirn

By

Steve Keirn
with Ian Douglass

DARKSTREAM

Copyright Steve Keirn 2023. All Rights Reserved.

Published by:
WOHW/Darkstream Press

www.darkstreampress.com

All rights reserved. This book may not be reproduced in whole or in part in any form without written permission from the author.

This book is set in Garamond.

10 9 8 7 6 5 4 3 2 1

ISBN 979-8-218-17210-7

This book is dedicated to the memory of
Jack Brisco
September 21, 1941 – February 1, 2010

Thank you for being the best professional wrestling mentor that a young kid from Tampa could ever have.

Table of Contents

Foreword One	2
Foreword Two	4
One	8
Two	27
Three	44
Four	60
Five	78
Six	98
Seven	120
Eight	144
Nine	169
Ten	187
Eleven	210
Twelve	235
Thirteen	256
Fourteen	275
Fifteen	299
Sixteen	317
Seventeen	337
Eighteen	353
Nineteen	369
Twenty	385
Epilogue	399
Afterword	414
Author's Acknowledgements	417
Biographer's Acknowledgements	419
Credits	420

Foreword One

Having spent the majority of my wrestling career back in the golden age of the wrestling territories, I feel confident in saying that Championship Wrestling from Florida under the tutelage of Eddie Graham was at the pinnacle of that era. This breeding ground spawned many wrestling stars and the author of this book, Steve Keirn, is certainly no exception.

This bedrock of old school mentality forged the foundation of Steve's grit and drive that made him the success that he was throughout his career. I personally got to experience this first hand when he and I were partnered together in the early 1980s as The Fabulous Ones tag team in Tennessee.

The fact that the promoter who brainstormed the idea for this mat marriage, Jerry Jarrett, passed away today as I sit here writing this foreword makes it especially poignant and overwhelmingly sad. The Fabulous Ones were perhaps the most copied and emulated tag team in pro wrestling history thanks to Jerry's innovative videos and promotion techniques that carved a new MTV-rockstar-babyface genre on the wrestling landscape. I couldn't have asked for a better partner than Steve to share this experience with.

Traveling to shows seven days a week by car in those days afforded the opportunity to completely indulge all aspects of that person's mentality and psyche. I must say that I emerged a smarter and more well-rounded person by having that experience. Steve educated me not only about wrestling, working, and ring psychology, but also about life outside the ring including investments, finances, and business ventures long term. For that I am truly grateful.

I look back fondly on those days and know that I have been truly blessed to lead the life that God laid out for me. I'm thankful He allowed mine and Steve's life roads to intersect and join up in that time period of our lives.

However, let me implore the reader to please not think that Steve's life story is all about wrestling. Far from it! His entire life is so diverse, complex, and unique that the reader will be spellbound delving into it page after page.

Please join me in this read, as I am certainly looking forward to it as well.

Stan Lane and Steve Keirn – The Fabulous Ones

Stan Lane

Foreword Two

When I was asked to write the foreword for this book, I immediately said yes without thinking about it. To say I was overwhelmed, flattered, and downright confused why I was asked to handle what I consider a tremendous honor would be a gross understatement. Why did I agree to do this?! Why *me*?

Certainly, there are more qualified people. Maybe Stan Lane can't type, I thought. Maybe the Sheepherders can't read, I said to myself out loud. Sure, I'm a lifelong student of the game with immense respect for the wrestling business and those who paved the way for me, but after giving it some thought, I don't think it's possible for anyone – let alone me – to even begin to explain what Steve Keirn means to wrestling. Fortunately for both you *and* me, Steve happens to be an excellent storyteller.

I first met Steve – or Mr. Keirn as I called him back when I was stationed in Ohio Valley Wrestling – in Louisville, Kentucky in 2006. I was the new kid on the block with way more experience than anyone around me wanted to admit, yet I seemed to be one of only a handful of developmental wrestlers who was excited the office had sent Steve Keirn to us for the day. While I knew Mr. Keirn as one half of the Fabulous Ones, others questioned why Doink the Clown was sent to us and what he could possibly teach us that was of any value.

As athletes in a developmental program who had to train in a cold building with no heat (there was probably heat, but Nightmare Danny Davis ran a tight ship and would disappear anyone who touched the thermostat) we would often do whatever we could to not take bumps at 10 a.m. Mr. Keirn recognized this and promised us he didn't want to make us warm up and cool down and take unnecessary bumps. Instead, he spoke to us for four to five hours.

To me, this is what we were missing. You didn't learn in the ring, you learned in the car, driving from town to town while listening to veterans talk about what you did wrong and what you did right. This was taken from us when the territories collapsed, but now the office would send these human fountains of knowledge and I would drink it all up. Mr. Keirn talked about his time in Memphis, his thoughts on what heat was and how to get it, his countless tours of Japan, his struggles with the Road Warriors, and also about the way he acclimated himself to different territories and styles of wrestling.

My head was spinning as I took notes and tried to retain everything that was being thrown at us. After the fifth hour – after he had promised not to run us or make us take cold bumps in the arctic-like Davis arena – Mr. Keirn, with a sly smile on his face, said, "Okay. Get your gear on. Let's see some *matches*!" The legendary ribber got us, and I think I was the only one that knew what had just transpired. Good rib, Steve. Good rib.

That's right. Not only is Steve a great storyteller, but he's also a legendary ribber. That is to say he was known for pranking everyone around him. I'm sure some of the stories he can't tell due to the statute of limitations, but trust me when I say you always had to be on your toes when Steve Keirn was booked.

Anytime I've been fortunate enough to spend time with Steve, I feel I always bothered him with questions. This occurred mainly because I wanted to hear his stories. It was *always* about the stories: The life he has had; things he has seen; lessons he learned along the way. His father was twice shot down over enemy territory in two different wars defending this country. Yes, *please* tell me about that. I'd sit and listen. Getting started in the wrestling business under the tutelage of possibly the greatest wrestling booker of all time, Eddie Graham. What was *that* like? *Please* tell me! You were trained by legendary Japanese grappler Hiro Matsuda, and tutored by NWA champions Terry and Dory Funk, along with fellow NWA champion Jack Brisco and his equally impressive brother

Jerry – the incomparable, multi-time NWA tag team champions?! Holy shit! Share your knowledge with me!

Steve was always gracious with his time in placating the ultimate fan in me. I realize now that you are holding the answers to all of my super nerdy questions in the palms of your hands. How did Steve, along with his tag partner Stan Lane, help revitalize and redefine tag team wrestling in the '80s? Just like the wide-eyed, younger version of me who spent all that time pestering Steve, you now have access to those valuable tales.

There is a small part of me that wants to keep all the stories Steve has told me over the years to myself, but that would be criminal. It would also be criminal to not talk about Steve as a human being. Someone who I always saw give his time to others, ready to help those who needed it at the drop of a hat. Kind, but stern. Never afraid to voice his opinion and stand up for what he believed in. In the wrestling business, that's not always looked upon favorably, and there were times it could cost you your job. That didn't ever stop Steve from doing what was right.

Have I covered it all? No. Steve's final form is that of trainer. Mentor. He took all he learned from all the legendary minds I've already listed and did what so few have done at such a high level; he gave back. Steve took all the knowledge he had from Championship Wrestling from Florida and turned it into FCW.

Florida Championship Wrestling took over where OVW left off and trained many of the superstars you love (or hate!) in the present era of wrestling. You can see Steve's fingerprints all over such stars as Roman Reigns, Seth Rollins, Natalya Neidhart, Jon Moxley, Big E, Kofi Kingston, Sheamus, Claudio Castagnoli, Bray Wyatt, and countless others. There's a lot of us that are indebted to Steve and the contributions, sacrifices and lasting memories he has given us as wrestling fans.

I'm proud to say I'm a friend of Steve Keirn. Thankfully, I have lived a charmed life, and the biggest proof of that is that my heroes have become my friends. Steve is one of them, and I'm glad you all get to read his stories now.

CM Punk and Steve Keirn

CM Punk

ONE

On February 17th, 1973, I was sitting in a car at Maxwell Air Force Base in Alabama, awaiting a reunion with a father that I'd believed had been long lost.

It had been nearly eight years since I had been told that my dad had been killed in action in the skies over Vietnam and would be absent from my life forever. In those same eight years, I had been desperately attempting to determine what it meant to become a man while a war being waged 9,000 miles away had deprived me of Richard Keirn – the very same man who should have been guiding me through that process.

At the time I was born, my dad was enjoying the brief period between the two wars that would largely define his life. He had been a pilot in the Army Air Corps during World War II. My mom, Hazel Neal, was a Navy WAVE – or one of the Women Accepted for Voluntary Emergency Service – in World War II. It's incredible how much our very existence can seem to hinge on such random events. In my case, it came down to the scheduling of train travel.

The Fabulous Wrestling Life of Steve Keirn

My parents were both passengers aboard trains that pulled into a train station in Memphis, Tennessee while headed in opposite directions. While the trains sat there, my dad made a bet with his buddies and said, "Hey, I'm gonna go make a date with one of those ladies for after the war is over!"

Dad got off the train he was riding on, bought a bag of peanuts, and then boarded my mom's train with the peanuts in hand and asked all of the girls, "Do any of you girls not have a husband or a boyfriend? I'm headed off to war, I'm not married, I don't have a girlfriend, and I need someone to be my pen pal!"

My mom was the only one of the ladies who raised her hand, and the two exchanged the addresses of where they would be stationed. Dad gave mom the address from where he would be situated in England, and Mom gave Dad her address in Chicago. Once they had secured one another's contact information, Dad reboarded his train, and the two continued in their opposite directions.

Early in my 19-year-old father's service, his B-17 was shot down over Germany, on September 11th of 1944, in a battle called "The Bloody One Hundred." Mom ran a teletype machine in Chicago, and she immediately recognized when Dad's name came across the teletype machine declaring him to be missing in action, and also when he was later confirmed as a prisoner of war. Mom then contacted Dad's parents and corresponded with them the entire time my dad was a POW.

When my dad was eventually released from his German POW camp in May of 1945 and returned home, his parents told him all about the nice young lady he had met during the early stages of his service, and who had kept them apprised of everything that had transpired during his imprisonment as a POW. Right after that, my parents met up in Chicago, went out a couple of times, started dating, and got married two months later. It was a classic love story, and the beginning of a marriage that would last 55 years.

My older sister Sherye was born in 1948, and then I came along three years later in 1951.

My dad departed from the Air Corps and joined the Air National Guard. His first love had been flying, but it was now second to his family and his need to support us. He got into law enforcement as a highway patrolman in Ohio, but then transitioned into a boilermaker at a steel mill.

That form of making a living wasn't nearly as stable as it first seemed, and once the United States Air Force was officially created in 1947, my dad reenlisted in the military as an Air Force pilot, and the family accompanied him from one Air Force base to the next. We started out living in a low-income projects area in Amherst, Ohio, and then we moved to Langley Air Force Base. That was promptly followed by two years living on a base in Okinawa, Japan.

Young Steve Keirn on Kadena Air Force Base in Okinawa

Life on military bases was heavily regimented for my sister and I, even as kids. Dad was very strict about our manners because we were intermingling with everyone from the sergeant's kids to the captain's kids on a regular basis, and we needed to reflect well on our parents in all circumstances.

We moved back to the United States to the Seymour Johnson Air Force Base in North Carolina when I was about seven years old, and that's when I first got introduced to athletics by playing football for the children's team on the base. I also received my unforgettable introduction to pro wrestling by watching the action that aired out of Raleigh. I only managed to steal a couple of viewings of it, but Rip Hawk and Johnny Weaver were very memorable characters. Our television options were so limited at the time that we might have had a maximum of three channels available to watch, and as the youngest person in the household, I rarely had any sort of control over what was displayed on the television screen.

Richard and Hazel Keirn

In the early 1960s, Dad got transferred to MacDill Air Force Base, which is located on the south end of Tampa, Florida, and the rest of us went along for the ride. I started in the 6th grade in Tampa, and went straight from 6th grade into junior high. My dad became certified to fly many of the different aircraft, and wound up flying the fastest jet fighter commissioned at the time, which was the F-4. He was on call at the base during the Cuban Missile Crisis, but thankfully was never called to take action.

The Fabulous Wrestling Life of Steve Keirn

   Our house was also at the south end of Tampa, right by the base. Due to Dad's military service, I had never been in one place long enough to establish a stable friend group, but that was finally changing. For the first time ever, I was able to meet kids that I would eventually become long-time friends with. Life progressed in a relatively straightforward fashion as I advanced through Monroe Junior High. Suddenly, as I was preparing to begin my 9th grade year at the young age of 13, everything in my world was unsettled by a drastic, devastating change.

   It was July 24th of 1965. My dad had been shipped to Vietnam due to the escalation of the conflict with the Vietcong. I had just been out playing with some friends and enjoying the summer afternoon, and then I returned home once we had all had enough. When I approached our front yard, I noticed that the driveway and the street in front of our house were uncharacteristically full. Several military vehicles were parked in front of the house, including an Air Force Security car, a chaplain's car, and a base commander's car.

   The house was pretty small, so when I entered the front door, I was standing in a multipurpose area that was simultaneously the kitchen, the living room, and the main gathering area of our home. I walked through the door to find my mother sobbing inconsolably at the kitchen table, while the chaplain was holding her and desperately trying to calm her.

   Before I could even utter a single syllable, the stone-faced colonel snatched me up abruptly by the arm and asked me, "Which room is yours, son?"

   I pointed toward the end of the hall, and the colonel steered me away from my mom, then pulled me toward the far end of the hall and through the door to my room. He sat me down on my bed, stared into my eyes and said, "Today your dad was killed in North Vietnam. He was shot down with the first SAM missile ever used in the war. His plane *exploded*."

   I immediately began crying at the thought of my father's violent death. I'd barely squeezed out the first few tears when the colonel grabbed my shoulder with one hand and shook it.

"Son… *stop* crying. Today, you became the man of your family," the colonel said. "There are no other men in your family; *you're* the man now. Your dad wouldn't be proud of you if you were upset and crying like a little kid. You're a man now, so you have to accept that responsibility."

It was such a jarring moment in my life and something I'll never forget. I immediately began to wonder what it meant to be the man of the family at only 13 years of age, because I had no clue.

When the commotion of the day concluded, the Air Police departed from our home along with everyone else, leaving only my mother and I remaining to console one another since my 16-year-old sister hadn't returned from working on the base yet. The two of us just sat there, staring blankly, and not knowing what we should talk about or what we were going to do. All we knew was that my dad was dead, and he was *never* coming back.

When my sister came home, we broke the news to her, and we all sat there feeling lost. The house was still ours, but we had no idea how we were going to pay the bills. As the newly promoted man of the house, I immediately quit the junior high football team and acquired a job on the base. I rode my bike out to the officer's club every day and served there as a busboy, cleaning the tables and serving them celery and other appetizers until the club shut down at midnight, and then I'd ride my bike back home.

I knew it was my obligation to provide an income for my family. My mom didn't work, so my sister and I both maintained our jobs even after school began in September. I was engrossed in my junior high school physical education class that October when my coach hurriedly approached me.

"Steve, you've got to go home *right now!*" he said. "Your mom needs you!"

Fearing that some other unimaginable tragedy had befallen the family, I raced straight home on my bike, pumping the pedals as fast as I could.

This time, the scene in the front yard was much different, and far more active even from a distance. Representatives from *The Tampa Tribune* and Channel 8 News were standing there, frantically shouting about something. Standing dead in the middle of a full media gaggle was my mother. In her hands, she held a photo that I couldn't recall seeing before, and when her eyes fell upon me, the expression on her face contorted into something midway between sadness and joy.

Mom quickly grabbed me and we darted straight into the house and down the hallway. She pulled me into my bedroom, which was across from hers, and she thrust the picture she was holding right into my face and simply said, "Look!"

What mom held in her hands was a photo of my dad that I had never seen before. I stared at it with a quizzical expression, confused as to why Mom would be holding a photo of Dad and why all of this would be of such interest to the local media.

"This was just sent to the media from a teletype machine in Hanoi," said Mom. "A Red Cross volunteer in Hanoi took a picture of Dad being marched through the streets. It took three months to bring him in. He was shot down 40 miles south of Hanoi. They took him to villages all over the area and tortured him. The media asked us to identify him."

Being an experienced military spouse, Mom was wise to the situation. When the media contacted her, she didn't respond to them directly. Instead, she called the Air Force base and informed them that the press was sniffing around. As mom and I emerged from the bedroom, the front door swung open violently. In walked the Air Police, accompanied by agents from the FBI and the CIA. They introduced themselves by the departments they represented, and then they started snatching away cameras and any recording devices being held by the reporters who were trying to write stories about the reemergence of my dad.

Colonel Keirn (far left) being marched through the streets of Hanoi

"Have you made a statement?" one of the men asked my mom.

"No. I haven't said anything," she replied.

With that, the agents turned their attention back to the media.

"Get away from this house!" said one of the men who stepped forward and took charge. "Leave this family alone! They're not identifying *anybody*! They're not making any statements!"

The agents then sat all of us down at the table, and they explained to us that because the war in Vietnam hadn't been declared a war, they didn't know what should officially be done with the knowledge of my dad's survival. They confirmed that they had also identified him from the photo, but they couldn't have the knowledge of his survival publicized. It *had* to remain a secret, and we weren't allowed to tell anyone that my dad had been captured, or that he'd gone from "missing in action" – or

MIA – to technically being the 14th American POW of the Vietnam War.

Again, given the technicality that no war had officially been declared, there was therefore no Geneva Convention to govern the conditions of my dad's treatment while he was imprisoned. The government agencies also weren't quite sure what to do with our family. Because of anti-war activism that had been gradually spreading throughout the U.S., they didn't want my dad's circumstances to become a rallying point for protests from conscientious objectors.

With the secrecy surrounding my dad's survival preserved – at least temporarily – I finished the 9th grade, then went to Robinson High School for 10th grade. I kept the secret. Nobody knew my dad was a POW, and everyone I'd grown up with believed my father had been killed in action, because that remained the official story at the time.

Robinson High School is where the flow of students from the two junior high schools converged at the south end of Tampa. This is where I met my classmates Dick Slater and Mike Gossett. Mike's father Edward was one of the owners of the Championship Wrestling from Florida organization headquartered in Tampa, and he wrestled under the name Eddie Graham.

Mike was an only child, and when I told him that my dad had died over in Vietnam, we became very good friends and got along exceedingly well. I hadn't been watching wrestling all that much, but once Mike became my best friend, I began to watch it religiously to follow the exploits of my new friend's famous father.

Ultimately, my grandmother in Ohio spilled the beans with respect to my father's identity when the media came to her house and showed her the photo. She enthusiastically identified her son to them as the POW in the photo. Just like that, it became public knowledge that my father was the 14th American POW in Vietnam. Afterwards, things began to lighten up and I was allowed to speak about my father's circumstances more openly.

The Fabulous Wrestling Life of Steve Keirn

When I mentioned to Mike Graham that my dad was a POW, Mike immediately passed that information along to his father. Meeting Eddie Graham made quite an impression on me. I was a skinny, young teenager, and Eddie had a bodybuilder's physique and bleach-blond hair at the time, so he looked like an absolute *monster* to me. Like my dad, he was also a pilot, and when you combined that with his muscles and his fame, Eddie was like an action hero come to life.

Eddie was unbelievably nice to me, and I began to frequently hang out with both Eddie and Mike together. Every time Eddie took Mike and I out somewhere, people on the street approached Eddie and asked him for his autograph. People without pens at the ready were content to simply shake Eddie's hand. It was hard not to admire Eddie, since he was a well known celebrity in the area. I was honored that he had taken such a liking to me.

In part because I wanted to develop a physique like Eddie's, I frequently joined Mike at the Grahams' house to work out and lift weights. Eddie also helped me to land my first job away from the Air Force base, which was at Eddie Graham Youth Camp, where I spent the summer teaching both wrestling and weightlifting to the kids. The Graham family also took me fishing and hunting, and Eddie helped me to sort out any life questions I might have had.

As a teenage boy who was rapidly growing up, I had a mountain of questions that my dad wasn't around to provide me with answers to, so I resorted to asking Eddie instead. Very quickly, Eddie turned into a father figure for me. He even allowed me to ride in the plane alongside Mike and some of the wrestlers as he flew us to the Bahamas to watch the wrestling events they held in Nassau and Freeport.

Once I turned 16 years old and became licensed to drive, Eddie would send me to fetch the incoming wrestlers from the airport. If someone like "Cowboy" Bill Watts flew in, I would pick him up from the airport, drive him to his hotel, take him to the Fort Homer Hesterly Armory for the show, and then drop him back off at the hotel when the show concluded. I did the same thing with other superstar wrestlers like Terry Funk and Dory Funk Jr., and I even provided the same chauffeur services for boxing legends "Jersey" Joe Walcott and Joe Louis when they came to Tampa as special referees.

I was *so* excited when I was speeding to the airport to pick up Joe Louis, but once the former world boxing champion got in the car, he started talking about all of the unfortunate events that had transpired during his post-athletic life, like his indebtedness to the IRS, and how he had to resort to accepting whatever opportunities he could to earn any money at all. By the time I'd absorbed all of the tragic tales Louis told me during the drive to the show and then the post-event trip to his hotel, I was ready to go home and start crying because I felt so sorry for him.

Eddie was very kayfabe about the professional wrestling business, which is to say that he didn't expose anything to me about the real nature of wrestling as a predetermined, cooperative enterprise. I wasn't allowed in the dressing rooms, and I couldn't sit in on general conversations between the wrestlers when they were discussing their bouts. Still, Eddie accepted me and looked after me like I was his extra son. As time progressed, he asked me if I wanted to go along with Mike to be a ring announcer at the shows in Fort Lauderdale where Mike was working as the promoter. I even got paid for it, which was infinitely better and more exciting than the sorts of low-level jobs I had been obligated to do to get paid back at the Air Force base.

It certainly wasn't very hard to stand there and introduce wrestlers by reading what was in front of you on an index card. Also, there weren't many factors present to leave me with a sense of stage fright. The audiences in Fort Lauderdale weren't very large at the time, by any means.

Finally, Eddie asked me, "What do you want to do with your life? What do you want to *be*?"

That was the number one question in my life at the time: "What do you want to be when you grow up?"

It might have seemed like the logical answer should have been, "I want to be involved in the wrestling business." Yet, despite having such rare and privileged access to the unquestioned king of professional wrestling in Florida, and despite my immersive introduction to the wrestling business, I still had absolutely *zero* interest in being involved with it professionally.

One of the things about the wrestling business that gave me considerable pause about getting involved in it was the fact that I could see the wrestlers up close when they returned from their matches. Their heads and faces would be beaten up, and often bleeding from cuts to their foreheads. Their bodies were banged up and bruised, and at the time, I liked to think of myself as being pretty cute. I didn't want my face to go through that type of abuse on a nightly basis. I said, "Man… I'm too *pretty* to do this!"

I enjoyed being around it, but did I want any part of the in-ring action? No thanks. I didn't even consider myself to be nearly tough enough to become a full-time pro wrestler.

That isn't to say I wasn't at least *slightly* tough. I started developing a bit of an attitude during my junior year of high school. I started getting a little too cocky, and I began to hang out with a gang of guys that simply liked to get into fights. It's not like we controlled a block or were part of an organized criminal enterprise. However, we did call ourselves "The Junior Mafia." All of our members pitched in and purchased space in our high school yearbook to print an additional photo of all the guys in the Junior Mafia together.

Several of the JM's members were military kids like me, because we all at least had family members who worked on the Air Force base even if we weren't all related to active military personnel. It was a fairly low-income area. Just north of us was the high-income area where Mike Graham grew up, and that is where more people went to Plant High School instead of Robinson High School.

The Junior Mafia would go out on Saturday nights to the all-night Royal Castle, or Crystal, or other local hangouts just to pick fights with unsuspecting attendees. It was never anything as violent as guns and knives, but there was *plenty* of sucker punching and brawling that would ensue until the altercations were broken up, and then we would be thrown out. That was our *favorite* activity.

**The Junior Mafia of Robinson High School;
I'm second from the left on the stairs**

Without a doubt, the most accomplished fighter in the Junior Mafia was Dick Slater. He was easily the toughest guy I grew up with. In fact, Dickie's reputation for toughness stretched all over the Tampa Bay region. The funny thing is that Dick didn't look the least bit impressive in a physical sense. He was a husky kid, but he had no obvious muscularity to his body. Yet, if you examined his hands, you would see that he had *colossal* fists that gave off the impression that Dick was wearing boxing gloves even when he was barehanded. Dickie also had a natural instinct with punching, and almost every time he was in a situation where he was able to get a punch off, the fight reached its conclusion instantly, or shortly thereafter. He was one of those fighters whose fists came preloaded with the dreaded "Touch of Death."

The Junior Mafia had a memorable incident during Tampa's Beach Week. At the end of the high school year, the local teens would rent rooms in the hotels along the beaches. Four or five guys would be in a room, and the girls would be in separate rooms, and we would just hang out at the beach and unwind. There would be plenty of parties and beer drinking to engage in on each day of the week.

During this particular Beach Week, the Junior Mafia was staying at a place in Redington Shores called the El Morocco Motel. The motel offered cheap rooms that six guys would squeeze into, and most of us slept on the floor. The only accessories that accompanied us into the rooms during the entire week were our cases of beer, and we simply drank, partied and slept all week long.

That week, one of our buddies from the Junior Mafia, Steve McCall, went hitchhiking to join us over at the beach, and he was picked up by some college students in Clearwater and bummed a ride from them. At some point while he was en route to the beach, Steve got into a serious argument with the students, so he invited them to return to the beach later that same evening for a brawl.

We were all relaxing by the motel pool when several cars pulled into the adjacent parking lot and a group of fairly large guys hopped out. I forget which college they were from, but it was from some place in the upper Midwest. Most of these guys had facial hair, and they were clearly older than our gang of high schoolers.

The one guy from their group who had been the most anxious to fight called out Steve McCall and said, "I'm here just like I promised I would be, you little bitch!"

Steve obliged the significantly larger college student by following him out into the parking lot, and all of the onlookers formed a ring around the pair so that we could clearly view the ensuing action. The college kid raised his arms, balled up his fists and held them as if he was engaging in a classic boxing match under Marquess of Queensberry Rules. The guys that I grew up with were pure sluggers. Classy combat wasn't something that any of us had been taught to emulate.

As most people would have expected, the fight ensued with Steve getting outclassed and thrashed rather soundly. He was getting pasted with jabs and hooks, over and over again. While the one-sided fisticuffs were in progress, I was stationed right next to Dickie, and taking it all in.

One of the largest college kids, who was clearly a football player, leaned down toward Slater to whisper into his ear.

"Pretty good fight, huh?" he snickered mockingly.

"Not as good as *ours*!" Dickie answered.

Slater rose up with a right hook and knocked the gargantuan guy out with a single shot to the jaw. As we all stood there frozen with surprise, Slater began to kick the motionless body of the fallen football star. Then, when those kicks were met with no resistance or response, Slater looked up, raised his fists, and just started decking the rest of the college athletes that had descended upon the beach, one after the other. They were all caught so off guard by the onslaught that they had no clue what to do. Slater mowed them down like insignificant blades of grass. He didn't lay out challenges or call them out individually; he just walked right up and drilled them, no questions asked.

In a panic, the college kids collected their fallen comrades, piled back into their car, and beat a hasty retreat. The police were quickly summoned, but when they surmised that a group of out-of-town college students had instigated a fight with a group of local high school kids, they weren't very sympathetic. Slater was officially minted as a legend.

On another occasion, we got into it with a different group, except this time they were fellow high school kids. One of the toughest kids from that group was drunk and shooting his mouth off, so Slater walked right up and promptly knocked him out. After that, the humbled kid and his friends locked themselves inside of their motel room, with Dick lurking outside, pacing like a tiger, and ready to lash out at anyone that emerged, whether they were looking to challenge his supremacy or not. Eventually, the imprisoned kids began passing messages to us through the door, asking for Slater's permission for them to leave their room.

Despite all of the altercations I saw Slater in, I never once saw him get hit, and I was in *a lot* of situations and scraps with him. If he connected with his fists, it instantaneously separated his foes from their consciousness.

Eddie started noticing me arriving at his house with marks on my face from all of the fights I was getting into, like black eyes and busted lips.

"What did you do?" he finally asked me. "Where did that busted lip come from?"

"I got in a fight the other night," I responded. "I got kind of beaten up."

"Next time you get into it, just grab him," instructed Eddie. "Don't swing your fists because you'll hurt your hand. Grab him by the hair, pull their head toward you, and bite their *nose* off. Do things like that. They won't be prepared for it."

I stared at Eddie like he had grown a third eyeball.

"Bite their nose off?" I asked.

"Or you can bite their *ear* off," continued Eddie, as he really started to get lost in his illustrations. "Or take their little finger and *snap* it like a twig!"

I started having nightmares in my sleep following that conversation with Eddie because I wasn't feeling empowered to fight; I was actually terrified about who else had heard this sort of advice. I might find myself picking a fight with the wrong guy and lose my nose or one of my ears over it. That wasn't something I was prepared to experience.

A lot of what I was doing by getting into all of these altercations was simply acting the way I perceived a real man should act. But can you really blame me? I was very young, and thinking I was the man of the family. Aside from Eddie Graham, all of my male role models were movie stars like John Wayne, Clint Eastwood and Charles Bronson.

I also loved the Hercules films as long as the guy playing Hercules was a bodybuilder. Steve Reeves was the best Hercules, and I loved the Sunday afternoon Steve Reeves films when they would come on. Even if they were technically bad movies by most people's standards, I still regarded them as awesome. It was the same thing with Tarzan films as long as the actor in the lead role was well put together, like Gordon Scott.

Acting the way I thought a man was supposed to act frequently got me in trouble even when I wasn't actively fighting. One of the times I got arrested was for underage drinking at a high school party. All of us were guzzling beer as the cops pulled up to my friend's house and raided it. Everyone who had been drinking beer took off running in different directions while I remained planted on the couch watching TV. I made it very easy for the cops, who simply scooped me up, handcuffed me, and loaded me into the paddy wagon.

The next thing I knew, I was downtown in a holding cell with 10 of my friends, and despite the seriousness of our predicament, we were all obsessed with seeing the toilet at the police station flush for some reason.

"You ain't gonna believe the *suction* on this toilet!" said one of my friends who'd been there far too many times.

The toilet flushed with such tremendous force; we all assumed its power had been ratcheted way up to prevent any inmates from plugging it. We all passed the time by standing there flushing the toilet repeatedly and admiring its power.

When it was my turn to make a phone call, the officers brought me over to the desk to dial my mom, and I had to explain to her why I had been arrested for minor possession of alcohol. Now my mom was having to bail me out of jail at half past midnight, and she didn't even know where the police station was.

"Honey, how do I get there?" said my mom, with concern for her wayward son saturating her voice. "I don't know where to go!"

"I don't know," I told her. "Just drive around and then ask a cop when you see one on the way! See if he'll point it out to you!"

My mom had been raised in a small town in Mississippi, and I can't imagine what must have been going through her mind as we rode home and she came to the realization that her only son now had a criminal record. The crazy thing was, I didn't even like the taste of beer. I've *never* liked the taste of beer. I've had to be peer pressured into drinking beer ever since I was in high school.

Failing to learn my lesson, I got arrested a second time when I was in a mall parking lot trying to steal hubcaps off of a '57 Chevrolet to go on my car, which was a '55 Chevrolet. Those hubcaps wouldn't even have fit on my car if I'd successfully stolen them!

The policeman who arrested me was a detective who'd been visiting a friend of his at the mall, and he just happened to see me out in the parking lot with my hood up and stealing hubcaps. He simply pulled over, grabbed me and arrested me, and I had to be turned over to my mother's custody once again.

"Ma'am, your son's not that smart," said the inspector.

"What do you mean?" asked my mom.

"He was stealing hubcaps that wouldn't even have fit his car!" he said.

My mom was caught between a rock and a hard place. She knew I wasn't a bad kid at heart; I simply didn't have any guidance, and I was trying to figure life out on my own. She didn't blame it on my influences. It wasn't like I'd been hanging out with a gang of mobsters. It was just a case of growing up as a kid in a rough part of town. You *had* to fit in. Whatever my friends did on Friday and Saturday nights, I did it with them.

Mom didn't have to lecture me or raise her voice at me. No words were required; I *always* felt awful, like I'd directly mistreated her when I did something wrong. If I hurt her feelings, she would give me the silent treatment, or she would cry tears of disappointment. Seeing her cry was infinitely worse than if she would have whooped me. But if she'd *really* wanted to hurt me, she would have made me eat the entirety of one of her dinners. She was *not* a great cook.

I didn't disrespect my mom. It's just that I got caught up in a couple of things. I'm not claiming innocence by any means. Here's the thing: I may have been caught doing something illegal on *one* Friday night, but I was doing those same illegal things on *every* Friday night. I'd go to someone's house and drink beer, then go to watch the high school football game before heading over to someone else's house and drinking even *more* beer before going home. Mom just happened to be made aware of the one night that I actually got caught. The only reason I got hemmed up on that occasion is because I just didn't feel like running anymore.

No less than *five times* that same month, I'd been in situations where someone yelled, "The cops are here!" and I'd been the first one escaping through the sliding glass door in the back, and then hopping chain link fences and getting my head taken off by people's clotheslines. One time, one of the neighbors had a ladder on the side of his house, so I climbed the ladder along with a buddy of mine, pulled the ladder up after us, and then sat on the roof as we watched the police chase everyone else around while we just waited for things to calm down.

No matter how you slice it, I was simply a troubled, fatherless kid who was in desperate need of some advice, guidance and direction, and I was about to find all of those things from several sources that were both beneficial, and detrimental.

TWO

Once high school reached its inevitable conclusion, Mike headed directly into the wrestling business, and Dick Slater joined right alongside him because of the bond they had formed. I still wasn't convinced that wrestling was a good fit for me. Despite working out frequently, I only weighed 165 pounds at the time of graduation. I may have thought I was somewhat tough, but I was nowhere close to being an acceptably big guy.

This was still at a time when I was a pretty ballsy kid who was great at running his mouth and then following it up with a few punches, but then I was on the receiving end of a solid sucker punch that taught me a valuable lesson about not standing around running my mouth when it was time to fight. The smarter move is to just start throwing punches if that's what you're there to do, because the person who lands the first solid shot usually won. Regardless, I still believed wrestling was 100 percent authentic combat, and I knew I wouldn't make it very far simply on guts alone, and without any size to back it up.

I decided my best bet for life success was to attend college and try something different. I went to junior college in Clearwater and St. Pete at Hillsborough Junior College. At no point did I gain any clarity as to what I wanted to be while I was there; I was just drifting along and hoping something would stick. This was the educational path that my mom preferred for me to take, but there had been no planning in my life that would have prepared me for a high-skill profession. I'd simply had no guidance along those lines while I was in high school.

While I was enrolled in junior college, we were visited by a cousin on my mother's side of the family, which was from way out in the northeastern section of Mississippi. He become a radiologist, and he had been visiting us far more regularly after my dad became imprisoned in Vietnam.

"You should consider becoming a doctor, Steve," he told me. "You'll earn a healthy living."

When I started thinking about what professions made the most money, doctor and lawyer always appeared near the top of the list, so it didn't take much to convince me that I'd be best served by becoming a doctor.

From there, Mom's cousin convinced me to attend his alma mater, which was Mississippi College in Clinton, Mississippi.

"It's a great place to get your medical license," he insisted. "It's a good, small college."

In pursuit of an acceptable pre-med degree, I transferred to the college in Clinton, which is just outside of Jackson, Mississippi. Once I set foot on the campus, I immediately fell in with a group of police officers who trained as members of their department's powerlifting team 10 miles away from campus at the YMCA in Downtown Jackson.

One of the guys on the team introduced me to steroids in the form of a pill called Dianabol. He told me to take just one a day while we were training with the group. Well, between the steroids, my training, and my diet, I grew *astronomically*, shooting from 165 pounds to 245 pounds in a span of only three months. So you could say I was majoring in chemistry, but not the type that looks impressive on a medical school application.

Just because I was now in college didn't mean I'd left my troublemaking tendencies behind. One weekend night in Jackson, a football player from Southern Mississippi named Bruce Duck showed up in the street. He was drunk out in a parking lot, hollering and screaming about how he was going to kick everybody's ass.

"Who are you?" I asked as I walked toward him.

"Bruce Duck!" he said.

I stuck out my left hand for him to shake it, and then I said, "Steve Keirn!"

When Bruce clasped my left hand with his, I immediately jerked him into the haymaker right that I threw at his chin. He *never* saw it coming, and it immediately put him to sleep. Was it fair? Absolutely not. Did I win? *Undeniably*. No one ever asks if you cheated to win a fight; they only ever ask if you won it.

While I was attending Mississippi College, Mid-South Wrestling promoter Bill Watts found out from Eddie Graham that I was living out there, got a phone number for me, and called me one night to invite me to a show. It was the funniest thing because Bill thought I was smart to the business and already knew all of its secrets because of all the time I'd spent around Eddie and Mike.

Bill walked me straight into the Mid-South dressing room, and I nearly crapped my britches. Sitting right there in front of me were Dusty Rhodes, Dick Murdoch and Porkchop Cash.

"Introduce yourself, kid!" said Bill. "Hey everybody! This is one of Eddie Graham's kids from Florida!"

Some of the guys knew me from passing through Florida, and as they said hello, several of them gave me the worker's handshake, where they would shake hands like their hands were dead fish. I was all jacked up because I'd been on steroids and been powerlifting, and I shook each of their hands like a normal human being. Afterwards, Watts told me that a few of them approached him and said, "Hey, this kid is *stiff*! He's just like all them guys from Florida! They're *all* stiff!"

Watts walked me around and let me listen to conversations as the guys planned out their matches and went over what the finishes to their bouts would be. All the while, I was thinking, "Man, if Eddie knew I was seeing and hearing this right now, his head would *explode*!"

Powerlifting served as a welcome distraction from some other events that were transpiring in my life and causing me to panic. I had been classified as 1-A by the U.S. military – as number 112 in the draft – and at the time there was no deferment for the sons of POWs. My father was still a captive of the Vietcong as far as we knew, and the only deferments being granted were for sole-surviving sons or individuals in similar situations. In other words, if my father was dead, I would have been granted a deferment, but since his status was far more tenuous, there were no deferment options available for me.

At a portly weight of 245 pounds, I had to travel to Jackson to take a physical. It was held inside of an emergency room at an Air Force base, and I was the sole draftee lined up with several volunteers. We were all standing in a single-file line in our underwear, and the medical staff immediately fixed me with a red tag after weighing me.

"You're *way* overweight for a guy who's six feet tall!" they said.

Next, they commanded us to stick our arms straight out, rotate them to the left and right, put our hands straight up, put our palms up, and wiggle our fingers. When they got to the part where we were supposed to stick our palms up, there was a perfect row of flat palms with the lone exception of mine. My left palm was flat, but my right hand was sitting at a 90-degree angle.

Both of the large bones in my right arm had been broken just above the wrist when I was playing football for my junior high school team. During that fateful game, I took a hit, spun around, fell backwards with my arm extended straight out, and snapped the two bones.

At the time, the Air Force doctor had simply pulled the bones apart, set them, and put my arm in a cast, but they didn't do anything elaborate to address it, like put pins in it.

Of course the military guys who were evaluating me thought I was messing with them because I was a steroidal monster standing with a bunch of skinny kids from Mississippi, and they figured I would have needed a fully functional arm to get that huge. I also had long hair for that era, so they probably had this preconceived notion that I didn't want to go off to Vietnam, which was 100 percent true. I didn't want to go *anywhere*. I just had the look of a classic troublemaker, and they assumed I was simply being a smartass.

One of the military men walked up, gripped my arm with both hands and physically tried to twist it into place.

"Sorry, man. It just doesn't twist over anymore," I told him.

So, I got another red tag for that.

From there, they sent all of us to receive a simultaneous psychological evaluation from the staff psychiatrist. He wanted to know if there was anyone who felt like they shouldn't be there, and I raised my hand.

"My father is a prisoner of war right now," I told him. "He's been there since I was 13. That's been five years. I don't mind getting drafted if he comes home, but not until then."

"I understand," he said, before slapping me with a final red tag.

That left me with a collection of three red tags hanging off of my underwear. Based on three separate criteria, I'd flunked my military physical. All the same, that didn't mean I would be shielded from getting drafted into military service.

I was asked to take a second physical, which was conducted at the college infirmary, and I flunked that one as well. This time, the primary tests being conducted were the measurements of my blood pressure and my heart rate. Those had been two of my biggest red flags, with my blood pressure reading being through the ceiling. When it was time for me to take my follow-up exam, I intentionally *ran* all the way to the infirmary. Unsurprisingly, when I arrived at the exam location, my heart rate was elevated even higher than before.

"Lie down on the table," ordered the nurse. "We'll get a resting blood pressure for you."

The nurse left me alone to give my blood pressure time to lower itself. As soon as she exited the room, I began to crank out push-ups, one after the other, right up until she returned. Is it any surprise that I was able to maintain a high blood pressure reading all the way through the exam? I was doing everything in my power to deliberately flunk it.

As luck would have it, businessman H. Ross Perot was touring the country at that time, and he was visiting cities to promote his plan to provide additional aid to the military. The POW issue was a particular favorite of his.

My mom called me and told me that Ross Perot was having a POW rally, and they'd contacted her to see if she wished to attend.

"My son is right outside of Jackson," my mom told them. "He's at the college in Clinton."

Steve at the Ross Perot assembly for POW families

So I was invited to the Ross Perot rally in Jackson even though I had no clue who he was. When I got there, my name was on a list, and they put me right up on stage as the son of a two-time POW. There was also a lady on stage with me whose husband was a POW.

As I sat on the stage with Perot during his speaking engagement, he actually leaned over and greeted me.

"Hi, son! How is your life going?" Perot asked me.

"It's going all right, but they're trying to draft me," I told him. "I flunked two physicals, and I don't plan to pass my next physical either, but my mom is a little upset with me because she doesn't want me to get labeled as '4F.' I'm *still* going to flunk the physical. I know I'm going to flunk it because I'm going to *try* to flunk it."

"Well, I've got a lot of friends in high places," said Perot. "I'll see what I can do to help you out."

The next thing I knew, a congressman or senator in Texas passed a bill that stipulated that you couldn't be drafted into the military if another one of your family members was an active POW. So I became the first person ever classified as 1-H.

At this stage, it seemed like the war in Vietnam had been dragging on forever. My dad was 39 when he was shot down in Vietnam, and most of the pilots in the early stages of Vietnam were grown men who had children. I'd been a young teen when that happened, and now I was being sought to fight in the same war that had claimed my dad. It felt like time had caught up with me.

When the moment arrived for me to fly home for Mike Graham's wedding over Thanksgiving break, I'd grown a full beard, and my hair had lengthened by several inches. Combined with the fact that I was 80 pounds heavier than I had been before I left for Mississippi College, this made me totally unrecognizable to anyone that had interacted with me before. I walked straight past my mother at the airport, and she didn't even squint in my direction.

I circled back around to her and said, "Mom, don't you know me?"

Mom looked at me and flipped out because I'd gone from a lanky large to a bulky extra-large in all sizes of clothing. The difference was striking.

All of my former friends were stunned by my appearance when they saw me in my tuxedo at Mike's wedding, but no one was more enamored with my new look than Eddie Graham.

"How did you get so *big*?" asked Eddie.

I explained my growth secrets to Eddie, right down to the deadlifts and the Dianabol tablets.

"Well how is college going for you?" inquired Eddie.

"Not too good," I replied.

I told Eddie all about how they'd attempted to draft me into service in Vietnam, along with what the outcome had been.

"Let's do this: Why don't you do some summer work for me as a referee?" suggested Eddie. "I'll teach you some things about the wrestling business."

"Sure," I told him.

I wasn't thrilled about being away at school, and I knew I would need a job if I was going to move back home. I also assumed I would be safe from getting beaten up by the wrestlers if I was just a referee.

Those three months I spent as a referee are what got me highly intrigued about the idea of pursuing a career as a full-fledged wrestler. At the beginning of the summer, Eddie said, "I want to break you into the wrestling business, but first we need to find out if you've got what it takes."

The Tampa Sportatorium at 106 North Albany served as the home building where the Championship Wrestling from Florida territory taped its weekly television program. It was like a furnace in there due to the lack of air conditioning. There was one ring in the center of the building, and it was set up for a one-camera shoot. Gordon Solie served as the legendary announcer of the television program, coloring the action with his unmistakable, gravely voice.

I was already intimately familiar with the Sportatorium by that time. In fact, I was *uncomfortably* familiar with it. I'd sat in the building's bleachers with Mike a few times to watch what happened when guys attempted to break into the wrestling business after Eddie had already decided that they had no future in it. I'd sit and cringe while the would-be wrestlers were brutally stretched and pummeled, and then physically discarded back into the parking lot.

The majority of the unwitting victims were guys like bodybuilders and football players who were interested in becoming wrestlers. Once inside of the Sportatorium, they would be ushered inside of the ring with shooters – guys like Bob Roop, Jack Brisco, Hiro Matsuda, and a few other wrestlers who really knew how to fight well.

The interactions would commence with the would-be wrestlers getting stretched, and then the level of violence would drastically ramp up and culminate with the applicants getting beaten relentlessly. There was also no escape; the Sportatorium doors would be chained shut to prevent them from retreating to safety. I had well-founded fears that some of the poor suckers might actually die.

"Eddie... no offense... I want to try this, but I don't want to get the crap beaten out of me," I admitted. "That's what I've seen."

Eddie shook his head.

"Those are guys we needed to make examples of," explained Eddie. "I'm gonna break you into the business the *real* way."

"The real way" began when Eddie sent me down to the Sportatorium to meet with wrestler and trainer Hiro Matsuda, who I'd already known for several years. Workouts were initiated when Matsuda would break out a deck of cards, shuffle it, and then flip over the top card. Whatever card came up corresponded to a number of free squats.

After several exhausting rounds of squats, we'd graduate to sets of other basic exercises like back bridges and push-ups. Finally, after I was already half dead from the calisthenic training, we'd get in the ring, and Matsuda would want to wrestle. I didn't have any amateur wrestling background at all to draw from, so whenever I tried to grab Hiro, he would slip away and stretch me ruthlessly. There was no such thing as tapping out in those days. I was forced to scream, yell, or holler, "I quit!"

Adding to the discomfort of the training was the fact that we were meeting in the Sportatorium in the middle of July.

That's when the heat would climb to about 100 degrees in the center of the ring when you factored in the additional warmth radiating from the light that was beaming down on top of you. I was sweating like crazy in there, but I was doing the best I could because I wanted to make a favorable impression, and I didn't want to let Eddie down after he'd shown so much faith in me.

Whenever I came home from training with Matsuda, I had mat burns all over my entire body, from my forehead and my nose down to my elbows and knees. I was also exhausted, horribly sore, and savagely beaten. I was stretched so hard during each session that I felt like I was getting taller by the day.

When my mom caught me dragging myself back into the house each day looking like I'd been mugged, she asked me what was going on.

"They're teaching me to be a pro wrestler," I groaned.

"A pro wrestler?" mom asked. "But I thought pro wrestling was fake!"

"Hey, so did I!" I remarked.

"Are you *sure* you want to do this?" she asked.

I *wasn't* sure I wanted to do it. In all honesty, I did want to quit at the time, but I would have been too embarrassed to do so. Eddie had become directly involved with the entire training process as well, including getting in the ring and wrestling with me. I didn't want to disappoint him. After all, he was like a father to me.

My training continued with its savage consistency for somewhere between four to six months. At times, I considered leaving the state of Florida simply to hide from Eddie so that I wouldn't have to continue training, and also to avoid graduating to an *actual* wrestling career where I might get placed in the ring in front of a live audience and beaten up even worse.

Fortunately, after months of training, Eddie pulled me aside and clued me into the reality of what had been happening to me.

"You've proved to us that you respect our business," said Eddie, proudly. "You stuck with it. You gave it your all. You never questioned anything. You never asked about the realism. You just did what you were told. *Now* I'm going to teach you how to work."

"Work?" I asked. "What are you talking about?"

I didn't know what he meant, but it didn't sound good. One of the reasons I wanted to wrestle was because I hadn't wanted to become a construction worker or perform any of the tasks I associated with actual work.

"I'm gonna teach you how to wrestle another guy," said Eddie. "When you refereed, I told the guys to kayfabe you because you weren't smart to the business. You never really saw what they were doing in that ring; all you knew was to count to three when you had to."

"What was that word you used?" I asked.

"Kayfabe? It means that we need to give the impression everything is real because someone is around that doesn't know that we're workin'," said Eddie. "Come on… I'll show you."

I followed Eddie's lead and we both climbed into the Sportatorium ring.

"I'm going to show you a collar-and-elbow lockup," said Eddie.

We applied the familiar face-to-face tie up with our arms, and then Eddie backed me into the corner. Then he pulled my arms down to my sides.

"Let's see what this feels like to you," said Eddie.

Out of the blue, Eddie whacked me so hard right in the neck with his fist that I felt the goosebumps shoot straight down to my butthole. It was like a bolt of lightning had blasted its way right through me.

As I was staggering along the ropes trying to recover from that sudden right hand to the neck, Eddie said, "Now *that's* how you punch. I punch to the side of the neck with my whole fist. Now, if I was to grab your throat…"

In a flash, Eddie lurched forward, grabbed my throat, and started squeezing it to the point where he was nearly crushing my Adam's apple.

"... how do you react to *this*?" continued Eddie.

I began flailing with my arms and waving them around in a panic like I'd seen plenty of guys do during prior wrestling matches that I'd viewed. In response to this improper reaction, Eddie clamped down on my neck even harder so that I instinctively reached up and tried to pry his hands from my throat.

"*That's* the way you've got to do it," said Eddie. "You've gotta react the way that you would react if it was real, to communicate to the audience that it is real. That's how you sell."

I'd swear that's the exact moment my voice changed. It went from a quality singing voice to being a lot more coarse and gravely in response to Eddie clamping down on my throat to give my first lesson in selling a chokehold.

From that moment on, I was no longer getting stretched and then forced through an endless battery of calisthenic exercises. Instead, I was stepping into the ring and working out by learning how to work during wrestling matches, along with learning up to 10 very basic moves.

It was during this period of my training that I was also working out with Jack Brisco – an NCAA Champion wrestler, and one of the most exciting pro wrestlers in the world that I most looked up to a great deal. Eddie informed me that my first match would be coming up shortly, and I was feeling nervous about how I would look to the crowd during my first showing.

"I don't know how I'm supposed to wrestle," I revealed to Jack. "I only know a few moves."

"Steve, there's somethin' you need to know: It ain't all about moves," advised Jack. "You don't need to do a bunch of moves to be successful in this business. It's all about how you get along with the rest of the boys in this business. That will be the main thing that determines how good you get to look to an audience."

"What do you mean?" I asked.

"A lot of it has to do with how you're accepted in that dressing room," added Jack. "Always be humble. Walk over to each individual, shake their hand, and introduce yourself to them. When you talk to your opponent, ask them, 'Is there anything you want me to do? Is there anything you want to do?' Also, tell them, 'If you're hurt, please tell me so I don't go over to that area.'"

"So I'm just supposed to do what other guys want me to do?" I followed up.

"Steve, right now, you are a *giver*. You have nothin' to offer to nobody," explained Jack. "When you're in the beginning, all you do is give, give, give, give. You don't want nothin', you don't take nothin', you listen, and you pay attention."

"Pay attention to what? I asked.

"You go out and watch *every* match," ordered Jack. "If you're in the first match on the card, don't shower. Put your towel around your neck, and then go stand out there and watch every match. See what the guys are doin', see what moves they're makin', see what the people want and what they're excited about. For sure you want to watch the main event and figure out why those guys are in the main event and what they're doin' different from everyone else. You have to be like a sponge, because you're a minnow in a sea of sharks. And if you don't like somebody, *never* let them know it. Be kind and humble."

All of this advice would end up being invaluable to me throughout my career, and it's no surprise that it all came from Jack Brisco. He was a major mentor of mine in this business, and a true stud. I absolutely idolized him.

When I ultimately had my first match, it was against Chris Markoff in Arcadia, Florida, inside of an armory. I was terrified the entire time I was in the ring. Fortunately, there were probably only 15 people in the building to view my discomfort firsthand.

"Listen to me, kid!" Markoff kept telling me after the match was underway. "Listen to me! Slow down! Don't move too fast!"

Markoff kept me grounded throughout the match, and we somehow got through the night despite my trepidation. It was nothing worth writing home to mom about, but we navigated that first match successfully, and then the ball started rolling. I became the type of guy who would occupy an enhancement roll on TV right off the bat. My job was simply to wrestle and get beaten on camera to make the established wrestlers look good. Then I'd drive to towns all throughout Florida and get beaten. Pretty much all I did was "jobs," which is a shorthand way of saying that my "job" was to get beaten in every town I wrestled in.

Every once in a while I would get to wrestle my opponent to a Broadway, which was a time-limit draw. Those were pretty much arranged so that I would get an extended 15-minute match with somebody more experienced so that they could instruct me in the ring, and guide me through the process of working a longer wrestling match. And if I did get a win, it was because some old timer I was wrestling against felt sorry for me.

Most of my education about movement in the ring came from watching other guys, or by reviewing films and tapes of prior matches. I also slowly added to my repertoire of moves. I didn't go through 900 moves and learn each move; I just picked out what I thought I could do well, and then adapted my arsenal as I went. Physically, my body was average in appearance. I was strong, but I was on the round and pudgy side. I still retained much of my baby fat from being a powerlifter. Wrestlers with clearly defined muscles were said to be "cut"; I used to say that my body had as many cuts as an M&M.

If I had been entertaining any fantasies about roaring out of the gate as a major winner during my wrestling career, Eddie quickly expelled all such thoughts from my mind.

"Here's what you need to know: You're just starting your matches while you're 20 years old. People aren't gonna buy you as a serious wrestler," said Eddie. "They're not gonna pay money to see you. You need to mature. You need to be at least 30 before you're able to draw money, *if* you have the potential to draw money. That's when they'll respect you as a man and won't think of you as a kid anymore."

Getting my neck squeezed by Gorgeous George Jr.

In other words, there weren't any imminent plans to turn me into something special, or even into anything respectable to the fans. I did jobs in very basic matches in most of our stops across Florida. I didn't get to wrestle in the Tampa Armory too much because I'd grown up in the surrounding area. A lot of my friends would come to watch the matches, and Eddie didn't want me to be portrayed as not being very good in front of my hometown friends, at least not with any regularity. The company was running shows in two towns on

Tuesday nights: Tampa and Fort Myers. I always went to Fort Myers, which was easily the smaller of the two markets.

The Florida territory was a tough cycle to work through. On Monday nights we'd drive to West Palm and back to Tampa, which was 200 miles each way. On Tuesday nights we would find ourselves in either Tampa or Fort Myers. Wednesday night was reserved for the Miami Beach Convention Center, but we also had TV tapings to record early that morning. If you were important enough, you had your weekly interviews taped, or you simply climbed straight into your car and drove to Miami. At the conclusion of the show, we would drive all the way from Miami back to Tampa, only to turn right around and depart for Jacksonville the next day.

On Friday, we would be in Fort Launderdale or Tallahassee, and on Saturday we would perform within a 60-mile radius of Tampa, in St. Petersburg, Sarasota or Lakeland. Then on Sunday nights, we were in Orlando.

We spent the majority of our waking hours driving from place to place, and I had a tough time keeping my eyes open on the road during many of those return trips. We never had any nights off. We basically never had *time* off. We wrestled Sunday through Saturday, and twice on days when we had TV tapings, so that was ordinarily eight times per week.

Some of those stretches of road were rather treacherous. The road from Yeehaw Junction to Lake Wales was about 80 miles of two-lane travel. Going down there wasn't so bad, but on the way back home, we were driving right toward other cars going 80 to 100 miles an hour. It was straight and wide open, and it didn't take much to send you careening off the road. All it would have taken to cause a wreck at that speed would have been a slight swerve to avoid an alligator that was lying in the middle of the street. We also had some terrible rainstorms, and on those stretches of two-lane roads, it was very easy to hydroplane your car.

When I recall my life, I think of all the times I fell asleep at the wheel when I was on the road. There was at least once when I fell asleep and woke up just as I was about to run up underneath the tires of an 18-wheeler. I slammed on the brakes in sheer panic before I drove my car into that trailer and got crushed. There was also an occasion when I was jolted awake just after sliding off the road, and someone honked at me before I hit them in the opposing lane.

It was so hard to stay awake as the driver, and you often didn't have anyone else there who would ensure that your eyes remained open. When I rode with the old guys, I was usually the assigned driver. They would get in the cars, drink two beers, fall asleep, and wake up in Tampa after I'd parked the car.

Regardless of my low status in the CWF organization, at least I was fully integrated into the roster and fully accepted by the boys. Little did I realize that I was about to get an impromptu lesson about what it was like to fly *completely* solo.

THREE

Out of the blue, Eddie Graham presented me with an opportunity that sounded so off-the-wall that I initially thought he was joking.

"We've got this thing we want to send you off to do," said Eddie. "I'm gonna send you to wrestle in Guatemala. You're gonna be there for five weeks, and they're gonna pay you $350 a week. The name of the promoter is José Azari."

"You're *serious*?" I laughed. "Guatemala?"

Eddie *was* serious. I was headed off to wrestle in Central America. The negotiation for my services had already taken place in my absence. All I had to do was hop aboard a plane.

"Also, don't sell any of the acrobatic shit they do down there, and don't try any of it either," warned Eddie, as he handed me my one-way plane ticket. "You're too big to be flyin' around like that. Take them down, ground them, and wrestle them."

So now I was headed off to wrestle in a Spanish-speaking country. The only times I had been outside of the United States before that was to watch wrestling in the Bahamas, and when I'd lived in Okinawa.

My plane landed in Guatemala City, and I felt hopelessly lost the instant I stepped into the airport. No one was waiting there to pick me up. I also had no phone number to call anyone on, so I was stuck sitting inside of the airport all day long. My Spanish vocabulary consisted of just one word; I'd learned to pronounce the word "luchador" so that if anyone asked me who I was or what I did for a living, I could point to myself and say, "Luchador."

I sat at the airport for an entire afternoon and evening, and still no one came to collect me. That night, I slept at the airport with my body draped on top of my suitcase because I was afraid someone might steal it. I chalked it up to miscommunication on the part of the office, and that maybe they had been off on the scheduling by a day.

Well, the next day arrived, and once again I sat at the airport for an entire day. Just like the prior day, no one came to retrieve me. It wasn't until the clock struck 6:00 p.m. that I finally began to panic in earnest. I was wondering if this was an elaborate practical joke – or rib – on Eddie's part to send me to Guatemala and leave me abandoned at the airport the entire time just to see how I would react to it.

As I was sitting there, I experienced one of my first moments that I truly began to reconsider my newfound line of work. If getting abandoned in the airports of developing nations was a basic job function of a professional wrestler, I wasn't certain that I still wanted to be involved in in the business at all.

By the time 7:00 p.m. rolled around, my anxiety had swelled to the point where I was now in a full panic. I paced around the airport and screamed for help.

"Does *anybody* speak English?!" I yelled at the top of my lungs.

From behind one of the rental car counters, a man finally emerged and said, "*I* speak English."

"Thank God!" I said. "I was sent down here from Florida to wrestle. This guy named José Azari is in charge of a wrestling company here. He was supposed to send someone to pick me up, but I've been waitin' around for two days and no one has come to get me!"

This guy calmly picked up a phone book, opened it to the 'A' section, and easily found José Azari's phone number.

The man who was assisting me spoke a few sentences into the phone in Spanish, and then looked up at me and said, "José says you're not supposed to be here until tomorrow."

I was so fortunate that the man at the car rental counter spoke English, or I would have been sweating things out at the airport for an additional night.

José arrived at the airport to get me, and then he drove me from the airport to a hotel in Downtown Guatemala City. We didn't speak a word to one another during the entire drive because I didn't know any Spanish, and he didn't speak any English.

Once we reached the hotel, José helped me check in, and then he made a gesture of pointing at a calendar and counting on four of his fingers to communicate that he would be back in four days to pick me up. At that time, I would wrestle on Saturday and Sunday, and then I would stay in the hotel the rest of the time. The room had a lightbulb hanging from the center of the ceiling. There was no air conditioning, television, or anything else inside of it other than a bed.

The Black Angel works over his downed opponent

As if that hadn't been bad enough, José also gestured to me that I wasn't to travel anywhere else within Guatemala City because the police were crooked and they would arrest me and hold me for ransom. According to him, the military was okay, but the police could not be trusted.

I learned how to order food so that I wouldn't starve, but I did as José instructed me and never wandered outside of the safe haven provided by the hotel. It wasn't until José finally sent someone to pick me up and take me to wrestle that I learned they wanted me to wrestle under a mask.

"I don't wear a mask," I told them, before pointing to my face. "I just wrestle like this."

"No, you're going to wear a mask," my driver told me. "*Everyone* wears a mask in Guatemala, so you will, too."

Our first stop was at the shop of a mask-maker, and he crafted a mask for me out of primarily black materials.

"You are going to be called 'El Angel Negro,'" my driver told me. "You are 'The Black Angel.'"

"Okay. Whatever," I shrugged. Jack Brisco had advised me to go along with the program wherever I went, so I was willing to do whatever was asked of me in order to fit in and fulfill my obligations.

My first night of wrestling was at an outdoor TV taping. The building had a concrete wall around it, similar to the configuration of Nassau Stadium in the Bahamas, only without any chicken-wire strategically positioned around the ring to catch the debris that was being hurled at the wrestlers from fans seated all over the arena.

I watched a couple of the matches while they were in progress to try to figure out their structure, and while I was conducting my analysis, the local promoter came up and tried to explain to me that I was supposed to completely dominate and crush the guy they were putting me in the ring against that night. That's when I learned they intended to build me up rapidly over the course of my five weeks so that it would be a big deal when someone beat me on my final night in Guatemala.

When I stood in the center of the ring for the very first time in Guatemala, I kept seeing objects flickering in and out of the light. Initially, I assumed they were bats. That delusion was violently shaken when rocks began crashing to the mat all around me. I instantly realized that the fans were lobbing rocks into the ring, and trying to draw blood from El Angel Negro. They landed in the ring all around me, occasionally accompanied by other objects like apples and oranges.

This was definitely a new experience for me. I was an inconsequential wrestler in Florida, but I was instantly a despised villain on my very first night in Guatemala. Fortunately, the throwing of objects subsided once the babyface arrived and the match got underway. I beat him quickly and got out of there before the fans could pelt me with any other debris.

The very next night, I was in the Colosseum, which was a huge building that had originally been built for a sports festival of some kind. It was shaped like it was primarily used as an indoor soccer stadium. It had a spacious open flooring configuration, and had a chain-link fence on the top of the outer wall that stretched to a height of about 10 feet. I walked out into the arena and looked around, staring at the chain-link fence, and wondering what it had been built for. It had obviously been built with a purpose.

That night, I was a nervous wreck sitting in the dressing room and thinking about wrestling in front of such a large crowd. These two wrestlers from Mexico who were exceedingly kind came over to me, and they gestured toward their eyes and then out toward the ring to indicate that they wanted me to see what was about to happen when they walked to the ring. I heard the introduction to the match, and then I was able to hear, "... de México," to signify that the next wrestlers approaching the ring would be from Mexico.

When those two guys hit the door and entered the arena, they ran out about 10 feet, slammed on the brakes, and then backpedaled to the door. As they were stepping backwards, they were pointing out toward the fans, and I could see stuff flying from the cheap seats all the way down to the arena floor. The people were throwing everything they could get their hands on at these two guys, including the rocks and fruit that I'd already been introduced to during the prior night.

It seemed like the two guys were waiting for the people to reload, and that's when they seized the opportunity to sprint toward the ring. I could recognize that the fans would stop throwing things if they ran the risk of hitting their fellow fans seated closer to the ring, so that's when I successfully identified where the safe zones were.

"Okay, I see what's going on here," I told myself. "I've *got* this!"

When the announcer said, "... de los Estado Unidos, El Angel Negro!" I burst out of the dressing room door like I was going to run to the ring, but I skidded to a stop just like the Mexican wrestlers had done. On cue, the shower of debris pelted the floor where the fans presumed I would have been if I hadn't halted my own progress. Then these four little guys from the back came up to me and said, "Protection! Protection!"

The men ran alongside me, which I appreciated, but I was also thinking, "*These* guys are my protection?" They were so tiny standing there next to me that the fans could easily see me towering over them and pick me off with ease!

We successfully made it to the ringside area, and that's when I felt safe enough to break into my cocky strut, which is what I figured an arrogant American heel was supposed to do. I got near the ring and began to look around, but then I felt stinging sensations all over my body, as if something hot was repeatedly striking me in the legs, back and arms.

"What on earth are they hitting me with?!" I wondered. "Do they have pea shooters or something?"

Then I noticed that the area around me was littered with lit cigarettes that the ringside fans had all been flicking toward me. I quickly climbed into the ring and the cigarette flicking ceased. The match started, and I once again demolished my Guatemalan opponent and swiftly retreated to the dressing room.

After my first weekend of in-ring action, photos of my masked face began to circulate in Guatemalan newspapers, along with the description of me as an American wrestling heel. Clearly, with my size, shape, and lack of Spanish comprehension, I stuck out like a sore thumb in a city like that, so I needed to disguise myself somewhat everywhere I went. I also had to learn how to catch cabs because they didn't have typical American-style cabs; you had to haggle over the price of your trip with any driver who had a flag sticking out of his car window.

My second-to-last weekend in Guatemala, I was booked to have a big battle in the ring, and they asked me to "get color" – or bleed. Not only had I never done that before, but I also had to navigate the process of getting color for the first time while wearing a mask.

The bleeding "El Angel Negro" displays his anger

"We'll have him rip your mask open," the promoter told me. "We'll cut the thread a little bit to make it easy to tear, then he'll cut you, and you go crazy."

Reluctantly, I went along with their proposed plan, but when my opponent finally cut me, he gashed my head so deeply that the gaping wound in my head wouldn't stop bleeding after that match was over. They drove me straight to a nearby hospital from the arena and rushed me inside.

As I was sitting on the medical table bleeding profusely, the hospital staff was attempting to ask me questions about things I was allergic to or medications I couldn't take, but I had no idea what anyone was saying to me because I couldn't speak Spanish. Unable to communicate, I wound up receiving several sample shots I probably didn't need, which the staff circled with a pen at the injection sites to see if I had any allergic reactions before they finally administered the care I required.

Somehow, despite what I was convinced were the Guatemalans' best attempts to kill me, I arrived on the day of my final show. As I sped off to the arena seated in the back of an old Buick with holes in its hood, I was thrilled at the thought of going home and telling everyone back at the CWF office about all the adventures I'd had. The Buick I was in looked like a tank, and I sat slumped over in the back seat, having learned to wait until I'd arrived at the arena so as not to be identified ahead of time. I would wait until I arrived at the arena before donning my mask and exiting the vehicle.

At long last we pulled up the long driveway that led to the entrance the wrestlers utilized at the rear of the arena. As usual, I pulled my black mask over my head, sat upright, and prepared to exit the vehicle. Suddenly, the car came to a screeching halt.

"*Ahhhhh!*" came a scream from the front of the vehicle.

My driver had been watching me in his rearview mirror, and when he saw me sitting up with a mask over my head, he thought he was about to be mugged. Either that, or he was horrified at the thought of what the villainous Black Angel might do to him. Regardless, his screams caused a commotion and drew the attention of nearby fans, who surrounded the Buick and began to pound and kick at its sides, while others rocked the car from side to side.

Now that my mask was on, I had fully committed to the gimmick and made myself a juicy target. To make matters worse, I couldn't afford to remove the mask because then everyone would have known what I really looked like, and then I wouldn't have been safe in that city under any circumstances.

In the midst of that ruckus, the driver dove for cover on the floor of the Buick.

"Drive!" I screamed at him. "You *have* to drive!"

The side-to-side rocking of the Buick became more extreme, and I thought to myself, "Ain't no way they're gonna flip this thing over!"

I was wrong. The crowd forced the Buick all the way onto its left side, which resulted in me assuming a standing position with my feet on the car's side window. Facing imminent death, I reverted to being the 20-year-old kid that I was and I began crying my eyes out. I then worked my way into a position where I was standing on the dome light of the car, and I could see the springs of the front seat from where I was situated.

"Wow. I'm going to die," I said, reaching the only logical conclusion I could draw at that moment. "Right here in Guatemala. This is it. That's what I get for trying to become a pro wrestler."

Out of nowhere, the car was rocked by a deafening bang as if a bomb had gone off. This was followed by the sounds of grunting and groaning, and then everything fell silent.

"Oh, I'm not falling for this!" I told myself. "They're waiting for me to stick my head out, and then they're going to decapitate me!"

I maintained my position and stood in the vehicle's center. In the silence, I could hear the sobs of the old cab driver, who was still crawling around and crying at my feet. Then I looked down, and I watched a white-gloved hand reach into the Buick through the back door. It was followed by a khaki sleeve, and some military boots.

"Come out! Come out!" a voice said to me.

I looked again and saw a chrome helmet. The gloved hand belonged to a member of the Guatemalan military. Assuming I was finally safe, I crawled out through the back of the car, and I saw bodies strewn about on the road. Guatemalan military personnel had waded into the fray and gunbutted and clubbed men, women and children to get to the Buick and save the Black Angel's hide.

When I reached my feet and grabbed my bag, the military guys motioned for me to follow them. That's when I was ushered into the building by a group of men holding fully automatic weapons.

"What was that all about?!" I asked myself.

ESTE ERA BLACK ANGEL
STEVE KEIRN
HIJO DE UN HEROE
MILITAR DE EE.UU.

Somehow, despite being in literal fear for my life just moments prior, I made it through my final appearance as El Angel Negro, losing both the match and my mask in the process. The next day, the local newspaper ran an article with my unmasked face, revealing that I was really Steve Keirn, the son of an American military hero.

Relieved to have the entire experience behind me, I gratefully boarded the flight back home to Florida, and I went straight from the Tampa airport to the Sportatorium to chat with Eddie and tell him all about what I suffered through there.

"It's all part of your education, Steve!" chuckled Eddie. "Wrestling ain't always a sane, safe place for on-the-job training. I knew you would either get tough or die in Guatemala, and you survived it! You learned about blading, riots, crowd control, and gettin' around without being able to speak the language. It's just another obstacle you stepped over!"

Everyone else at the Sportatorium was patting me on the back and heaping praise upon me for everything I'd dealt with in Guatemala, which left me wondering how they'd managed to hear about everything when I'd only just returned. It turned out that the promoter had been keeping Eddie apprised of every stumbling block I'd contended with along the way.

Even though I'd essentially been a main-event wrestler during my brief stint in Guatemala as El Angel Negro, I went right back to being an enhancement wrestler in Florida. As if I'd needed a reminder of what my place was in the pecking order, I even wrestled the legendary "American Dream" Dusty Rhodes alongside two other wrestlers on television while Dusty was a heel. Dusty stacked our bodies on top of one another like firewood and simultaneously covered us all for the pinfall victory. Scenarios like that meant that it didn't take long for me to relearn what my purpose and place would be in the pecking order.

During that time period, I really started becoming more educated. I sat in the crowd just like Jack Brisco had advised me to, and I watched guys doing moves I'd never seen performed before, and then I asked them to teach me how to do them.

So many great wrestlers enjoyed coming through Florida, and that provided me with a golden opportunity to rub shoulders with many of the best wrestlers on the planet. I became friends with the Funks and the Briscos. Heels and babyfaces were kept separate, and since I was booked as a babyface, they were the primary folks I spoke to. I rode primarily with the old guys as they drank beer coming to and from the towns, and I listened to all of their stories and soaked up the information. I wasn't a big beer drinker, but I pretended to be for the sake of making them feel comfortable hanging out with me. I wound up secretly chucking more cans of beer out the window than I actually drank since I secretly hated it so much.

I was *elated* when I was finally assigned to ride with "The Great" Boris Malenko, who was a certified legend as a heel wrestler in the state of Florida. Despite my excitement, our inaugural trip together quickly devolved into a miserable disappointment shortly after I slid into the driver's seat and placed the key in the ignition. Within moments of our trip to

Miami commencing, Boris pulled his sweatshirt up to his mouth, reclined his seat, pulled his hood down over his eyes and said, "I'll see you in Miami."

I'd been expecting to hear exciting tales of Malenko's decades-long feud with Eddie Graham. Instead, Malenko dozed straight off to sleep, so the only thing I got to listen to was the sound of him snoring. As if by magic, Malenko awakened automatically when I turned south to head out of Yeehaw Junction.

"Hey, let's stop and get some pie and coffee at the rest stop," Boris said.

"Pie and coffee?" I thought to myself. "I've been driving for four hours already while you've been sleeping, and you want pie and coffee now?"

Of course I did it exactly as Boris requested. As a rookie wrestler, I was obligated to run off and fetch whatever food or beverages that any of the veteran wrestlers had a taste for. Outside of the ring, I got the veterans whatever they wanted, and inside of the ring, I did whatever I could to make them look good. That's the attitude that helped me to earn the respect of my peers; I accepted whatever treatment I received and rapidly acquired a reputation as a guy that was just happy to be involved in the wrestling business in any capacity.

Somebody eventually suggested to me that I should run off the road while Malenko was sleeping, and that he'd wake up and want to drive, and then I would be able to talk to him. Taking this advice to heart, I eased off the pavement and got in the grass along the highway a little bit. Malenko shot straight up in the passenger's seat and stared at me.

"I can't keep my eyes open," I told him.

"Pull over. I'll take it," he said.

From there, Malenko dutifully drove the rest of the way.

I was deathly afraid at the thought of having to deliver interviews and promos during the earliest stages of my career, and I was thrilled about not having to do them. Eventually, Eddie asked me to sit next to Gordon Solie to give an interview. As a general rule, ordinary babyface interviews from the 1970s were as exciting as watching paint dry. They were boring and lifeless. Most young wrestlers would sit next to Gordon and say things like, "Yes, Mr. Solie; I'm going to do whatever it takes to become the next champion, and when it's all said and done, all I can say is may the best man win."

Gordon watched the monitor during those interviews, and it was funny because whenever he asked me a question and the camera would pan away from him, he'd put his finger in his mouth to pantomime like he was throwing up as he reacted to my boring babyface responses to his questions. Either that, or he would pretend to nod off to sleep due to the sheer boredom produced by my generic answers.

Truthfully, I had no desire to *ever* do any interviews, and I wasn't in any hurry to be slotted into a main-event position no matter how much additional money would have wound up in my pockets at the end of the week. The main event of a show was what everyone in the dressing room pointed to and either credited or blamed it for the success or failure of a show. If the attendance for a show was lower than expected, "Who's in the main event tonight?!" was a frequent question that would be asked throughout the evening. You didn't want to be the guy who had to answer, "Me!" because then several of the other wrestlers would say things like, "Well, your shit can't even draw flies, brother!"

All of the wrestlers depended upon the financial success of the show to support themselves and their families. I didn't want to be responsible for someone coming home to their wife with less money than they'd expected; I just wanted to fit in. I was more than content to be confined to the first couple matches on the show and deflect any responsibility for a show's failure.

As humorous as it might sound, it wouldn't be much of a joke to say that the first music that ever signaled my entrance to the ring was the U.S. national anthem. The anthem would play to start the show, and then I would jog straight out to the ring to be sacrificed to the heel in the first match of the evening.

When I was finally allowed to wrestle in Tampa, I looked out into the audience during one of my earliest bouts and saw a tall, muscular, long-haired blond guy sitting in the crowd with his bare arms exposed. I immediately recognized him as Terry Bollea. He and I attended the same junior high and high school, except he was two years younger than me. Terry had been causing quite a stir locally by playing in Tampa's clubs with his band, Ruckus. After seeing me in the ring a few times, he approached me on the beach one weekend with a question cued up about an altogether different form of entertainment outside of the music world.

"Hey Steve! How do you get into wrestling?" Terry asked.

"Man, I don't know," I told him. "By the way, you *don't* want to do this; I only make 40 bucks a night and have to pay for my own gas! You're a bass guitar player in a band. Stay in the band! There's *no* money in this!"

I would eventually live to eat those words.

Along with the in-ring education came the understanding of the wrestling lexicon. Then we learned a carny language, which was essentially a pig latin where you would add a few letters to each word to change it just enough that it would be very hard for folks who weren't prepared to hear it in that setting to decipher what was being said, especially over whatever other competing noises were traveling through the crowd.

In the beginning, I wasn't very good at speaking carny. That was unfortunate, because there were important words that I *desperately* needed to be able to hear. This was especially true whenever a guy would shoot you into the ropes, because it was critical for you to know what was expected of you once you came off those ropes. Sometimes I'd be in the ring repeatedly asking the guys, "What? What? What?" because I couldn't hear, and it was so *vital* to understand what was coming next.

Perhaps the most important word to know and remember was "dizuck" or "duck." Obviously, that meant someone was going to throw a blow – usually a punch – right at your face with full force. If you didn't duck for whatever reason, you simply needed to pray that your face could absorb a punch without receiving too much damage, or that your opponent was able to blunt the force of the impact somehow.

I started trying to alter my appearance a little more to appear more athletic as opposed to simply being big and round. I also got into understanding the quality of matches a lot more and wanting to get better at them, so I would talk over my performances with the veterans on the way home from shows.

I also asked the guys I respected the utmost if they would take some time to watch my matches and give me some advice. If I was going to get better, I needed to know if I did anything particularly good so that I could do it over again, and also needed to know when I'd screwed up so that I could eliminate that from my routine.

Believe it or not, guys usually enjoyed being asked to critique your matches. They liked being respected at that level by their peers, and they also relished the thought that their opinions were valued. On the flipside, some guys would offer me their advice whether I'd asked for it or not, and a few of the guys were workers that I had so little respect for that when they gave me advice, I'd think about it for a second, and then it would go in one ear and out the other.

"Why didn't you do what I told ya?" Chris Markoff asked me when I didn't do something he'd advised me to do.

"Oh, I'm sorry. I forgot," I lied. "I guess I'll just have to try to remember next time."

It also helped that I'd started feeling more at home in the dressing room, and that was partially owed to the fact that I had stories to tell that other wrestlers actually wanted to hear. Guys were interested in hearing about my trip to Guatemala, and the fact that my father was a prisoner of war.

As fate would have it, my life was about to undergo a massive upheaval, and I was soon going to have an important climax to add to the story of my father's imprisonment.

FOUR

The Vietnam War was finally coming to an end, and we suddenly received word that my dad would be flying home. I hadn't seen him in eight years, and he had been spending that entire eight-year period as a recipient of daily torture by the Vietcong.

When the war ended, my father was granted priority as the 14th POW taken during the war to be on one of the very first planes headed back to the U.S. They gave him a choice of seven different hospitals that he could head off to first to get evaluated, and he chose the hospital in Montgomery, Alabama, because that was the closest to Tampa. The Air Force brought the entire family up to Montgomery and provided us with rooms in a hotel by the base.

In the eight years since my father had left, I'd gone through nearly a full decade of different developmental phases, including growing straight through and out of my teenage years, being a member of a street gang, being a draft-dodger, enrolling in college, becoming a powerlifter, and then eventually starting a career as a full-fledged professional wrestler. I was already thinking that I'd developed into an authentic man at this point, especially because I'd been told I was the man of the family at age 13. Now the man I thought I had been replacing in my household was coming home to reclaim his rightful place.

Eddie Graham gave me the time off I needed so that I could be present to greet my returning father upon his arrival in Montgomery. I was standing there in the hotel room, and a military guy came in and explained to us how he wanted everything to go.

"This is how this is going to happen," he began. "We're going to put just the wives in a car and take them out to the runway. When your husbands get off the plane, they're going to say a couple words to the press, then get in the car and come straight back here to the hotel."

I was a little too assertive by that point to not voice my disagreement.

"That *ain't* the way it's gonna work here," I interrupted.

"What do you mean?" said the colonel, clearly surprised by my challenge to his authority.

"*I'm* gonna be in the staff car," I told him.

"No, no, no!" said the colonel. "Only the wives will be in there; we aren't going to have any family coming with us."

"Oh yeah?" I said. "Well here's the deal: I was 13 when I last saw my dad and I was standing on that runway. I'm 21 and I'm gonna be standing on that runway when he gets off that plane. Whether I'm in that staff car, or if I have to walk to the end of that runway, I'll walk over there. I *guarantee* you I'll be on that runway when he gets off that plane. I'm gonna be one of the first people he sees."

The colonel and I went back and forth, and he clearly thought I would bow down to his authority, but I'd grown up with an officer as a father, so I wasn't intimidated by any of that.

"I'm not in the military, so you're not givin' me orders," I told him.

The colonel finally relented.

"Okay, so *here's* what we'll do," he started over. "You get in the front seat. We'll drive out there. When your dad gets off the plane, you get out, open his door, he'll come over to you, you'll hug, shake hands or whatever you want to do, and then let him get in the car and then we're gone."

"Gotcha," I replied.

When we got out there, it was in the dead of night, at 12:30 a.m. Dad's plane landed, and I had several thoughts looming in the back of my mind: What do I even say to my dad? Look how much my life has changed and who I am now. Dad wanted me to be a fighter pilot like him; a pro wrestler is a *far cry* from a fighter pilot.

The last time I'd seen my dad was when I was 13 years old standing on the runway at the airport in Tampa and watching him fly off to Vietnam. Now I was a 21-year-old,

240-pound professional wrestler, and I was standing in about the same place on a different runway awaiting his return.

Reunited with Dad after eight long years

I saw my dad get off the plane, and I shifted my gaze from my dad over to the colonel who had given me such strict instructions about how I was supposed to conduct myself. Then I looked back at my mom. Then I opened the passenger-side door and just took off in a dead sprint toward my dad. Some members of the press spotted me running from the car.

Meanwhile, my dad was staring into a spotlight being asked questions by the media.

"What are your thoughts about Vietnam?" a reporter asked my dad.

"All I can say is Old Glory is the most beautiful sight of all," replied Dad.

Dad barely got those words out of his mouth before I had him locked in a tight bearhug. I jerked him clean off of his feet, and I began running while carrying him, with tears streaming down my face like a baby. The emotion of the moment was more than I could handle. I couldn't even get a word out of my mouth.

"Son! I hope that's you!" laughed my dad.

He had no clue how big I'd gotten, and here I was running with him and carrying him down the runway. As soon as we reached the car, Dad climbed into the backseat to sit with my mom.

"*Now* my life can really begin," I thought to myself. "My dad is home, my mom is safe. Now it's time for me to move out and be the man I'm supposed to be."

Having my dad home after all that time was incredible, but it also attracted the attention of some lunatics. The phone rang one morning, and I answered it just like I would have answered any other phone call.

"Hello?" I said into the phone.

"You and your family will pay for the crimes your dad committed in Vietnam," threatened the voice over the phone. Then the caller hung up.

The implication was that my dad had committed some sort of war crimes while he was in Vietnam. In some circles, *anything* the Americans did in Vietnam was regarded as criminal activity to many anti-war activists. I had to repeat the statement that was said to me over the phone to the FBI, U.S. military officials, and plenty of other government agents over the course of the ensuing months. I'm sure atrocities were committed by American soldiers against the North Vietnamese people over the course of the conflict, but my father obviously wasn't involved in any of that.

Despite the fact that our lives were being threatened, I still had wrestling shows to get to. The FBI drilled me about things to watch out for, including people who might be following me.

"Don't turn around and stare at the people you suspect to be following you," they warned me. "If you pull into a gas station and someone pulls in that doesn't look like they're really there to get gas, you should probably get back in the car and keep going. We have no idea who these people are, what they're planning to do, or the lengths they'll go to in order to lash out at your family. You're one of the oldest sons of a POW, and you're an active professional wrestler. That makes you an *excellent* target for these people."

In theory, the FBI was following me for my protection, but it got to be annoying very quickly, and when I was with the Briscos, they thought having the FBI on our tail created a perfect opportunity to dick around with them.

The Briscos sped out of Yeehaw Junction all the way to Lake Wales at 120 miles per hour, and then they would stop and piss on the side of the road. It was hilarious, because the FBI's cars would actually match speed to keep up with us, and then stop at a respectable distance away from us while we relieved ourselves at the roadside. Then we'd go 50 miles per hour again for a while, and then Jack would pipe up and say, "Okay, take it up to 100 again!"

We were inside of a small building in Arcadia, and Gerald said, "Hey, Steve, take a look at this!"

Jerry directed my attention over to a car in the parking lot, and sure enough, there were two men in black suits standing there who stuck out like sore thumbs.

"They don't look like they belong in Arcadia to me!" Gerald chuckled.

It was fun in a way, but it was also something that was constantly in the back of my mind. The FBI would follow us until we stopped at the Sportatorium where we parked our cars. When we grabbed our bags and swapped cars, the FBI would resume tailing me all the way back to my apartment. I don't know if they sat in the parking lot of the apartment all night; I *never* went out to look.

Whenever we hit the road, the FBI was always there, so I was certain they had a copy of my booking sheet and knew exactly where I was scheduled to wrestle. I also didn't immediately notice when they stopped tailing me altogether. My guess is that they kept up the surveillance of me on the road for a total of two months.

"Hey, where's the FBI?" Jack finally asked.

"Beats me," I answered. "I think they're done followin' me."

"Shit! Does this mean *we* gotta protect you now?" asked Jack. "All we got is some bows and arrows!"

The humorous thing about this was that I was basically a jabroni who was in the middle of the card, trending toward the bottom. In the context of what we were doing, it was odd that a nobody like me had his own government-funded security team. It was a bit of an overkill. I never had any significant fears because the people didn't come right out and fully threaten my life, or vow to kidnap me.

That isn't to say that I was totally unknown, or that I wasn't becoming widely known to a lot of people. The regular Florida wrestling fans certainly began to recognize me, and that obviously came with increased attention, including from women. As a wrestler, you get more opportunities with ladies because you're perceived to be something special. Honestly, though, I just wasn't the kind of guy who wanted to go out of his way to get together with the ladies who attended wrestling shows.

I heard plenty of wild stuff from other guys in the dressing room, and a lot of those stories would just have you shaking your head and asking, "Really? You did *that*?!" It's not that I was naive, but I certainly wasn't as educated in those types of situations as a lot of other guys were.

To be honest, the girls who were showing up looking for me weren't exactly the best-looking ones to begin with; *that* group was usually lined up trying to get to Jack Brisco, Paul Jones, and the upper echelon of wrestlers. I might have been interested if the girls trying to talk to me were better looking, but when the girls winking at me weighed close to 300 pounds, there wasn't much temptation being thrown in my direction.

Also, I generally felt pretty sorry for these girls. They weren't exactly models. You got the sense that they didn't have many options on the dating market, and a lot of them were clearly desperate for attention from any place they could find it.

All things considered, even though I was losing almost every night, I thought wrestling was a dream job. It never felt like I was going to work. Instead, I was going out in front of an excited group of fans, gaining a lot of attention, having a fun match, and I was still getting paid to be in the thick of it all for some reason. That was the true allure of wrestling; I was being paid to have the time of my life.

To give me an opportunity to play in front of a different audience, Eddie sent me to Pensacola to work for Lee Fields and the Fields family in their Gulf Coast territory.

The first arena I went into for the Fields was in Crestview, Florida. When I walked in, I was greeted by the sight of a *bear* sitting on the floor of the dressing room with a chain around its neck.

"So what's with the bear?" I asked.

"The bear's workin' tonight," said one of the guys.

Nobody had told me *anything* about wrestling against bears.

"This job gets weirder every day," I said under my breath.

It was in Pensacola that I met Ricky Gibson. We were the same age, but he had been in the wrestling business since he was about 16. He was well-educated, and Lee put the two of us together as a team. That's when I first received an education on how to function in a tag match, and where I first got to experience a bit of visual success. Ricky and I won the tag titles in Pensacola, and defended them against guys like Ken Lucas and some other guys who were being rotated through the Southern wrestling territories.

Colonel Keirn standing between the Gulf Coast tag champs Steve Keirn and Ricky Gibson

The very first ribs in my career were very simple ones, and they were pulled on me by Ricky Gibson and Ken Lucas in the Mobile territory. They were extremely rudimentary, but I fell for them because I was so young and naive.

"Hey, do you feel that?" Ricky asked while I was driving.

"No. What's the problem?" I answered.

"You *don't* feel that?" he said.

"No! *What*?!" I said again.

"Just feel your dash right here," insisted Ricky.

As I went to feel the dash, Ricky brought his fist down and smashed my hand. It was so simple and stupid, but it technically counted as a passable rib.

Ken Lucas liked to pull a rib where he had young guys lie down on the floor after claiming he could hypnotize them.

"I can hypnotize *anyone* here!" Ken would boast.

Someone would always be dumb enough to fall for it.

"You can't hypnotize me!" they would say. "Show me!"

"Lay down on the floor!" Ken would say. "I'm gonna put my towel over your face, and I'm gonna walk around you. I'll bump you on the arm while I'm walking around you, and I'll talk you into a state of hypnosis. Then I'm gonna give you a command, and when I give the command I'm gonna rip the towel off you and see if you'll follow the command. If I've hypnotized you properly, you won't be able to follow the command I give you."

Ken would walk around the guy doing his best to sound like a hypnotist. Then at the right time, he would stand over the guy, pull his own tights down, and squat over the guy's face.

"One… two… three… sit up!" Ken would shout while ripping the towel away from his victim's face.

Every single person would immediately sit up to prove that they weren't hypnotized, and they would raise their face smack into the combination of Ken's balls and ass.

My first experiences in the wrestling business taught me that you need to accept being the butt of the joke on a few occasions if you're going to survive in the dressing room in a figurative sense. My next experience in a faraway land was about to teach me that sometimes quick thinking and divine intervention would be required if you wanted to survive leading a wrestler's lifestyle in a *literal* sense.

Eventually, Eddie assigned me with my first regular tag team partner in the form of Stan Hansen, a big Texan. The two of us were almost identical sizes at the time, and we were ranked *way* down the card as a tag team.

Hansen had just been cut from the Detroit Wheels of the World Football League and got into wrestling in Texas before he came to Florida. He arrived on the scene piloting a car that had no air conditioning, which meant that riding with him was a miserable experience. We had to ride with the windows down the entire way. If we drove from Tampa to Fort Lauderdale, I was worn out just from having the heat beating on me throughout the trip.

Tagging with Stan Hansen

As far as our team was concerned, we weren't very good at all. We were both rookies, so neither one of us was an effective leader at that point.

During one of our car rides back to my apartment in South Tampa, Hansen posed a question.

"Hey, you ever get color in a match?" asked Hansen.

"Yeah. This one guy cut me in Guatemala, but I never bladed on my own before," I answered.

"I ain't gotten color neither," said Stan. "Do you think we should practice just to try?"

"I don't see why not!" I said.

We stopped at a pharmacy and bought some Gillette razor blades, and then we drove straight to my apartment. Once we arrived, we sat there chopping up the razor blades just as we had watched the veterans do it countless times before in the dressing room. Then we went about deciding which blade-carrying tactic suited each of us the best. Stan taped his blade to his finger, and I put mine in my mouth.

Satisfied that we had accomplished all of the easy work, now we'd reached the critical point when it was time to draw our own blood.

"Okay… they say we're supposed to go to the bone for the business," I stated, repeating the phrase I'd heard that established the principle for proper blading.

Stan and I each stuck the blades in our own foreheads up to the tape, which resulted in a stream of blood spurting forth and trickling down our faces.

"Cool! We bladed!" I said.

"Hey, you got anything to wipe this off with?" asked Hansen.

I *didn't* have anything available to wipe it off with, but in my brief search for answers, it dawned on me that my apartment was situated very close to the pool of the complex.

"Let's just jump in the pool!" I suggested.

The two of us ran out through the door and bolted over to the pool of the complex wearing our wrestling tights. When we reached the pool, we ignored the other people from my complex who were enjoying their daily dips in the water and dove straight in, as two bleeding maniacs wearing wrestling gear.

As we surfaced and began treading water, we looked around at the people in the water and on the pool deck that were aghast at what they had just witnessed.

"Howdy, folks!" said Stan, as he reached his hand up to wipe away whatever blood remained on his face.

After that, we applied bandages to our foreheads before driving to that evening's show. The veterans in the dressing room all looked at us with great puzzlement. None of them could recall wrestling in a match with us where we would have been required to blade ourselves. Eddie finally approached us and asked, "So, when did *you guys* get color?"

"We did it at my apartment!" I answered proudly.

"You did it at your *apartment*?" Eddie answered.

"Yeah! We wanted to see how it was so we tried it out!" said Stan.

"Boy, you guys are really gettin' prepared, aren't you?!" laughed Eddie.

News of our blading practice session made its way around the locker room, and the older guys all laughed at the thought of us practicing the art of getting color before we'd even advanced past the point of being in the second match on the card. They took verbal jabs at Stan and I over it for a while. We didn't care, though. We were just two kids who were gung-ho about playing any role in the business.

Despite having Stan Hansen as a partner, I was still just the guy getting beaten on TV and at most of the house shows. I was wrestling guys old enough to be my grandpa, and we were doing Broadways every night. So it was usually one fall with a 15 or 20 minute time limit, or as long as the guy could handle without having a heart attack. I'd go out there, and the veterans would just take me to school. and I was led by those guys and they taught me what to do.

The heels always led the matches in those days. It was a rule of thumb in the regionalized days for that to happen unless you had a far more experienced babyface wrestling against a less experienced heel.

One guy led the entire match. Because we were confined to separate dressing rooms, we went out to the ring knowing the finishes to our matches, and how much time you were supposed to go.

As time progressed, I kind of lost touch with most of the people from my previous life in high school. Some guys came to see me who were close friends, but it was like coming home from college, moving off to your job, and no longer being connected with most of the people you'd once socialized with. Many of the guys I'd known would come to the matches every once in a while, but no one was coming there specifically to see *me* wrestle; they were there to see the stars. Also, since they knew I'd just recently broken away from them and had no experience, they knew I couldn't be that good, so they weren't exactly shocked to see me getting beaten convincingly.

One face that maintained its familiarity was that of my former schoolmate Terry Bollea. Even though I hadn't told him how to break into the wrestling business, he was *still* coming to the Sportatorium and planting himself in the same seat every Tuesday night.

Terry happened to be present one night when I was wrestling against "Superstar" Billy Graham, a bleach-blond powerhouse with a bodybuilder's physique and massive arms. There was no doubt in anyone's mind who would be winning the match, as I had yet to win a significant match in Florida, and Billy was a household name in several wrestling territories, and also a fake family member of Eddie Graham's.

Billy's reputation was built on the fact that he was a great promo guy with a fantastic body, but he wasn't the type of wrestler that most guys relished the idea of working with. His style was so loose that you couldn't really feel anything he did in the ring. It's hard to get your teeth into that as a worker when the guys you're working with have such a light touch that you can barely sense that they're around.

As soon as the match began, Billy raised his hands to indicate that he wanted us to lock hands and perform a test of strength. It was a common practice for wrestlers of Billy's size and musculature to do this so that they could get over just how powerful they were to the viewing audience. This was no surprise, and I obliged him by locking hands with him even though the results of the strength competition would never be in doubt. Graham's physique was so ripped and muscular that he looked like a million dollars, and I looked like 50 cents.

When we first locked up, I prepared myself for the sign that Billy was going to overpower me, and that I was to drop to my knees beneath the might of his hands. Undoubtedly, that's what *would* have happened if it had been a true test of strength between us. Instead, Billy *immediately* dropped to his knees and cried out like he was in agonizing pain.

I almost crapped my pants right then and there! I had no idea Billy was going to put me over as if I possessed herculean strength. Meanwhile, the authentic muscle man Terry Bollea was sitting just a few feet away from us, and he folded his giant arms in front of his chest. Along with some of my other friends in the audience, I could see him shaking his head as if to say, "What the hell?! This is *bullshit*! There's no way *Steve* is stronger than Billy Graham!"

"Get up! Get up! Don't do that!" I pleaded with Billy

I tried to cover up my pleas as best I could, but there was no way for me to hide my mouth.

Billy laughed at me a bit and then worked out of it. Everyone watching knew that wrestling couldn't possibly have been legitimate competition when he did that. That moment didn't do *me* any favors either. I was already at a point in time when many of my past friends would approach me around town, and they would eventually end up asking me, "That wrestling is all fake, right?"

"We can wrestle right now and you'll find out *real fast* if it's fake," was my usual response.

I'd been programmed and brainwashed to protect the business, and friend or no friend, parent or no parent, anyone who had anything to say about wrestling not being real, I'd been taught that it was my obligation to defend it.

If you came through wrestling in the state of Florida, that was the typical route you went through, and you got whooped by your trainers. Eddie's theory was that people were going to come up to you all the time and say, "Wrestling is fake!" and you needed to be prepared to say, "If it's all fake, then let's go outside and discuss it and then see who's still able to walk back in through the door!" He always wanted us to have the confidence to physically stand up for the wrestling business and protect it with our fists if necessary.

One day during a show, I was approached by Florida's booker Louie Tillet, a short, fat, French-Canadian guy.

"What do you think about moving to Georgia?" asked Louie.

"Why?" I replied.

"Because you *are*," he answered. "We're gonna finish you up in two weeks. We'll hurt you or do something to you so that you leave and disappear from our television show, and then you'll move to Atlanta and start working for Jim Barnett."

Once the promoters started grooming young talent that they thought would go on to benefit their territories for a long time, they started sending them to tour other territories and gain experience – often for periods of several years – and then they would bring you back in as a well-traveled wrestler who had upgraded your skills since the last time the local fans laid eyes on you.

Promoters generally wouldn't help you acquire a position somewhere if they didn't think someone could use you, or they didn't foresee future value in you. Still, Eddie was very intelligent and slick about the way he handled these transitions. Unless Eddie had some sort of a problem with a wrestler, he wouldn't be the one who would deliver any news to a talent that might cause an argument. That's why Louie was the person who was tasked with sending me my orders to ship out.

That was typical of how things worked. It wasn't something most guys resented. When I relocated to Georgia in May of 1974, I simply loaded up the U-Haul and hit the road. There weren't many things I needed to bring to Atlanta with me. The closest things to furniture that had been inside of my apartment had been a few bean-bag couches, and some concrete blocks that I had fashioned into shelves by putting boards on top of them. I'd only needed an apartment as a place to temporarily crash in between drives to wrestling towns, so I hadn't required a plush living environment.

My first stop in Georgia was at the home of my uncle Don Hull and his wife Betty. Uncle Don was an L-1011 pilot with Delta, and I stayed at his place for my first few nights in Georgia until I could get my bearings. When you first went into a territory, you never fully understood how it operated until you went on the road, and then you could figure out what form of permanent accommodations would be best suited to you.

In this case, I had to go straight to the NWA office in Downtown Atlanta to check in, and also to provide them with all of my contact information. From there, I was given a booking sheet to let me know where I was supposed to be for the next seven days. My first few nights, I rode to the show by myself, but once I got into the dressing rooms, I saw guys that I knew either from Florida or Pensacola.

At the early shows, I also saw guys I knew who were working on the other side as heels, like Bob Orton Jr., or other guys I'd wrestled against in the past. I familiarized myself with the guys and then tried to get everyone's contact information to ensure that I could get in touch with them.

I managed to link up with Ricky Gibson right away because we knew each other well, had ridden together before, and had also briefly been the tag team champions in Pensacola. He was a great worker and I learned a lot simply by having him as a tag team partner and watching him up close every night. Ricky quickly showed me where to get an apartment in Atlanta, and told me everything I needed to know about the towns we would be appearing in.

The dressing room was an important place for an incoming young wrestler to be interactive and attentive. You had to learn to fit in. Not every place was the same, so it might take you a couple nights to figure it out. First you needed to learn who you needed to make look good when you wrestled them. Then you needed to learn who the old timers were that you could ride with that could educate you with stories.

"Bullet" Bob Armstrong was a great example of an old-timer you wanted to ride with, and so was "Mr. Wrestling #2" Johnny Walker, except he would wear his mask for the entire road trip. Even when we went into a store together, he'd wear the mask, and I'd be thinking, "Really? You think someone is going to see the two of us together and magically deduce that you're Mr. Wrestling #2 if you're not wearing your mask?"

The name of the game was adaptation, because adapting was what you had to learn to do. Every time you switched territories, you had to become a chameleon and learn to fit in with the people and the expectations. They didn't want people coming in trying to be the round pegs and inserting themselves into square holes. If you didn't adapt to the territory you were in, your best option was to get the U-Haul packed and keep on moving.

One thing that helped me to adapt quickly was that Florida, Georgia, and the Carolinas were all hotbeds for NWA wrestling, and they all had the same basic style. They were big on wrestling, and low on theatrics and entertainment, but then they would occasionally throw a curveball at you with a charismatic or comedic guy like Dusty Rhodes or Buggsy McGraw just to shake things up sometimes. The whole card was usually filled with pretty serious wrestling, and almost everybody could work.

I very rarely saw matches or had matches of my own that I walked away from saying, "Oh, man; that *sucked*!" The only thing you could really complain about would be some guys' characters, and whether or not you thought they were too over-the-top. Aside from that, you knew you were getting in the ring with talented guys that you could trust not to hurt you.

The primary objective, even ahead of entertaining the people, was never injuring someone. Those were black marks on your resume that would *never* get erased. If someone knew you hurt someone with your carelessness, folks would be less likely to trust you with their bodies, and when that happened, it would eventually hurt your match quality.

Jim Barnett was running the Georgia territory while I was there. He seemed to kind of like me, but that was purely owed to the fact that Barnett liked *all* of the young guys.

People had explained to me that Barnett was a homosexual before I got there; it was no secret. Everyone talked about everything, and Barnett's penchant for young, male wrestlers was a frequent topic of conversation.

Some guys had to be very smooth in the way they worked around Barnett's sexual preferences. I was in a locker room full of young guys, which included Ted Dibiase, Bob Orton Jr., Tommy Rich and others. It was like a smorgasbord of young talent that were trying to climb the professional wrestling ladder.

Catching Barnett's eye wasn't the only reason you might get booked to wrestle in Georgia. A lot of guys in the wrestling business owed big favors to one another, so if one promoter called another and told them to take care of somebody by getting them booked, giving them a push, or even giving them a championship run, that may have been a favor being repaid.

The opposite could also be true: One promoter might call another and tell them that the guy they just acquired needs to be put back in his place.

"He's got it in his head that he's worth something, but he's not going to be worth anything if *you* don't make him worth something," they might say. "Just keep him at a medium level."

Unbeknownst to me, I was about to become all too familiar with the sleazy side of the wrestling business, while also receiving a glimpse into just how far some young wrestlers had been pressured to go in the pursuit of fame.

FIVE

Someone who had worked as a main-eventer in front of sellout audiences throughout Florida and drawn money could easily find himself starting all over again from the bottom in Georgia and the Carolinas, and having to work his way back up the ladder.

Just like in Florida, our schedule required us to work Monday through Sunday, with TV tapings held in Atlanta at 9:00 a.m. on Saturday morning. Then we did a second afternoon TV show, which was a live event for promoter Fred Ward in Columbus, Georgia. That same night, we'd come back through to Atlanta and either wrestle in Carrollton or Griffin.

In total, Saturday was a three-shot day where you were traveling and wrestling three different times in three different towns. This was at the conclusion of a week in which you were usually working nine times in front of a crowd.

Ricky Gibson took me under his wing outside of the ring as well as inside of it. He introduced me to a guy in Atlanta named Lil Al, who was well known for taking wrestlers' pictures. It was at Lil Al's studio that I took my first promotional photos as a professional wrestler.

"Pose," Al ordered with his camera at the ready as we stood in his studio.

Under pressure, I couldn't think of any poses to do, so I just did little lame things like smiling and holding up my fists.

"Turn around; face me," Al instructed me.

I arranged my body in exactly the way Al commanded me, but the photos were pretty horrible. I wouldn't have made a *dime* trying to sell any of them to fans.

Ricky helped me cap off my first successful week of touring through Georgia by taking me out on the town. We went to one of the local bars that was accustomed to having wrestlers milling about, and then we found a vacant pool table and started shooting pool.

"Let's get some tequila!" suggested Ricky.

Indeed, we rounded up some tequila shots and brought them back over to the pool table.

"Hang on! We gotta do this the *right* way!" said Ricky.

I simply stood aside and followed the leader. I watched as Ricky took three shots of tequila, strategically arranged them on the pool table, and then placed a shot of 151 rum behind the tequila shots. Ricky then added a mug of beer behind the shot of rum before finally igniting the shot of rum with a lighter.

One of my original pro wrestling promotional photos

"Okay, you do the three shots of tequila, blow out the fire, drink the 151 rum and chase it with the beer," Ricky instructed.

I wasn't a big drinker, but I was determined to be a chameleon and fit in with what the veterans were doing. Whatever the situation called for, I needed to change my colors to match.

I dutifully pounded down all of the alcohol as Ricky had directed me, and then we returned to our games of pool, which we played with a level of coordination that was now severely hampered by alcohol.

"Let's line 'em up again!" yelled Ricky.

"*Really?*" I said.

We repeated the process of the shots and the beer, and then resumed our pattern of pool playing and alcohol binging. I don't know how many cycles of that we drank our way through, but it was at least one too many for me. To say I was seriously feeling the effects of that alcohol before too long would be a gross understatement, and I decided that I needed to take a seat somewhere before I passed out.

"I need to find a place to lie down," I told Ricky.

"Come on outside to the car," he said.

Ricky had an early '70s Thunderbird, which was a monstrous two-door car. It also came with a seat that you needed to flip up and pull forward so that you could create ample space to sit in its back seat.

Ricky helped me climb into the rear of his Thunderbird, assisted me with getting situated, and then said, "See you later. I'm going back to the bar."

Abandoned in the backseat of a car with the Georgia humidity and the windows rolled all the way up, the inevitable happened. I puked *all over* the back seat of Ricky's Thunderbird.

The next day, which was a Saturday, we had our 9:00 a.m. television taping in Atlanta. I was so sick that I was struggling just to pull my wrestling boots onto my feet, and I was thinking that I was going to vomit some more if I made just one errant move. Meanwhile, Ricky was strutting around like he was in perfect working condition.

"Man… *how* can you do that?!" I huffed. "You drank as much as I did!"

"Nope. Not even close!," laughed Ricky. "*My* three tequila shots were *water*!"

So every time we were going through our drinking routine, Ricky and I were both having a shot of 151 rum and a beer, but I was the only one who was drinking three additional shots of tequila during each cycle. For every two drinks Ricky was consuming, I had been downing *five*.

The irony is that while Ricky might have accomplished what he'd sought out to do by ribbing me, he'd *still* been the one who had to clean my vomit out of his Thunderbird's interior.

During that ill-fated TV taping, I wrestled Jody Hamilton in his Masked Assassin persona.

"Jody, I'm *really* hungover," I told him.

"Oh yeah? How did *that* happen?" Jody smirked.

I informed Jody of everything Ricky Gibson had done to me, and Jody just laughed. He was a kind man and an all-around good guy, but he was also a badass, and I was hoping that he would take some sort of pity on me.

"I don't know what you were planning to do out there, but I *really* don't want to throw up during the match," I continued. "I'm pretty weak right now."

"Hey, no problem, kid!" said Jody.

I thought we had an understanding that we would take things slowly, but when we got out there, Jody immediately said, "Grab a headlock!"

Once I secured the headlock on him, Jody ordered, "Now take me down!"

I got Jody over from the headlock, assuming that his plan was to slowly waste time until we executed a quick finish the match. Instead, Jody immediately hooked me and rolled me onto my back. I had to kick my feet to keep myself from getting pinned. Once I was sitting upright, Jody immediately rolled me onto my back again, and forced me to kick my feet out once more to avoid a pin.

It was like Jody was shaking up a martini, and my unsettled stomach was the shaker. He was clearly doing this intentionally, and he knew this simple maneuver was all it would take to really jostle my innards. He did it three times in rapid succession.

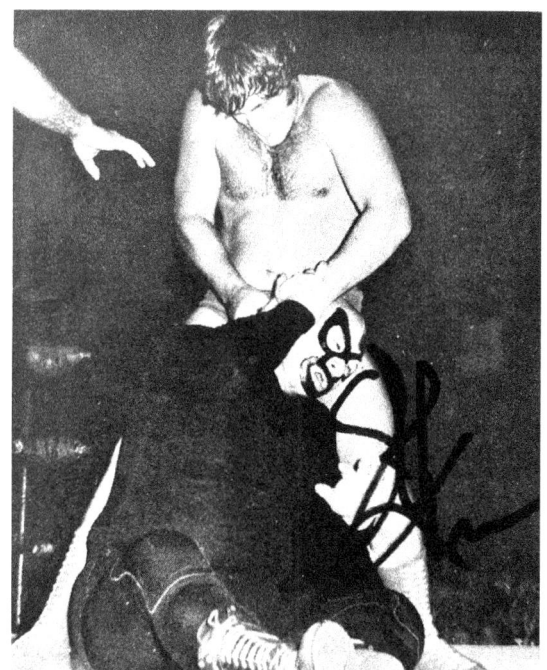

Clashing with "The Masked Assassin" Jody Hamilton

I looked at the top of Jody's mask and said, "Jody… if you do that *one* more time, I'm gonna throw up!"

I could feel Jody's entire body writhing with laughter. He had been waiting for me to beg him not to do it again.

One of the highlights of the Georgia territory, aside from the short trips and long work weeks, was the introduction I received to CB radios. We were driving every night, so any advantage we could gain on beating traffic and not getting ticketed by the police, we took it. All of the guys installed CB radios in their cars for that purpose, and of course I had to have one of my own.

We would all pass the time in the cars talking to each other on the CB radios, and when we went home at night, we would let each other know about road conditions and where the patrolmen were hiding. We had all the lingo from CB exchanges worked out, and we developed our vocabularies by also talking to the truck drivers. It was as if all of the wrestlers had been accepted into the larger CB radio brotherhood even though we only owned them to figure out the most opportune times to break the traffic laws.

I got to be buddies with Bob Orton Jr. even though we had separate dressing rooms. We had similar interests, right down to having the same taste in dogs; we both owned Weimaraners. I talked to him on the CB radio quite a bit, and the funniest part about his communication was that he stuttered quite a lot.

During one round of travel, Orton attempted to explain to me that there was a highway patrolman up ahead with a radar gun. He tried to tell me the mileage marker where the cop was stationed, which was 222. But Orton's efforts to get the words out resulted in the funniest thing I'd ever heard on a CB radio.

"Watch out at mile marker ta-ta-ta-ta-two, ta-ta-ta-ta-ta-two…" stammered Orton.

"*What?!*" I said, laughing hysterically.

"I said marker ta-ta-ta-ta-ta-two…" Orton tried again.

Before Orton was ever able to get the whole thing out, I was already flying by the mileage marker myself and getting radared by the patrolman, who promptly hit his lights and was pulling up behind me. Orton was still trying to warn me as I was moving off to the side of the road with the officer behind me.

"Mile marker ta-ta-ta-ta-two, ta-ta-ta-ta…"

"Yeah, Bobby," I said as the officer pulled me over. "Mile marker two-two-two. I got it. *Thanks.*"

During another memorable road trip, Ricky Gibson and I were driving to the third of our Saturday shots after wrestling in Atlanta during the morning and then again in

Columbus in the afternoon. Now we were headed to Carrollton along one of the many two-lane roads Georgia had in those days.

"Hey, man, I'm gettin' tired," said Ricky. "Do you mind takin' the wheel for a while?"

"Yeah, no problem," I said.

The two of us made the switch, and I assumed control of the car. Before long, we reached the top of a long hill and began to descend into a valley. I could see a car coming toward us, and the driver was flashing his headlights. I looked over at Ricky to see if he was noticing this as well, but he was sound asleep in the passenger seat while I was steadily rolling us down the hill at about 80 miles an hour in a Thunderbird that was built like a tank.

"This guy must think I have my brights on," I thought to myself.

I flashed my high beams right back at the driver, but he continued to shine his brights at us. We continued to exchange the flashing of our brights right up until we passed one another. Well, when I ascended and reached the top of the next hill, I discovered what the guy had been trying to warn me about the whole time; there was a *monstrous* deer standing dead in the center of the road. I veered to the right, which was unfortunate because that was the direction the deer had attempted to flee in. I absolutely *drilled* the deer head on, and it was at this very instant that Ricky awoke from his sleep to see a deer's butt on the hood of his Thunderbird.

"What the hell did you do that for?!" screamed Ricky.

"Did what?!" I answered back.

"You ran off the road to hit a deer!" he accused me.

"No I didn't! I was trying to *miss* it!" I said.

Ricky kept cursing me out about the deer as we stopped the car, climbed out to assess the damage, and also took a look at the corpse of the deer that was now lying in a ditch. As we were surveying the scene, a car pulled up behind us. It was the driver who had tried to warn us about the deer in the first place.

"You boys hit that deer?" he asked us.

"Sure did," I told him.

"That's what I was tryin' to warn you 'bout," he said, shaking his head. "Welp… you guys want him?"

I looked over at Ricky, who was a bit of a con man and probably thought he might be able to make some money by selling the deer to somebody at the matches that evening.

"*Yeah*, we want him!" answered Ricky.

"All right. Then take my knife," said the stranger. "You have to cut his scent bags off of his knees, and then cut his throat so that he bleeds out."

The old guy escorted us down into the ditch with a flashlight, and we cut the scent bags off the deer and cut its throat, and then we picked it up and moved our wrestling bags from the trunk into the back seat and dumped the deer carcass in the trunk. Afterwards, we continued with our drive to our small spot show in Carrollton.

"Damn deer bled all over my trunk," complained Ricky. "Let's set it out in the parkin' lot and see if one of these marks wants to buy it."

"Who wants to buy a deer that got hit by a car?" I asked him.

"I'll bet we can find somebody in there who wants it," said Ricky. "I'm sure there are folks from 'round here who would pay decent money for a deer. All we have to do is go in and ask people if they want to buy it."

We dropped the dead deer in the parking lot off to the side of the car, and then we went into the building. While the show was in progress, Ricky was wandering through the crowd of people asking, "Any of y'all want to buy a deer?"

As this was going on, the guy who was parking cars out in the parking lot walked into the building and yelled out, "Hey, who killed that deer in the parking lot?!"

"We did!" Ricky replied.

"I'm a game warden by trade," the man said. "I just park cars here on the side. You guys gotta get that deer outta here! I'm not supposed to see a dead deer out in a parking lot like that!"

After going through all that difficulty, Ricky wound up having to give the deer away for free to some guy in the crowd. He'd gotten the trunk of his car soaked in deer blood and received nothing for his efforts.

After Ricky had been traveling with me for a while, I started riding with some other people. That included Ronnie, Jimmy, and Terry Garvin, who all lived in an apartment complex close to where I was staying in South Atlanta. I did jobs in the ring for the Garvins at shows all the time. I was also working with guys who were pretty much on my same level, like Bob Orton Jr., Steve Olsonoski, and Dennis Stamp, who came out of Minnesota.

Ronnie Garvin liked to fly small planes, and I would always agree to come along whenever he asked me if I wanted to fly with him because driving was so tedious. The most attractive flying option was whenever he offered to fly me to Savannah, which was the longest trip in the territory at the time. Ronnie's only shortcoming as a pilot was that he didn't have instrument ratings; he could only fly as long as the skies were clear. When we got down around Waycross, Georgia, Ronnie decided he was going to fly, and he took me, Ricky Gibson, and midget wrestler Cowboy Lang along for the ride.

Early in the trip, Ronnie decided to mess with Lang.

"Oh, no! We're gonna *crash!*" said Ronnie, as he pushed the controls forward and caused the plane to dive.

"*Ahhh!* We're gonna *die!*" screamed Lang.

Ronnie immediately pulled the handles back to level off the plane, and burst into laughter.

"Gotcha!" he said.

"That shit isn't funny!" the enraged and tiny Lang told Ronnie.

Justifiably rattled, the chain-smoking midget wrestler lit up a cigarette.

As we were flying down, conditions grew ever cloudier, and Ronnie began to radio back and forth with the guy in the traffic control tower.

"I don't have instrument ratings," Ronnie told him.

"That's fine. Just land the plane in Cordele or Waycross," the traffic controller told Ronnie.

"Once we land we can just rent a car from the airport and drive to Savannah," Ronnie told us. "It'll be fine."

Cowboy Lang was now totally freaking out now that we couldn't land, and he began to burn through cigarettes one right after the other. Aware that his diminutive passenger was scared, Ronnie started exaggerating the movements of the plane as he dove in and out of clouds trying to find a clear spot.

Meanwhile, I was trying to play it cool and act like I was totally calm the whole time, but inside I was probably just as scared as Lang was.

Ultimately, Ronnie decided landing in Waycross would be our safest option, so he radioed the tower and told them where he would be putting the plane down. He got all the necessary clearances, and set his course. Everyone in the back of the cabin was sweating bullets, but Ronnie successfully landed the plane. We all relaxed as Ronnie taxied the plane in. That's when Ronnie looked at the aircraft hangar and a sudden realization came over his face.

"Oh shit!" said Ronnie.

"What?" I asked. "What's the problem?"

"I just landed at the *wrong* airport!" said Ronnie. "They're going to think we crashed because I didn't land where I said I was going to land!"

"Well get back on the damn radio and tell them you made a mistake!" I urged him.

"I don't want to do that!" said Ronnie. "I don't want to get in trouble!"

"But they're gonna send out emergency vehicles to look for us!" I continued.

Finally Ronnie hopped back on the radio.

"I just landed. I thought I was on the approach for Waycross, but I landed in Cordele," said Garvin.

It all got worked out. We rented a car and made it to the show in Savannah, but we couldn't fly out that night because the weather was so lousy. Instead, the four of us rented a hotel room, and after everything that had transpired between them, Ronnie and Lang were forced to share a bed together.

"You know, I've never slept with a midget before," joked Ronnie.

"Oh yeah?" answered a pissed-off Lang. "Well I've never slept with an insane Canadian lunatic before either, you *asshole*!"

The foremost problem that came from riding to and from the shows with the Garvins had nothing to do with aviation emergencies. Instead, it involved withstanding the advances of Terry Garvin, who was a well known homosexual. Terry never bothered me on the way to the towns. In fact, he rarely even spoke to me before a show. However, on the way back from the towns, he always made it a point to sit in the back seat with me and make sexual advances toward me.

"Come on, man! Just let me *see* it!" he would say as he was propositioning me. "Let's pull over and pee. I just wanna watch you pee!"

"Stop, man!" I'd answer. "What are you doin'? Get away from me! There ain't no way!"

"It's no big deal, man!" said Terry. "There's nothin' wrong with being a little gay."

"Hey, Jimmy... Ronnie... Can you please get this guy off of me?!" I'd request.

I suppose Terry thought he was ribbing me, but I was so homophobic at the time that I didn't find it funny at all. I never became violent with Terry in response to his advances, but there were times when I got out of the car fuming, and wishing that I'd punched him in the face.

On subsequent occasions, Jimmy Garvin would come up to me and say, "Don't worry about Terry. He's not gonna mess with you."

I'd take Jimmy's word for it, but as soon as we were in the car after the show, Terry would be sliding in right next to me saying, "Come on! Just let me touch it! Just let me *touch* it! I'm not gonna *do* anything to it. Just pull it out and let me touch it!"

With Jim Barnett being the owner of the territory, and with everybody knowing his sexual orientation, I didn't exactly see him as someone I could confide in to crack down on Terry and make him stop. On top of that, if I ever reacted violently toward Terry in response to his unwanted solicitations, I couldn't expect Barnett to be sympathetic toward me in that situation. If anything, I would have been likely to lose my job.

It was all overwhelming for me, and it got worse. Terry and I had both been on a flight with Ronnie, and as we were standing out on the runway afterwards, Terry walked up to me with an indecent proposal.

"You know, kid… your career could skyrocket," he said. "You could be taken care of for the rest of your wrestling life. You'd be put over, and they'd make you a champion like *that*! All you've got to do is let somebody *do* something to you."

Even though Terry had propositioned me before, I got the sense that he was fishing on behalf of Jim Barnett without openly mentioning his name.

"How many of these guys do you think have gotten to where they've gotten on their own?" he continued.

From there, Terry mentioned specific names of guys, with the implication being that they had either given or received homosexual favors in exchange for favorable booking in the Georgia territory. And on the one hand, he had a point. The guys he was mentioning had received pushes, but there was nothing truly special about them that should necessarily have singled them out and separated them from other people in the industry.

In all reality, *anybody* can be booked to look like a star. I'd seen guys that couldn't work at all who had come into Georgia and been booked right to the top because they had been made to look amazing.

"Listen to me carefully, kid," began Terry. He then began to lay out a very intricate scenario in which sex acts would be performed on me in exchange for favorable booking, but the acts would be performed in such a way that I wouldn't even know who had done them, and could even have pretended in my mind that it was a woman.

"There's *no* way!" I told him in response.

All I could think of in my mind was that if I let someone do that to me just one time in order for me to get ahead in the wrestling business, that was going to stick with me for my entire career, and probably for my entire *life*. I knew that was wrong, and I was already totally unwilling to suck up to people to get ahead, let alone let someone perform a homosexual act on me. There was no way I could justify it.

Later on, I was driving down the road with Ricky Gibson, and I was explaining to him how much Terry Garvin was bothering me with these propositions.

"You know, you should probably call his bluff," remarked Ricky.

"What do you mean, 'Call his bluff?'" I asked.

"Tell him you'll do it, but see how much they're willing to pay you for it!" said Ricky.

Ricky lived down the street from a Chrysler dealership, and a new Chrysler Cordoba had just been released. Ricardo Montalbán had done a commercial for it, and I was in love with its black-on-black look and "Corinthian leather." I drove to the dealership with Ricky, and they had a shiny new Cordoba sitting right on the showroom floor.

"I've *got* to have that car!" I said.

"You know what I'd do if I were you?" said Ricky. "The next time Terry or Barnett makes you an offer like that, tell him that you'll do it as long as they give you the keys and the title to that car!"

"Are you serious?" I asked him.

"Hell yeah!" said Ricky. "You should say, 'Okay, Barnett. If it means *that* much to you that you're willing to buy me that Chrysler Cordoba from right off the showroom floor, I'll accept your offer!'"

That's exactly what I did. Terry Garvin came to me just a few days later and asked me if I'd reconsidered the offer.

"I thought it over, Terry, and I've come up with a plan," I said. "There's a car sitting on the showroom floor, and I want that car. If I get the keys *and* the title, I'll do it!"

Terry looked at me for a second like I'd spontaneously sprouted another head, and then he went off on me.

"Who the *hell* do you think you are?!" he said. "You expect someone to mess around with you and *then* pay you for it with a brand new car?!"

Hilariously, Terry was so offended by this, like I had vastly overpriced myself. The funniest thing was that he actually quit bothering me as a result of it. Even though my response had essentially been a joke, the terms I'd extended to him for accepting the deal had been sufficient to turn him off to the idea.

About a month later, there was a big party at Ronnie Garvin's place, and Louie Tillet – the booker from the Florida territory – was present for it. In front of everyone, Louie Tillet looked at Terry Garvin and said, "Well, do you owe me $50 or not?"

"I owe you $50," said Terry, sounding defeated.

All of that propositioning by Terry Garvin had been the result of a $50 bet between Terry and Louie to see if he could get me to "turn gay." Thank God I hadn't accepted that deal; I would have compromised my entire career and my integrity over a $50 bet between two French-Canadians.

Even if none of that had ever happened, I still would have felt like I'd needed to be somewhat on guard when I was around Barnett. He was still the boss in Georgia no matter what, and I felt somewhat uneasy around every boss I ever had. You had to appeal to Barnett in some way because his opinions of what sells and draws money influenced whether or not you got to stay employed.

Barnett was going to tell his booker whether or not he wanted you pushed to the top of the card. It's like being a movie star; you're chosen on the basis of what some producer or some director thinks your potential is. That can be based on appearance, style, or anything else that might contribute to fans handing money over.

Barnett also had a thing called an "arena rat report." Every Friday night, when you worked in Georgia, Barnett would come into a meeting with the boys, and he'd say, "Hey, boys… who's in charge of the arena rat patrol?"

Well, they put me in charge of it one time, and the focus of the report had to do with how guys were interacting with the girls in the towns we were visiting.

Barnett's concept was that the more women came to the matches, the more men would follow them into the buildings. There was a connection there, but half the time you were making up the details of the report. It's not like I was writing down whether or not I saw Ted Dibiase with one girl or Steve Olsonoski with another. You just had to make up a story and make it entertaining for Barnett.

Despite not allowing Jim Barnett or Terry Garvin to perform sexual acts on me in exchange for a push, I was still earning enough money that I felt comfortable buying a black-on-black Cordoba for myself. I was making a little more money than I'd been making in Florida, and wrestling guys on TV like Hawaiian strongman Don Muraco, who they'd put me in matches with just to let him kill me.

Outside of Guatemala and Pensacola, I still hadn't won any major matches yet even though I'd been in the business for about three years. That didn't matter to me, though. I was still perfectly content with the idea of getting beaten every night. I had no motivation to get into the main events, and I still didn't want that sort of pressure hanging over me. I knew I still had a lot to learn before I ever dreamed of getting close to sniffing the main event of a show, let alone actually headlining one.

Jerry Brisco had arrived in Georgia, so of course I invited him to ride with Ricky Gibson and I. We had completed our usual round of a TV taping followed by a show in Columbus, and we were now headed straight to Griffin. When we were within hailing distance of Griffin, Ricky reached into his pants pocket, pulled out a plastic bag, and said, "Hey, let's smoke some pot!"

Posing with Gerald Brisco

"What?!" I asked from behind the steering wheel. "Let's smoke some pot," repeated Ricky.

"No, I heard you the first time," I said. "I can't do that; I'm driving, and I *just* got this car."

"Yeah, I'd been meaning to ask you about that," said Ricky.

"Ask me about *what?*" I answered.

"Your new car," said Ricky. "Why don't you let *me* drive it? After all, you wrecked my Thunderbird. The least you could do is let me drive your new car."

With that sort of suspicious phrasing, I *really* didn't want to let Ricky drive my car, but I also felt guilty about hitting the deer with his Thunderbird, so I caved to the pressure and let Ricky get behind the wheel.

Once he was in the driver's seat, Ricky prepared a joint, and we all took a couple hits off of it. Now we were very close to Griffin, and out of nowhere we got lit up by a local Sheriff's deputy.

"Oh shit!" said Ricky. "Toss that out the window!"

I tossed the lit marijuana joint out of the passenger-side window. Ricky pulled the car over, and then he turned and looked at me with a ghostly shade of white in his face.

"I don't have a driver's license!" he said. "Give me your driver's license!"

I looked at him like he was crazy.

"I *don't* have a license; *give* me your license!" he repeated. "We're not gonna get in trouble!"

In those days, a Florida driver's license was just a piece of paper. It had no photos on it; it only had a general description of the driver, like your height, weight and where you were from. I pulled out my wallet, extracted my driver's license, and handed it over to Ricky.

The deputy came up to the car and said, "You guys were really speedin' back there. I'm gonna need to see your license."

Ricky handed my license over to the deputy, who examined it and then asked him, "Are you Steve Keirn?"

"Yes," said Ricky.

"Well then you need to follow me into town," said the deputy. "We have somethin' to talk about. I can smell somethin' funny comin' from this car, so follow me on into town."

Now I was *totally* freaking out. I'd never been in any type of legal trouble before, at least not since I'd become a wrestler. This wasn't the sort of trouble I wanted to start with.

"Oh shit!" said Ricky. "What are we gonna do?!"

"We?! *You're* the one drivin' the car!" said Jerry. "You're the one that just *had* to smoke pot! This is all on *you*!"

We followed the cop all the way into town, parked the car in the lot, and then walked into the Sheriff's office.

"Y'all stay in here. I'm gonna search the car," the deputy told us.

We still had plenty of beer and wine in the car, along with whatever marijuana Ricky had brought into the car with him. I figured Ricky was going to be getting hit with a DUI, along with whatever additional charges the Sheriff's deputy wanted to pile on top of him. Then it dawned on me that the only one potentially being arrested was the person the deputy knew as Steve Keirn, who was *actually* Ricky Gibson.

"Is there any way we can call one of our friends on the CB radio to get them to come help us in case we have to bail him out?" I asked the deputy, since neither Jerry nor I had any money on us.

"That's fine, but I need to come with you," the deputy said.

Under the supervision of the deputy who remained stationed behind my car, Gerald and I climbed into the vehicle, and we pretended to contact our friends on the CB radio. In reality, we were doing our best to hide the alcohol bottles under the car seats to make them more difficult to find. Meanwhile, the deputy was running the license, the plate and everything else through his system. Finally he said, "Now we're gonna search the car."

Jerry and I now knew that there was no marijuana in the car, because whatever pot had been in there had either been smoked or tossed out the window, or it was physically on Ricky's body, and it wasn't much.

We walked back into the building and sat on a couch in the Sheriff's office while the car was being searched. Ricky was nervously hovering over the office desk, because he was sure he was about to be booked.

Finally, the deputy came in.

"Now we've got *another* problem," said the deputy.

He opened his hand and said, "I found *this* in the trunk."

In the deputy's hand was a glass tube designed to increase the potency of marijuana as it was being smoked.

"*That* wasn't in the trunk!" I protested.

It's not like we could prove that the deputy had planted evidence in the vehicle. The deputy arrested Ricky – under his temporary alias of "Steve Keirn" – and sent him off to jail. They even fingerprinted him and took his picture. Almost as an afterthought, one of the deputies walked over to Gerald and I and asked us what our names were.

"Jerry Brisco," said Jerry.

Then the deputy looked over at me and said, "And what's *your* name?"

"I'm *Ricky Gibson!*" I declared proudly.

I didn't know who else to be at that moment.

"Well, your buddy Steve Keirn is under arrest, and he's going to be spending the night in jail if he doesn't make bond," said the deputy.

The bond was $300, and the fine for the possession of marijuana was $1,500. Between us, we reasoned that the Sheriff's office needed a new bass fishing boat or something like that in their little redneck town, and so they planted the pipe in the trunk in order to have the grounds to fine us.

Once we bonded Ricky out of jail, there was no major fallout. Tom Renesto was the booker, and he knew it wasn't a big deal. He was confident that none of us were serious drug users, and Jim Barnett decided that he didn't care either once it became clear that the incident wouldn't be receiving coverage in any of the local newspapers.

In a lot of ways, I'd passed my first crucial test in staying true to myself and not compromising my morals as a young wrestler. Now, my career was about to receive a needed surge in the form of a major national award. The inscription on the plaque might have said one thing, but it could just as easily have been viewed as a reward for maintaining my integrity. Either way, I was about to enjoy my first true taste of success as a professional wrestler.

SIX

In Georgia, I felt like I was truly beginning to catch on and learn my craft. I was learning a lot from watching guys like "Mr. Wrestling #2" Johnny Walker. For a guy wearing a mask, he received incredible reactions from the crowd. He was agile and had cat-like movement, but he was also crisp with his moves. In the ring, I was also working with guys who were quite a bit better than me, and I was traveling with guys closer to my own age, as opposed to being in Florida and traveling with guys old enough to be my grandpa.

In the process of improving, I was also adding to my list of injuries. I've broken every finger on both hands during my career at one time or another. I actually broke both of my thumbs at the same time while reaching to grab a guy's foot while he was kicking. I just taped them up and would do whatever was necessary to go out to the ring, perform and get by.

One of the most painful afflictions I ever had was when I had a boil come up on my achilles tendon when I was in Atlanta, and I could barely walk.

Jim Barnett came up and said, "What's wrong with you, my boy?"

"I have a boil on my tendon. Every time I put my boot on it hurts really bad," I told him.

Barnett sent me to a doctor to get it treated and get some medicine, but the bottom line is that if I didn't work, I wouldn't have gotten paid. So as a wrestler, you will work no matter what, and if you have to take pain medication to get through it, you'll take it and suffer the consequences the next day. That's exactly what I did. I accepted what I was, and I accepted what the downsides were.

Gordon Solie was one of the other familiar faces I came across in Atlanta. He was the announcer for the Georgia Championship Wrestling program just like he was for the Florida show. Because he had that familiarity with both territories, Gordon knew my entire background, and all about how I had grown up.

I was having a casual discussion with Gordon one Saturday morning, when he suddenly said, "By the way, they're giving you the award for 1974 Rookie of the Year today."

"What?" I asked. "That doesn't make any sense!"

I'd already had a couple of practical jokes played on me, so I was at the point where I didn't buy anything that anyone told me when they first uttered it.

The 1974 Rookie of the Year plaque

"The wrestling magazines are giving you Rookie of the Year," repeated Gordon. "It's quite an honor. You're in Atlanta, which is important for the NWA, so this is good for you. We're giving you a plaque today on the show."

It all seemed crazy to me for a couple of key reasons. First of all, no one outside of Guatemala and Pensacola had ever seen me win a major match. Second, I had already been wrestling for the better part of three years, so how could I win an award reserved for rookies as a third-year professional wrestler?

"How can I be Rookie of the Year?" I asked Gordon. "I've never even won a serious match!"

"I've got a feeling you're going to win one *today*," winked Gordon.

He was right. The funniest thing about the whole ordeal was when my opponent asked me, "What do you do for a finish?"

"*What* finish?" I laughed. "My usual finish is to lie on my back while the ref counts to three!"

It was funny, because the people there all knew me as the guy who lost nearly all of his matches. Well, they put me up against a guy who lost even more than I did, so when I won, it wasn't all that surprising. After that, I went over to the announcer's desk. Gordon gave a big speech about my background and asked me a couple questions, and I dribbled my way through an interview that probably wasn't particularly memorable to anyone who watched it.

I was simply dumbstruck by the fact that I was actually getting to win an award and might possibly be receiving a push as a result of it. Other wrestlers and promoters were reading these magazines, along with the fans, and this award would provide me with something I could list on my resume as I was advancing from territory to territory.

Even if I had no other accomplishments that anyone could use to promote me to an audience, at least I could say I was professional wrestling's Rookie of the Year in 1974.

The award was unexpected, as so was the setting when we wrestled in a Georgia town called Milledgeville, which was known to be the home to the state's mental institution, the Central State Hospital. The bizarre thing about the show in Milledgeville is that we actually wrestled *inside* of the Central State Hospital itself. In that match, I faced the brother of legendary American Wrestling Association wrestler Nick Bockwinkel. The matches were held in the insane asylum's gymnasium.

I'd never been to a mental hospital before, and the gymnasium had been uniquely configured for the event. There was a ringside area with folding chairs surrounding the ring, and there were bleachers on two sides of the ring that were reserved for patients who were suffering from dementia and Alzheimer's disease. Several of them were picking things off of one another while the matches were in progress, almost like monkeys picking lice off of each other's backs. What ensued was one of the rare instances where it was more entertaining to sit and watch the audience than it was to watch the actual wrestling matches.

Above the bleachers sat a separate caged-in area at the very top of the elevated perimeter of the building that overlooked the wrestling ring. That seating section was reserved for the criminally insane. We all watched as the inmates requiring close supervision were escorted in by armed guards and then collectively chained to a humongous eyebolt in the floor. The inmates were howling and screaming throughout the event, even when there was no action taking place in the ring.

The ringside area was reserved for the hospital's guards, the family members of the guards, and some of the everyday citizens who lived in the neighboring Milledgeville area. I figured it took a lot of bravery for that group to place themselves in the middle of an audience that was primarily composed of people who ranged from mentally challenged all the way to criminally crazy.

I attempted to do my usual routine of going out and watching the matches and talking to the fans before the show, but this was an *atypical* environment, and I was in for some additional surprises during those conversations.

"I've been waiting a long time to get here," said one of the first people I spoke with. "My dad is the King of England, and he gave me a Corvette, and I drove it all the way here from the UK just to see these matches."

It didn't take any special effort on my part to deduce which group of fans *he* belonged to. However, the health problems weren't isolated to the audience on that particular evening. Bockwinkel's brother had a drug issue, and it eventually played a key role in our match. I took him down and began to work over his arm from a kneeling position, and as I was cranking away at his arm, I noticed that I wasn't getting any sort of resistance out of him.

"Hey!" I whispered.

I received no response. I thought to myself, "There's no way he just fell asleep on me."

Just as soon as that thought crossed my mind, I began to hear what sounded like snoring coming from his face.

Without trying to be too obvious, I leaned over and asked the referee, "Hey, is he awake?"

The referee poked his head in and took a look.

"I think he passed out!" the ref said.

I almost panicked, because I didn't know what to do with an opponent who was totally unconscious, let alone the *heel* who was supposed to have been calling the entire match for us.

"What do I do?" I whispered to the referee.

"Shake him a little bit!" the ref advised.

I started tugging on his arm, and I still received no response. After waiting a few more seconds, I simply rolled him over and covered him for three. Trying to hide my disappointment, despite the fact that I had easily won the match and should have been thrilled, I got my arm raised by the referee and then walked straight back to the dressing room. The referee was eventually able to wake him up and help him out of the ring.

This was another one of those situations that left me wondering what kind of business I'd opted to get into, and also left me a little bit nervous as to what I was going to encounter next. It was simultaneously exciting, and more than a little bit scary, because *anything* could happen in this business.

Speaking of rare occurrences in the wrestling business, that period in Atlanta was the lone time I was asked to come down to a building and "stretch marks" – or beat up mouthy guys who wanted to break into the wrestling business. Harley was booking at the time, and he requested that Bob Orton Jr., Ricky Gibson and myself head down to the building where we filmed our show.

"I want you to do this just like you do it in Florida," explained Harley once I got there. "These smartasses want to be wrestlers. I want you to really hurt 'em *bad*."

I think Harley had gotten me confused with someone else. I wasn't a shooter *at all*, but was I going to tell Harley I couldn't do it? Absolutely *not*. That left me in a position where I was thinking I was really going to have to fight dirty and sucker punch whomever Harley put me in the ring with.

Orton Jr. got in the ring with the first guy, and he stretched him all around, crossfaced him, and rode the mark all over the ring like the fantastic wrestler that Bobby was. He smacked this guy up and down and made him regret ever speaking an unkind word about the wrestling business. When it was over with, the humbled mark left the ring and retreated to a seat in the bleachers to lick his wounds.

Now it was *my* turn. I was looking at the guy and thinking to myself, "What am I going to do? I can't wrestle!"

I may have learned shooting moves and hooks while I was learning to wrestle in Florida, but as the trainee, you were *usually* the one that the holds were being applied to. You were taught those holds primarily in case a mark ever jumped into the ring, because you would be responsible for inflicting horrific damage upon the mark.

It wouldn't be acceptable to simply remove the mark from the ring. If his head came through the ropes, your job was to ensnare him, drag him the rest of the way into the ring, and make an example out of them. The mark needed to be bleeding by the time he got out of the ring, or you would be in *deep* trouble with all of the boys in the back. You wanted to deter anyone who thought it might have been a smart idea to climb into the ring at any time, let alone while a wrestling match was in progress.

"Bobby didn't hurt his guy enough," Harley whispered to me. "I want you to *really* hurt your guy."

Meanwhile, I'm looking at my guy thinking, "Shit… I hope *he* doesn't hurt *me*!"

After devising a plan, I walked over to my guy and tried to put him at ease.

"Okay, relax," I said, as I approached with my palms raised. "Here's what we're going to do. Do you know how to lock up in the ring? Let's lock up. I'll push you back into the corner, and then we'll break. When we break, put your arms down, step out, and I'll step back."

The guy just followed me unquestioningly, totally oblivious to the fact that I was leading him straight to the slaughter. I knew *exactly* what I was planning to do with him.

I backed him into the ropes as we'd discussed, and then he lowered his arms and stepped forward. That's when I waistlocked him while simultaneously capturing his arms in my grasp, and suplexed him right onto his face with a belly-to-belly suplex. His legs did the scorpion movement where they flailed up and over his back when his face got planted in the mat.

He wasn't unconscious, but he *had* been knocked senseless. That's when I started to put the boots to him. My mind blanked on any wrestling moves or holds I could do to him at the time, so I just started kicking him. That was sufficient to hurt the guy, though, because he rolled out of the ring and quickly took off running. Harley got up from where he was sitting and began to chase the guy around the building. Realizing he was being pursued by the toughest man in wrestling, the mark made a beeline for the door, then burst through it and out onto the street with Harley hot on his tail.

The sports arena we were in was in the middle of Downtown Atlanta. It was right across the street from where the police department's vehicles were dropped off for maintenance. All of the police cars were over there, but that was no deterrent to Harley, who fearlessly chased this guy down the street. I was right behind them, wondering what was going to happen, and terrified about how much trouble we were about to land in.

Harley caught up to the guy and tackled him to the ground like he'd just chased down a running back on the gridiron. The guy's head struck a glancing blow against the curb as he hit the pavement, and he began to yell, "Oh no! Oh no!"

Harley took the guy's arm, reached beneath it from behind, jerked the guy's shoulder back, and very calmly *broke* the arm. I'd just reached them as this was happening, and there was a *sick* snapping noise. The guy screamed, and then being the renowned southpaw that he was, Harley took his left hand and drilled the guy in the chin to render him unconscious.

"Come on back to the building," Harley said coolly, as he stood up, dusted himself off, and left this guy lying unconscious on the street with a broken arm.

Whenever people spoke about Harley Race being a man's man, that was true, but I knew better than most people that Harley was capable of achieving a level of viciousness that few people could comprehend.

There's a legendary story about Harley that demonstrates how he would just as eagerly contend with opponents who weren't powerless to defend themselves against him. According to the legend, Harley and his wife were eating in a restaurant somewhere when two guys came in to rob the place. Once the robbery was in progress, one of the men watched the door while the other man moved quickly from person to person while holding a gun in front of their faces, and instructed each of them to hand over their watches, rings and wallets.

When the robber arrived at Harley's table, some words were exchanged, but Harley refused to hand anything over. Eventually, the guy glanced over at his buddy by the door, and that's when Harley charged the robber, pushed him into his accomplice, shoved both of them through the restaurant door, and then battered them *both* senseless.

I wasn't present to verify the veracity of this story, but when I heard it, I certainly believed it. Harley was one of the most respected guys amongst the wrestlers, and no one *ever* dared to challenge him.

Harley also liked to speed at well over 100 miles per hour whenever he drove from one town to the next, and he was usually behind the wheel of something like a Trans Am. Dick Slater told me the story about how they were driving back from Jacksonville, and the police started following them. Instead of pulling over, Harley opened up the throttle, got way ahead of them, pulled behind an overpass, turned back around, and watched as the cops flew by.

"I thought we were going to jail for sure!" Dickie told me later.

When it was time to rotate me out of Georgia and on to another NWA territory in February of 1975, Jim Barnett thought the best place for me to land would be in the Mid-Atlantic territory owned and operated by the Crocketts.

"We've got a kid here from Florida, and we'd like to send him up there to let him work for you," Barnett told them over the phone.

The Crocketts agreed, and I made the drive up to Charlotte and found an apartment. I located a place in the form of an apartment off of I-85 in Charlotte. Living there enabled me to easily hop on the freeway and get wherever I needed to go.

The trips in the Mid-Atlantic were a lot longer than in any of the other territories I'd been in, because they were regularly covering three states: North Carolina, South Carolina and Virginia. Paul Jones, Wahoo McDaniel, Blackjack Mulligan, Ole Anderson and Gene Anderson were all active names in the territory at the time.

When I started wrestling for Mid-Atlantic, I immediately started riding to events with Kevin Sullivan. He'd been around when I got my start in Florida, but he'd been Mike Graham's partner at the time, and Mike always rode with him instead of me.

I'd never spoken to Kevin much before, but I'd already decided in my mind that I didn't like him. I viewed him as the ultimate ass-kisser because of how much he would suck up to Mike whenever the three of us were around each other. He'd compliment Mike on everything from his wrestling ability to having the nicest, fastest boat in the water. It seemed pretty obvious he was using flattery to work himself into a position that would enable him to be the tag team partner of the boss, which was a pretty safe position for any wrestler to acquire.

As Eddie Graham's son, Mike wielded a lot of power. He was never going to get beaten up and destroyed on television week after week the way I had been early on in my career. Mike was working competitively with older guys and getting great experience while I was working in an underneath role and getting squashed.

In fact, simply by virtue of being Eddie Graham's son, Mike could bank on the fact that he could go to any territory and not have to worry about getting mistreated. Meanwhile, I had no family in the wrestling business; nobody owed me anything. I was Colonel Keirn's son, and that had nothing at all to do with wrestling.

When I started riding with Kevin Sullivan, I figured I had to be open and honest with him about my disdain for him just to clear the air. Our very first car trip was a long one, and I decided it was a good time to get my true feelings for him out in the open.

"Kevin, there's no use in hiding this," I began. "I always used to think you were a real *suckass* to Mike Graham."

"What?!" replied Kevin.

"You would kiss Mike's ass in the ring, out of the ring, in the boat, or wherever," I continued. "I couldn't *stand* it!"

Kevin looked over at me and just kind of smiled.

"You know something: You're right. I was," he chuckled. "But guess what: *Nobody* takes care of my family but me. So should I worry about you thinking I'm a suckass, or should I do what I have to do so that I can get as much out of this business as I can?"

It was hard to argue with Kevin's logic, and thanks to that conversation with him, he and I quickly became great friends. The two of us would spend time shooting frogs over on his pond at night and eating frog legs at his house. We would share stories about the guys we didn't like in different territories, and the result was that we both marked certain guys as being people we wanted to avoid working with or fraternizing with long before we ever met them.

Thanks to Kevin, I never looked at the wrestling business quite the same way ever again. That's not to say I became the type of guy who sucked up to the authority figures, but Kevin did convince me to try to keep my mouth shut and fit in without always feeling obligated to voice my displeasure over certain things.

It was a valuable lesson to learn at a crucial time. The Carolinas were a *very* clique-y territory. All the guys – including Wahoo McDaniel, Paul Jones, the Crocketts, and booker George Scott – would go down to the office on a certain day and drink coffee, and then they all drove out to play golf together. I didn't play golf, didn't want to play golf, couldn't stand golf, and had *no* interest in golf at all.

"What are we supposed to do here to blend in with the boys if we don't play golf? Everybody golfs here!" I complained to Kevin.

On top of everything else that annoyed me about the Carolinas, I didn't really like the Crocketts as people. I found Jim Crockett in particular to be extremely snotty towards me. Meanwhile, Wahoo was very brutal and straightforward with his criticism of everyone. He figured he should be in the main event every night. If he wasn't in the main event, and a show had sub-par attendance, he was the first one to pipe up and say, "Whoever's on top tonight can't draw worth shit! *I* should be on top!"

And heaven forbid that Wahoo was actually told that he needed to lose a wrestling match; he would throw a full-blown tantrum and start hurling chairs around the dressing room.

I thought that I would be able to get over in the Carolinas once I watched some of the other guys work. For instance, Johnny Weaver threw punches like a girl, and held his hand flat as it was coming at you. However, for the first few months I was in the Carolinas, I was working with Bunk Harris, who was an old, fat guy with a miserable disposition, and he was *horrible* to work with. I didn't want anything to do with him, and he was *awful* in the ring, which was made worse by the fact that he was constantly trying to give me advice.

"*This* is how you do it, kid," Harris would say. "I've been doing this all my life. Just listen to me; I've been doing this all my life!"

When you wrestled Bunk, he tried to make himself sound like a wise veteran who worked, but in actuality he had a very light touch. There was a group of guys when I started in the business, and one of the first things I noticed about them was their handshake. They'd shake your hand, and it felt like a dead fish. People called it "The Workers' Handshake."

I was in a generation where we kind of turned that around a bit. I was raised to shake hands firmly. I wasn't overly stiff with it. I couldn't just give a guy the tips of my fingers, or a loose hand as if that somehow would hint to them that I was this great worker, and they weren't because they didn't know they were supposed to keep their hand limp. It was *stupid*.

Bunk always worked on the first match, and he was always there for enhancements. His job was to lose every time, and to work with him was a huge letdown. After you'd driven a couple hundred miles and then found out you were working with Bunk Harris, you kind of wanted to throw up. I learned absolutely zero during my matches with him.

Bunk didn't want to take any bumps. He didn't even want to take a tackle. In fact, he didn't even want to drop down because he was too fat to get back up. He wanted to stop you by blinding you, raking your face, giving you thumbs, scratching your back, and other things that didn't take much effort. Then he would give you a little comeback and let you beat him.

The matches pretty much just sucked. If I had a list of the worst consistent matches of my career, anything I did with Bunk Harris would have certainly made it into the bottom 10 of the list. Bunk had no business being in the wrestling business.

Why was Bunk even allowed in the wrestling business if he was so bad? The only thing that kept him in the business was his penchant for trying to get other wrestlers in trouble. He always had his head up someone's ass, whether it was the owner, the promoter, or the booker. So not only was Bunk an unathletic, fat piece of crap, and he was a *stooge* on top of it. He was a horrible worker with a horrible body, and he was an equally horrible person.

In his role as a stooge, Bunk would try to find out things that guys had done that might be upsetting to the people in leadership, and then he would go to the Crocketts or George Scott and stooge them out. That was his reputation. He had the stooge title, and that isn't a label that gets attached to you easily unless you have a habit of actually doing it.

When you're sharing locker rooms and cars with guys for almost seven days a week for an entire year, they're eventually going to figure you out. If you're looking to get ahead by being up somebody's butt, it *will* attract attention, and then you'll get labeled. A stooge is about as close as you can get to being a thief in the wrestling business without actually being one, because a thief is the worst label you can get. If you're known to have stolen something because you're the only one that could have done it, *everybody* will find out. Word travels.

You don't even have to steal from one of the boys to get labeled a thief. Let's say everyone in the car decided to stop on the way to the matches to purchase some cases of beer, and you watch somebody stick some bologna or cheese under their jacket without paying for it. They pay for their share of the beer, but then when you get to the car, they have bologna, cheese, cold cuts, and other snacks they clearly didn't have the cashier ring up for them. That person is going to get a reputation for having sticky fingers, and the worst will be presumed about them. Once a thief, always a thief.

If a guy was willing to steal from a 7-Eleven, you have to assume he'll steal from you, too. If he'll steal minor things and risk getting busted for it in a situation where the police might get summoned, he'll *definitely* steal from you if he gets the chance.

As far as veteran advice went, everything Bunk would say was so obviously wrong, but I had to stand there and say, "Oh yeah! I get it! Thanks so much!" while I forcibly propelled it through one ear and out the other. I was an information sponge around Jack Brisco, Terry Funk and Harley Race, so when I heard advice that wasn't compatible with theirs, I simply rejected it.

It was pretty readily accepted that anyone who'd been in the business less than five years was going to be pretty green, and I was able to use that to my advantage. Every time I made a mistake and a veteran said, "What the hell, kid?!" I could just say, "Sorry; I'm still in my first five years," and they would be pretty quick to nod and let it go. In the case of Bunk, I could simply lie and say I'd forgotten to implement his worthless advice on account of still being green.

One of the specific things Bunk asked me to do was to sell his punches more, but his punches were so soft, feeble and unconvincing that they looked like they wouldn't break an egg. They were the polar opposite of the solid punches to the side of the neck that Eddie Graham had personally taught me to throw.

Every night of working with Bunk was about as comfortable as getting a tooth pulled. He was dominating every match because he figured I was too young and wasn't smart enough to hold up my end of the action.

I figured that somehow or another I had to get bumped up the card. At least I was going over every night, as beating Bunk Harris seemed like it was the Crocketts' way of ribbing me while introducing me to the fans in the territory.

111

I wasn't in Charlotte for very long before George Scott pulled me aside.

"I'm gonna team you up with Tiger Conway Jr.," said George. "With you being the Rookie of the Year, it should work out great. You guys would be one of the first Black-White teams we've had in the Carolinas."

With Tiger Conway Jr.

I didn't really know Tiger Conway Jr., but it sounded like a worthwhile opportunity to me. I certainly didn't think I was in any position to chime in and say, "Actually, I was thinking I should be Ole Anderson's partner." In wrestling, almost any opportunity that pays you money is better than not being used at all, and *anything* was better than working in singles with Bunk Harris.

Tiger Conway Jr. and I clicked together pretty well, and after periods of teaming with him, Ricky Gibson and Stan

Hansen as regular partners, I discovered that I *really* enjoyed tag team wrestling. It took so much of the pressure off of me from having to be responsible for carrying an entire match. If I went out there and I felt like I was getting lost for some reason, I could easily tag out and watch things unfold from the ring apron for a while. Besides, there was a limit to how flashy or extreme we could get during our tag matches back then, because leaping from the top turnbuckle was a disqualification. Most people in the NWA territories did variations of the same moves, and often the most aerial thing most wrestlers did was a dropkick.

I was *horrible* at dropkicks.

Speaking of dropkicks, while I was going through the learning phase and teaming up with Tiger, Gene Anderson pulled me aside and asked me if I could come down to the small building where they ran shows in Charlotte.

"I want you to help me train this guy," Gene said. "He's got *a lot* of muscle on him."

I went down there, and this muscular Black kid with unbelievable proportions walked up to me and said, "Hi, I'm Tony Atlas."

Tony was barely 20 years old, and Gene seemed to want me to work with him in part because I was a pretty young guy myself, and Gene assumed I could teach Tony how to throw a dropkick properly. It wasn't a move I particularly liked to do, but I went along with the program and handed Tony a stop sign.

"Hold this up for me," I instructed him.

While Tony held the sign, I jumped up and dropkicked it. It went sailing a good distance.

"It's not that hard," I told him.

We took turns throwing dropkicks, one after the other. To this day, if someone asks Tony Atlas about a dropkick, he'll tell them that I was the person who taught him how to do one. In reality, all I taught him was how to jump up in the air, throw his legs out, and land safely, but in some respects, I suppose that's all a dropkick really is. Seriously, asking me to teach someone to throw a dropkick made as much sense as asking me to teach someone how to be a shooter.

Working for the Crocketts was nowhere near as enjoyable as working for Eddie Graham, or even working for Jim Barnett. If you weren't a member of the leadership cabal or the golf brigade, they didn't really care about you. I fell into the latter category, and it was something that I was forced to be mindful of.

The Crocketts would usually show up for TV tapings in Raleigh, or they would show up to the big shows. If I saw Jimmy Crockett coming and said, "Hey, Mr. Crockett," he wouldn't say one word to me in response. Instead, he would stare straight ahead and keep on walking like he hadn't even heard me.

I got into the car with Tiger Conway Jr. once after a TV taping and asked, "What's the deal with Jimmy Crockett? Who the hell does that guy think he is?"

"He's an arrogant prick," shrugged Tiger. "Always has been."

It was difficult trying to be nice to a boss who you were certain didn't like you at all, and who you didn't even particularly *want* to be nice to. It was mentally exhausting just to be in the dressing room in Mid-Atlantic, but then we'd have to get in the ring with some of the guys in the Crocketts' clique.

Ole Anderson was a clique guy who was right in the thick of things because of his connection with the booking, but Gene Anderson wasn't. Any time I was wrestling against the Andersons, I had to be on edge because I knew that if Ole didn't like the match, he could run to the Crocketts in the office the very next day and say, "Well, that match sucked, and it was *all* Steve Keirn's fault!"

It took me a long time to be able to fit in with Ole. The only way to do it was to become a smartass with him, which was basically just a matter of mirroring his personality right back to him. The weirdest learning process to go through was trying to project the different personalities that would get the right people to look favorably upon you so that they might suppress their urge to bury you in the booking, and possibly even give you an opportunity.

Tiger and I began working against the Anderson brothers almost every night, and our program continued for a couple months. We went to the time limit with them once, but never won the tag belts from them. Ole was somewhat of a bully in the ring. He threw his weight around and would snatch people and drag them to whatever area of the ring he wanted them to be in. He had a very forceful way of dictating a match.

Gene was more of a teacher than Ole was, but there were specific things he wouldn't tolerate out of his opponents. If he grabbed a headlock on you, he didn't like it if you wrapped your arms around his waist. If you did, he would sock you with a potato punch to the head, and then pull your arms off of him. That was his way of swiftly teaching you what he didn't want in his matches. Even if Gene's lessons were tough, they really elevated the quality of my work. Whenever I got to spend time in the ring with guys who were accustomed to performing at a main-event level, I improved in the process.

In Mid-Atlantic, I felt like I was getting a handle on being able to work my way through matches without being spoon fed all of the time. If someone would lock up with me, I could anticipate what someone wanted me to do simply by feel and then begin to do it, and if they didn't want me to do it, they could simply stop me. I learned that I didn't need to be as much of a puppet, and I could take some initiative in the ring and be more hands-on. In my earliest stages, I'd been a minnow in a sea of sharks like Jack Brisco had said. Now I was beginning to feel like I'd at least reached the barracuda level.

If they put me in the ring with an underneath guy now, I could eat him up and get over, and not worry about how he felt about it quite so much. I was more aggressive about ensuring that Steve actually got to look good once in a while.

Outside of the ring, one of the foremost benefits to being in the Mid-Atlantic was that I got some opportunities to spend time with Andre the Giant. To me, it was an incredible thrill just to be in the same dressing room with Andre. It wasn't that I was a huge fan who'd watched him since the beginning of his career, and it wasn't out of admiration for his wrestling ability. It was just a matter of acknowledging Andre's uniqueness and wanting to be close to it.

With "The 8th Wonder of the World" Andre the Giant

Andre was so unique as a human being that he was one of those guys who it was going to be really challenging for me to connect with, and to show him that I was really legitimately wanting to be a friend of his. He only came into a territory for two weeks at a time. He rotated around the territories similar to the NWA world champion, so you only had a short time to be around him.

Thankfully, I made a connection early with Andre. He knew I was excited to meet him, but I was just like a little kid. I would sit and talk to him, and I didn't care about anybody else.

One of the first times I was with Andre in the dressing room in Tampa, I asked him if I could put his boots on. He looked at me as if to say, "Oh my God… what a mark!" I certainly did sound like one, but Andre seemed to think it was endearing. He gave me the approval, so I put Andre's boots on, then looked him in the eyes and said, "Can I put your tights on?" He looked at me funny, so I said, "I'm clean. I swear to God I'm clean. I took a bath and everything. Everything is cool. I'll put your tights on over my tights."

Looking tiny next to the Giant

Again, Andre gave me the nod of approval, so now I had his boots and tights on. I looked like a little kid whose dad was a wrestler, trying on his hero's clothing, and not coming close to fitting into his attire. I started parading through the dressing room with Andre's stuff on, and I was doing it primarily to entertain Andre. I realized the more I was doing it, the more he liked it, so I kept it up. Then I put Andre's ring on, which fit over two of my fingers.

Then I was all over him. "You're just the coolest," I told him. "You're a lot better than a pet monkey. You're *really* cool."

I made a connection with Andre that was significant enough that whenever he arrived in town, he made sure that he rode with me no matter where we were. I always made sure I had something he'd fit in. I even got a van one time, and he would sit on the floor in the back of the van, with his head propped up on the top. He had *so* much fun. He was just a normal guy, but most people treated him like a freak. I treated him like he was something special, which he was.

In the process of hanging out with Andre, I got smartened up to a lot of the things he would do. One of them was that he would speak French to you instead of English if he didn't like you or didn't want to talk to you. If we went into a bar and people came up to him and said or did a bunch of stupid shit when they were around him, he would speak French to them as a way of running them off. Or if we were in a place where he liked everyone, he would communicate with me first so that I could help communicate with them, even though he spoke perfect English.

He called everybody "boss." Everything was "Hey, Boss!" I don't know if that was because he couldn't remember everyone's names because he only saw people two weeks out of the year. I suppose it could have been like his own version of "brother," since all the wrestlers called each other brother, which *also* happened because wrestlers would forget each other's names all of the time. It didn't matter. I was a *real* mark for Andre.

I was with Andre once in the Playboy Club in Atlanta, and I said to him, "What have you been eating, man? Your *breath* is unreal!"

Andre laughed and jokingly backhanded me, but he knocked me clean off of the barstool and almost *killed* me.

In Richmond, Andre and I were walking next to a swimming pool as we were coming back from the bar one night, and I went to shove him into the pool as a rib.

"Watch this!" I assured myself. "I'm gonna be the only guy to ever push Andre into a swimming pool!"

As I went to push him, Andre backhanded me and knocked me right on my ass. It felt like getting smashed with a club. As I looked at him with a stunned expression, Andre looked down on me sternly and simply said, "I can't swim."

"You can't *swim*?!" I asked in disbelief. "Andre, you could sit down in that swimming pool and your head would *still* be above the water!"

"I'm terrified of the water!" said Andre, shaking his head.

"Wow!" I thought. "I would have pushed Andre the Giant into the water as a rib and wound up killing him because I couldn't save him!"

There would have been no faster way of getting blackballed from wrestling than being the guy who accidentally drowned Andre the Giant. The only place I might have been able to work after that is Japan; they would have called me "The Giant Killer" and booked me against Shohei "Giant" Baba.

While accidentally drowning Andre would have been a career-killer, my career had thankfully managed to survive years spent working in Florida, Georgia, the Carolinas, and even Guatemala. Now I was about to receive an education in what it was like to survive as a young wrestler in Japan.

SEVEN

Early in my career in Florida, I had ridden regularly to shows with both of the Brisco brothers, Jack and Gerald. The two of them talked *a lot* about wrestling in Japan for Giant Baba's All Japan Pro Wrestling company. When Jack stopped in to visit Mid-Atlantic when he was touring as the world heavyweight champion, we talked about it some more.

"I asked about goin' over to Japan when I was in Georgia, but they didn't seem to want to offer me any serious money to wrestle there," I mentioned during one of our car rides.

"Don't go to Japan cheap, or they'll always think you're cheap!" Jack warned me. "Hold off on goin' over there and make them offer you more money."

"I don't have anything much to offer them right now," I lamented. "At least nothin' they'd be interested in."

"Don't worry," Jack reassured me. "They'll get interested before long. Just don't fold up and decide to go in really cheap."

Eventually, someone put in enough good words for me in Japan – more than likely Jack himself – that All Japan Pro Wrestling decided to invite me over for the 1975 Champion Carnival tour right in the middle of my stay in Charlotte. Gene Kiniski, Mark Lewin, Dick the Bruiser, Killer Kowalski, and Bob Orton Jr. were all there on the tour with me.

In essence, the Champion Carnival was an annual tournament held in All Japan that enabled its winner to claim to be a world champion of sorts. The long-term NWA champions needed to be free to tour all of the other NWA territories, most of which were in the U.S., and no one from Japan was going to do that. However, Giant Baba *could* invite several of the most famous and accomplished wrestlers in the world over to Japan for a month every year and beat them all in a tournament, and that's precisely what he did.

Going to Japan required me to wrestle in a totally different style from what I'd grown accustomed to. Aside from my brief period as the Black Angel in Guatemala, I'd never wrestled as a heel before. In Japan, *all* of the Americans were cast as heels. This put me in a tough position for two main reasons: The Japanese wrestlers didn't speak any English, and I wasn't educated enough to run a match as a heel, which is what heels were expected to do.

Partnering with Dick the Bruiser in Japan

Luckily for me, Gene Kiniski – who was a former NWA World Heavyweight Champion – took a liking to me for some odd reason. I started off trying to wing it in the ring, but Gene pulled me aside and advised me as to how I should work a match as a heel inside of a Japanese ring, including everything from timing to reactions.

Mark Lewin also seemed to take a shine to me. He shared with me how he thought I should take care of myself in the wrestling business, and I really appreciated it coming from him. He was just a *cool* guy. He was like one of those guys that you grow up with who is just effortlessly cool. It was difficult for him to do *anything* that wasn't cool.

We worked every night in Japan, and I was in a lot of tag team matches with guys like Dick the Bruiser and Gene Kiniski. In those cases, I was definitely there to be the person who got beaten up. After all, they had to beat *somebody* in our matches, and it wasn't going to be a star like Dick the Bruiser. All the same, standing on the ring apron was one of the simplest ways to understand the expectations of how the matches were handled there before I tagged in, and if I got in trouble, I could tag out and bring in someone more experienced who could get the matches back on track.

The main reason we were in Japan to begin with was to get the Japanese wrestlers over with their home crowds. Some of the older foreign guys were able to put in a strong enough showing to maintain their reputations, and then they could throw in an agile, young kid like me to absorb the loss. When the older guys did lose, it was later in the tour, and typically against the foremost regular stars of All Japan, like Baba, and also the Destroyer and Jumbo Tsuruta.

During one match, I was partnered with Kiniski in a tag match against Baba and Tsuruta. They went to run our heads together in a headlock, and they brought Gene Kiniski over to me while I was already on the move, and we legitimately smashed heads into each other. It wasn't that bad, but I pretended I was knocked out cold to the extent that Gene Kiniski believed that I'd actually been hurt. He was so protective of me, almost like a grandfather.

Wrestling Baba was like wrestling a skeleton. Like Andre the Giant, he had been suffering from Acromegaly for his entire life, and even though Baba was a world-class baseball player in his prime, he was beginning to slow down. Sometimes he could barely raise his foot up high enough to boot you with it where he wanted to.

Beating up Giant Baba with Gene Kiniski

In the largest cities, we stayed in hotels that appealed to western tastes, but we also stayed in typical Japanese hotels during our visits to smaller towns. This meant we were required to leave our shoes outside of our rooms, we had to sleep on the floor, and the toilet was contained within the floor. I nearly starved to death because I hated rice, and I wasn't about to eat sushi either. Anything they put in front of me that was Japanese, I *wasn't* eating it; it just wasn't going to happen. The one thing I ate was a noodle dish called yakisoba, which I quickly got hooked on.

The cost of things could also be on the high side over in Japan, and I was hellbent on saving every cent I made. In that respect, Bob Orton Jr. was the polar opposite of me. He was so homesick that he would get on the phone with his wife Elaine and spend four or five hours talking to her every night. He basically spent every dime he made over in Japan on phone bills.

It was during my time in Japan that I first learned how to rib guys effectively. One night we stayed in a 10-story hotel that was shaped like a perfect square. Gene Kiniski was staying in the room next to mine. There was an expectation that you could go to your room after the shows, relax, and put your clothes on. Kimonos and slippers were standard provisions offered in all of the hotels. Hanging on the back of the door was this thing that looked like a miniature bat. It had a wooden handle, a flexible piece of metal, and a rubber ball on the end. It was a massaging tool that you were supposed to use by hitting yourself with the end of the bat that had the ball connected to it.

One of the other things that stood out to me was the little doorbells they had outside of the rooms, so you could ring the doorbell of each room and get the attention of the person inside of it.

Well, in Japan the television programming was entirely in Japanese, so I had a lot of time to myself to think, and my mind started cooking up ways to pull a rib on Gene Kiniski. Once I had a fully detailed plan in mind, I took a toothpick and the wooden handle with the rubber ball, and I walked out into the hallway. I took the toothpick and jammed it into Gene's doorbell so that it would continue to make noise incessantly, and I snapped the toothpick off in there so that the doorbell was stuck in its pressed-in position. It just kept beeping away while Gene was asleep.

When Gene finally came to the door and opened it and stuck his head out, I *blasted* him right in the head with the ball from the paddle as hard as I could, and then took off running. Gene was stunned for a second, and then he began chasing me straight through the hallway of this square hotel.

"Come back here, you son of a bitch!" came Gene's voice from behind me as he pursued me down the hallway as fast as he could.

By the time we made our first trip around the hall, I'd caught enough of a glimpse of Gene's body to recognize that he was completely naked. During subsequent laps around the hallway, I ran by Gene's room and pulled the door shut, and then I entered my own room and shut the door with myself safely on the other side of it. Poor Gene Kiniski was stuck standing stark naked in the middle of the hotel hallway.

I was dying laughing inside of my room, but I was also feeling triumphant. I'd just pulled my first major rib on someone, and I couldn't wait to pull more. Meanwhile, Gene was left outside in the hallway hollering obscenities, which got me thinking about ways to enhance the rib even further. I grabbed the phone and dialed the front desk.

In Japan with Killer Kowalski, Lord Jim Blears, Mike George, Bob Orton Jr., Steve Keirn, Joe Higuchi, Tim Woods, Dick the Bruiser and Mark Lewin

"Moshi moshi," said the desk attendant when he answered, which is a common Japanese phone greeting.

"There's a naked man in the middle of the 10th floor hallway!" I yelled. "Please send security!"

The desk attendant didn't understand a single word I'd said other than "security."

"Security! Hai!" the attendant replied.

A few moments later, I heard Gene grumbling with a security guard who couldn't understand a word he was saying, but the hotel staff was aware that there were a bunch of famous American wrestlers staying there, and they knew Gene was one of them, so they opened the door to his room for him and allowed him get back in.

Instead of harboring feelings of resentment over the incident, Gene kept putting me over with the rest of the guys throughout the remainder of the tour.

"You see *this* kid?" he told the rest of the guys in the American locker room. "He had the *balls* to whack me in the head with a ball and then lock me out in the hall naked! Who else on this tour would have the balls to do something like that to me – Gene Kiniski?!"

The Bruiser and Kowalski thought it was hilarious. Little things like that started to earn me more respect from the old-timers in the business and helped me to fit in. Even being willing to be on the butt-end of some of their jokes was crucial in getting them to like me.

Once I finally wrapped things up in Charlotte, the door was wide open for me to make a return to Florida, where I would be the only classic, white-meat babyface they had on the roster. Eddie Graham had Cyclone Negro, Omar Negro, Rocky Johnson and Pork Chop Cash on the babyface side. They had several Black and Puerto Rican wrestlers, but they didn't have a White, cracker-ass, apple-pie eating, American-flag-waving kid, and that was a role that I could easily play.

Obviously Mike Graham had been there the whole time, but that was part of the problem. The people in Florida were too used to seeing him, and he'd cooled off a little bit as an attraction. He was also relatively short no matter how much he worked out, and this compromised the believability of having him convincingly defeat men that were much larger than he was. No matter how much Mike trained, he was never going to get any taller.

My tour of some NWA territories outside of Florida had proven to Eddie Graham that I was prepared to be presented at a higher level. Jack Brisco had been the traveling world champion, and during his tours, he had seen me wrestling in Georgia and in the Carolinas. He had been feeding steady reports of my development progress back to Eddie Graham. Apparently the Andersons had also spoken up on my behalf when I left Charlotte and had plenty of good things to say about me to Eddie.

Back in Florida at the beginning 1976, they'd been making plans for me in my absence. I'd now been to four different NWA territories with significance: Florida, Georgia, Mid-Atlantic and Japan. I'd rubbed shoulders with the major talent that had been rotating through all four regions at all times. I also hadn't embarrassed any of the people who had vouched for me to the promoters of any of those territories. I went in and did as I was told, and they were pleased, so I didn't hurt anyone's reputation. Also, I got over with my peers in all of these places even if I didn't get over with the fans, and in a lot of ways that was even more important. After all, it actually isn't always your job to get over with the fans.

Eddie put me in matches to see what I could do, and slowly but surely he began to elevate me up the card. I was no longer competing in singles matches in the middle of the card, and guys who would ordinarily have beaten me in other territories were no longer beating me; I was winning regularly.

Finally, Eddie came to me and said, "We need to give you a really good finish; something that people really *believe* you have the ability to do. I'm going to have Don Curtis teach you how to use the sleeper."

Up until then, I'd been beating people with simple wrestling holds like inside cradles. However, once they had me beating guys convincingly on TV every week with a sleeper hold, I got so much more respect from the fans seemingly overnight. They also put over the fact that Don Curtis was the guy who taught it to me, which was true. The thing is, what Don Curtis had *truly* taught me was how to shoot on people with the sleeper and drain them of their consciousness for real.

"People will question it," said Curtis. "When they question it, you have to *really* be able to put people to sleep."

Once I started using the sleeper, Eddie quickly upped the ante in his promotion of me to the Florida public.

"I'm gonna put some pressure on you, kid," Eddie told me. "Starting this week, I'm gonna have the announcer tell people during the intermission that Steve Keirn is going to be demonstrating his patented sleeper hold, and that anyone who doesn't believe in it will get a chance to have it applied to them and get put to sleep. We'll let the audience pick who gets sent to you to get put to sleep."

So now the pressure was on me. I'd walk out to the ring first, referee Stu Schwartz would join me, and then we'd solicit volunteers from the audience. To my great surprise, we got so many people volunteering to get put to sleep that we had to narrow it down to the healthiest-looking fans in the audience just to make sure I didn't inadvertently *kill* somebody.

After the pool of volunteers had been whittled down to about five people, we would be left with a range of guys from short and skinny, all the way to men the size of typical nightclub bouncers. Whenever Stu Schwartz would place his hand over the volunteers' heads to choose the person for me to apply the sleeper to, the audience always picked the largest and most muscular guys. They always forced me to put *monsters* to sleep.

I'd step up behind the volunteer and say, "Okay. Relax. Don't get excited. I'm just going to wrap my arms around you. When I say 'go,' you try to get away. I'll squeeze with everything I've got, and we'll see what happens."

Once I yelled, "Go," I would start squeezing, and the guys would usually fall asleep within seconds. Some of them would fight, and some wouldn't, but regardless, they were usually being ushered off to dreamland very quickly. It established the legitimacy of my new finisher when the audience saw people who clearly hadn't been planted among them getting put to sleep, and they knew the volunteers weren't planted because they got to select them for me.

Don Curtis taught me several tricks for ensuring that things would go as planned during these demonstrations, and one of them was to have the guys lean back a little bit if they were taller than me. That gave me a far more dominant position if my head was situated higher than theirs. I'd secure my arm around their neck and get it hooked tightly, and then I'd put my other hand behind their head to protect my face.

Locking a sleeper hold on Don Muraco

Half of the guys would try to headbutt me in the face to break the hold. The other half would try to jack me up onto their backs and run off with me. I had to figure out just from

The Fabulous Wrestling Life of Steve Keirn

looking at the person what the most optimal position would be for maintaining my advantage in leverage. Most of the time, the wisest thing for me to do was to lean back a tiny bit so that the volunteers couldn't jerk me up off the ground. Even if they tried, I could quickly yank them right back down again. If they tried to headbutt me, the worst thing they could do was to knock my hand back into the side of my face, because my head would be turned to the side and the blow wouldn't make much impact.

The boys in the back all *loved* these sleeper hold displays, and they would come out to watch me every time. They thought it was so entertaining since it was the one part of our show without a predetermined participant or a preplanned outcome.

That's how I ultimately became a main-event wrestler down in Florida. I didn't get over as Steve Keirn the wrestler; I got over as Steve Keirn – the guy who can do the sleeper better than anyone else. I would sell for my opponent during the majority of my matches, and then when it looked like all hope was lost, I would lock my opponent in the sleeper out of nowhere, ride them out, and then put them to sleep.

As always, becoming successful creates additional opportunities. When Mike Graham realized I was getting over with fans, he asked the bookers to ease me in with him as his regular tag team partner. Even though we'd grown up together and had been close friends in school, Mike and I hadn't spent much time together on the road. Once the two of us began teaming together and riding together, we became inseparable friends once more. We'd come home from Tampa and head off to the bars together no matter what time of the night it was.

One of the nights after the sleeper had first caught on with the fans, Mike and I went to a bar that was directly across the street from the University of Tampa. The two of us went inside and had a couple beers and were just hanging out. Tampa had no professional sports teams back then to speak of, and so many people watched professional wrestling in that area that it was easy for us to get recognized. We were on local television every Saturday.

Nine different guys approached me inside of that University of Tampa bar and said, "We want you to put the sleeper on us!"

"Are you *sure*?" I asked them. "Well, if that's what you want…"

I lined those nine guys up next to each other along the bar like shot glasses, and I put them to sleep and dropped them to the floor one right after the other, and they *all* hit the ground. It was the easiest thing in the world, because none of them were trying to get away from me. They wanted to be able to brag to their friends that they had been put to sleep by Steve Keirn.

The last guy in line didn't go down quite so easily. Usually their knees were crumbling within the first five seconds, and shortly after that, they were out. I was squeezing as hard as I safely could without doing serious damage, but this guy didn't move at all.

"You know, it doesn't always work on *everybody*…" I started to say, as I began to offer up a prepared excuse.

Then I realized the guy was standing straight up, so I thought I should kick one of his legs out to try to buckle it so that I could bring him back and get more leverage. Instead of buckling, the leg shot straight out, and he plummeted to the ground. I woke the guy back up and asked him, "How come you didn't fall to the ground?"

"I have an artificial limb," he said, groggily. "I lost my leg in a high school motorcycle accident. It doesn't bend."

I couldn't believe someone who was missing a leg would have volunteered to get put to sleep in an environment like that.

Putting them to sleep was the easy part. The hardest part was waking them back up. They might have woken up on their own, but to speed things along I would rub their necks or hit them in the back. The cockier I got with the move, the more aggressive I became. If someone was a little more arrogant before they came to me to be put to sleep, I might lift them up by the hair and then slap them in the face to wake them back up.

"You were out pretty deep," I said to one guy that I woke up with a slap . "I had to work *really* hard to wake you back up."

"Hey, why does my *face* hurt?" he asked.

Every time I went to a bar, someone would challenge the validity of wrestling. One guy came into a bar in Ybor City and got a little rough with me.

"What do you think about a wrestler going up against a *karate* guy?" he said.

"So I guess that makes me the wrestler in this situation, right?" I replied. "So does that make you the karate guy?"

Even though I wasn't a shooter, I had to act like I was confident in my own wrestling ability so that guys would be terrified of fighting me.

"Okay. So what do you want to do?" I asked him.

"What do you *think*?" he said. "I'm *challenging* you."

"Well I think if we go stand in that phone booth out on 7th Avenue, the only person walking out of that phone booth is gonna be me," I said.

The guy looked at me for a few seconds, and then he decided to pass.

Executing the sleeper on everyday citizens in and out of the ring helped to build the legend of Steve Keirn's sleeper hold and to broaden my credibility with wrestling fans across the entire state. Even fans who knew I was young and inexperienced recognized that I had a very effective sleeper hold, and as long as I had that move in my arsenal, I was a threat to beat anybody on any given night.

It also helped that they teamed me with different guys who were established. In addition to Mike Graham, I also teamed with Jimmy Garvin and Bob Backlund. Mike and I spent the most time together, but when Bobby Backlund was around, he was in the early stages of his wrestling career, and was very green and almost robotic. He was a phenomenal amateur wrestler out of Minnesota, but that didn't mean much of anything to the fans when he first arrived in Florida.

Jody Hamilton was booking the territory, and while Eddie Graham was off working for Jim Barnett's World Championship Wrestling territory in Australia, Jody decided to inject some of my real life circumstances into my matches because he thought it would be appealing to the Florida public. The first angle that I actually made any serious money with, and that caused the audience to get behind me and buy tickets to see me, was when I worked against Bob Roop.

Bob Roop was a gigantic man, and a *true* shooter who finished 7th in Greco-Roman wrestling at the 1968 Olympic Games. He was also one of the primary guys that Eddie Graham put to work beating people up inside of the Sportatorium after hours.

Eddie would have the marks come and sign a deal that basically gave you permission to kill them during training. From there, Bob would brutalize guys and stretch them relentlessly until they were crying and trying to crawl out of the ring. He was an imposing specimen, to be sure.

"I've kind of got an idea for you, but I don't know how your dad would feel about it," began Jody. "It would involve mentioning how your dad was a POW."

"I could always ask my dad how he'd feel about it," I offered.

"We wanna have Bob go out on the interview and insult your dad for being taken prisoner. He's gonna call him a coward," said Jody. "He's gonna get really evil and *nasty* with it! I think this could draw a lot of money for us if we do it right. Eddie would never go for it, but if he comes back and sees that it's making money, he won't complain."

I sat down with my dad and explained the angle to him. To my surprise, he was *very* receptive to it. He didn't mind being mentioned on the wrestling program at all if I thought it would help my career.

On the fateful day when we kicked off the angle, Bob Roop brought up my name to Gordon Solie during an interview. Then he segued into mentioning how my dad was a two-time prisoner of war.

"I was in the military, and being in the military you learn a lot of things, but being a prisoner is *out* of the question!" snarled Roop. "I would've never let myself get caught twice! Actually, I think he's a *coward* for being a prisoner for so long!"

Putting Bob Roop to sleep with the aid of Jack Brisco

That was my cue to come flying out of the dressing room. We only had one camera for our shoots back then, and I sprinted right past the camera and jumped clean over the desk to get to Roop. At least that's what I'd *intended* to do. During my leap over the desk, I clipped my ankle on the desk's edge, and my ankle hurt so bad that I thought I'd broken it. I flew onto Roop, and I fought him like it was the real deal. Bob Roop was an authentic tough guy, and this was a day he *needed* to be tough.

    This angle required me to do something that I'd never done before. I had to emotionally move that audience to believe that this guy had gravely insulted the father that I'd been deprived of for eight vital years of my youth. Roop called the man a coward when I considered him to be a war hero, and I had to take things *way* past wrestling. I succeeded, and the crowd ate it up.

    To this day, my friend Terry Bollea tells me it was one of the most significant angles he ever saw during his days as a wrestling fan. He was right there in the Sportatorium when I sprinted past him and leapt onto Roop.

    Between the singles matches I was having with Roop and the irrepressible presence of Dusty Rhodes, the Florida territory was on fire by the time Eddie Graham returned from Australia. We could go to any arena, from the Miami Beach Convention Center to the Tampa Bay Armory, and the buildings would be packed to capacity. The towns we held our matches in were all major towns, and military servicemen were showing up to the matches in their uniforms to cheer me on. Meanwhile, Roop was receiving a steady stream of death threats, and had to contend with fans who were pointing guns at him in parking lots when he arrived at the buildings.

    To keep the feud going, Roop and I had steel cage matches, death matches, loser-leaves-town matches, and every type of gimmick match we could think of in order to prolong the violence and keep drawing money with it. There was a lot of blood and a lot of fighting in our bouts, but not a whole lot of wrestling. Everything was being driven by the emotional chord that Roop and I had struck with the audience. The fans fell in love with the believability of the angle, and I beat Bob Roop half to death.

Pounding on Roop in the ring every night of the week also helped me to reinvent myself as a hard-nosed street fighter rather than simply a garden-variety wrestler.

The feud with Roop enabled my career to reach a whole new level, like someone had suddenly flipped a switch on me. Now I was drawing money in the main event, and Dusty Rhodes was wrestling in support of my angle. That didn't always sit too well with Dusty, who wasn't accustomed to being in any position below a main-event level. I couldn't help but to needle him about that a little bit.

"Looks like at the show tonight it's Steve Keirn against Bob Roop… and *others*," I proclaimed sarcastically within earshot of Dusty, who flushed red with anger.

One of the things I now had to do was implement Eddie Graham's strategy for wrestling as a main-event babyface. This meant that I was to dominate my opponents at the beginning until my opponent had to start heeling and cheating to gain an advantage on me. From that point on until the point where I made a serious comeback, I was to sell, but *never* die. That way, the people would never lose interest in me.

Instead of kicking out of pinning attempts on the count of two, I was to kick out on *one*, and then I was to keep kicking out on one. I was to let the heels hit me with all of the punishment they could possibly give me without being pinned. In between moves and pinning attempts, I was to throw punches and fight back. I couldn't simply sit on my knees waiting for them to come get me. I had to stay active, keep resisting, and make the heels work hard and expend energy to stop me.

In Eddie's philosophy of wrestling, only after I had been beaten on for a while was I to even consider kicking out on two instead of one. That made perfect sense to me. After all, if a guy covers you two minutes into a match and gets a two count, and then he's still pounding on you 20 minutes later and still only getting a two count, it educates the fans that the prior

20 minutes meant nothing at all. By the time your opponent is getting a two count on you, that should signify that you're nearly *dead*.

With tag team partner and childhood buddy Mike Graham

As I continued my run on top in Florida, I added a big flying forearm smash as a prelude to the sleeper hold. I absolutely *blasted* guys when I caught them with it.

"That forearm is your *new* finish," stated Eddie after he watched me deliver it a few times.

"Really? *Why?*" I asked him.

"It looks great, and the sleeper takes a long time to set up," replied Eddie. "You can hit the forearm out of nowhere and have it be the finish at any time."

Between the sleeper hold and the forearm smash, I now had two convincing finishing maneuvers that fans knew would work in real fights, and I could also apply them to absolutely anyone.

Working in Florida's main events came with additional perks besides money. I started to receive a lot of attention from the professional wrestling press. Wrestling magazines were covering me with regularity, and promoters were talking about me all over the country. People rotating through Florida were seeing how much money could be drawn with me if my background with my father was showcased properly. In the end, that was the one thing that those promoters truly cared about: How can we draw money in the same towns 52 weeks per year?

Thanks to all of that attention I was generating, Don Owen in Oregon wanted me to head all the way out to the Pacific Northwest, and Bill Watts wanted me to work in his Mid-South territory.

I liked Watts, but there was no way I was ever going to work in Mid-South on a semi-permanent basis if I could help it. Before I worked in a territory, I always inquired about how long the trips were, because you might discover that you were spending large chunks of your time driving from place to place, and essentially being gone from home the entire time you were there. Driving was also one of the most dangerous times for wrestlers. Much of the travel was on two-lane roads late at night when guys were tired, drunk, or both. Plenty of guys got in accidents late at night for those exact reasons.

I'd been spoiled while working in Florida and Georgia, where we were capable of being home every night if we truly desired to be, even if we were working seven nights a week. One thing I learned about Watts' Mid-South territory was that the distances between towns and the way certain towns were scheduled made being home each night an *impossibility*.

The Fabulous Wrestling Life of Steve Keirn

The wrestling business in Florida was notoriously on fire during the summers. When school started, the box office tended to take a drastic dip. All the towns dropped off except for the Friday night towns. Everywhere else, people had to get up and go to school. The towns also dropped off during the holidays as many households started holding onto their money the closer it came to Christmas. We went through a time period when Bob and I had our angle where we just kept drawing substantial money even during the fall and winter months. My payoffs changed accordingly. I'd never made more than $300 a week during my first run in Florida, and things gradually increased when I was in Georgia and the Mid Atlantic. Now I was making anywhere from $1,000 to $1,500 every week, which was a huge uptick from where I'd been previously.

Because I was now a main-event wrestler, this also meant I was working with the world champions when they came to visit. The very first time I wrestled Harley Race, I was unbearably nervous. I really liked Harley, and I respected him immensely, but I was also *deathly* afraid of him. It's not like Harley ever did anything to me intentionally to make me afraid of him, but it was more of a respectful fear. If I didn't do something right around Harley, I knew that it would ruin me throughout the entire wrestling world. He traveled a lot, and I knew that he could bury me with everyone he came across.

"There's a kid in Florida named 'Steve Keirn,' and you don't want to work with *that*," is a sentence that I never wanted to escape from Harley's lips. I *dreaded* the thought of it. If Harley Race ever uttered those words, it would have been the kiss of death for my entire wrestling career.

On the other hand, I also knew that if I worked exceptionally well with Harley, he had the ability to hype me up to everyone he came across from Florida to Japan. Even if all Harley said was, "He's a good hand," or "I like the kid," that endorsement meant far more coming out of Harley's mouth than it did from anyone else. Any positive words being spread about you from Harley could be immeasurably beneficial to your future in the wrestling industry.

When Harley and I went out there to wrestle, we walked to the ring, got to the center of the ring, and the referee checked us for weapons and other things by examining our hands, waistlines, and the bottoms of our boots. That was when Harley and I had our first communication.

Harley looked like he was sizing me up. Even though I was actually intimidated in real life, I couldn't make it seem like my wrestling *character* was intimidated. I still had to play my role. One thing I'd been taught was not to simply stand there like a thumb getting ready to get stuck in a pie. I had to get out there and move around, and act like I was excited and intense. After all, I was supposed to think that I was actually wrestling for the world heavyweight championship. The audience needed to feel my excitement if they were actually going to be excited about what was unfolding in front of them.

I was absentmindedly pacing back and forth, and then I realized Harley was trying to tell me something. I'd never been told a long highspot at the beginning of a match before, and this was going to be my first experience executing something like that.

As I was getting my hands checked, Harley rattled off a prolonged sequence to me.

"Okay, kid. When we lock up, take a headlock. I'll shoot you off. Give me one tackle and drop flat," began Harley. "I'll hip toss you; you kick me off. Two arm drags. I'll scoot out onto the floor. You follow me out and around the post and back into the ring. I'll hit the ropes on the opposite side. You drop flat. I'll come off. You leapfrog me. I'll come off. You hip toss me. I'll come up. You armdrag me twice and get the headlock back."

"Ummmm… Can you say that *again*?" I asked him.

Harley looked at me and shook his head. He was also cognizant of the audience, too, but he gave me a look with added intensity to let me know he was only going to repeat himself once, and I'd *better* remember it this time. So now I was really nervous, and as Harley recited the sequence again, I was trying to focus, but my mind kept blanking out on me and I got lost once again. I was so excited just to be in the ring with Harley, but this was just another night for him, and he was focused on calling his first spot. He wanted the match to start off really exciting, but I was only half hearing it.

Despite my daydreaming, I successfully made it through Harley's initial sequence, but once it was finished, I was huffing and puffing so badly. It was like the first three minutes of the match, and we still had 57 to go. I was thinking to myself that there was no way I could possibly wrestle for an hour when I'd been blown up in three short minutes. Little did I know that Harley was smart enough to pace me through it, but I was feeling overwhelmed for the entire remainder of the match. Still, the match *flew* by.

Back then, the timekeeper would be sounding off with time cues like, "Ten minutes gone; 50 minutes remaining." I was sucking air. The Tampa Armory had no air conditioning. It was a July night, and it was more than 100 degrees in there with the hot lights beating down on you. People had been sucking air out of the building for hours by then, so it felt like the oxygen supply was limited. And there I was, nervous and young, wrestling the world champion and trying not to embarrass myself.

I was so relieved when the match was over, and I was especially happy when I returned to the dressing room afterwards. What I got out of it was a real education on carrying somebody. Harley taught me what I should be doing if I was ever in his position. He also taught me how to *build* a guy during a match. Harley was already built. He was the world heavyweight champion. He didn't need to get built up any further. I *needed* to be built up to make it look like I even belonged in the same ring with him.

Harley made it look like at any given moment I could beat him for the world championship, right up until the end of the bout. At the conclusion of the contest, he must have had me false-finish him 20 times in the last five minutes. I was inside cradling him, sunset flipping him, and doing every hooking movement I could to get his shoulders to the mat. He was kicking out, and then turning right into another pinning combination. Right when I looked like I had him beaten for good, the bell rang to signal that the time had run out.

The people collectively groaned as if to say, "Awww, man!"

It was so intense to have an audience follow you for an hour during a back-and-forth contest. By the time it was over with, they were just as worn out as I was from the intensity. They'd been sitting on the edges of their seats for the entire time thinking they were about to see the world title change hands.

The aftermath of that hour-long match with Harley was the first time I returned to the dressing room to be greeted by a roomful of guys were standing up applauding for me and patting me on the back. The highest compliment a wrestler can receive isn't from the fans; it's from your peers. When you come back through the dressing room door and the guys you work with are clapping for you and putting you over, and telling you that you just had a helluva match, that's the highest high that you can get as a wrestler. Then you get to the level when you're hoping to experience that every night, but you won't always achieve it because there are usually things that could have been at least a little bit better.

Guys didn't just automatically applaud one another. It was a response that needed to be *earned*. That was one of the first times I'd gotten that reaction, and it became my goal from then on to come back through the dressing room door and have at least one person that I respected tell me I'd had a great match.

A lot of people ask me what my favorite matches were over the course of my career, and I can't definitively pin them down. However, my favorite experiences involved working with guys like Harley Race, Jack Brisco, Dory Funk Jr. and Terry Funk. Everybody was different. They each had their own styles, and you had to learn it. You couldn't go out there and exclusively wrestle in their style. You have to keep working your own style, and try to intermingle it with what they do to forge a compromise. It created a real work of art if you could do it well.

The thing is, guys like Harley, Jack, Dory and Terry also needed to like you. If workers of that caliber liked you, they could make you look so good to the point where everyone watching believed you deserved to be the world champion. If they didn't like me, they might not be so generous.

Regrettably, no matter how much I might have wanted to, I couldn't work with wrestlers of Harley Race's caliber every night. Part of the chore of being a top guy in a territory was learning to work with guys you didn't necessarily enjoy sharing the same ring with from night to night. It was a lesson that every wrestler was obligated to learn on the path to the top, but the lessons didn't always feel – or *smell* – very appealing.

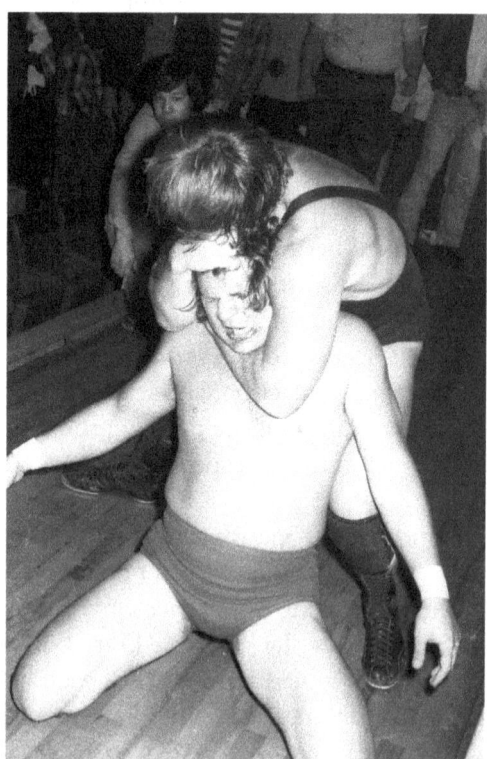

Securing a sleeper hold on Dick Slater outside of the ring

EIGHT

As a top territorial draw, you often found yourself squaring off against other wrestlers who came with plenty of name recognition, but whose in-ring styles didn't particularly mesh well with yours.

When I was younger, Ox Baker's mannerisms didn't really appeal to me. I'd quickly grown accustomed to exchanging holds with some undeniably great workers, and Ox was older, slower, and had substantially less movement to his act. He was best described as being a character and an attraction as opposed to being a worker, and I wasn't really used to sharing the ring with immobile characters.

Eddie put me in the ring with Ox, and I wasn't nearly as excited about seeing myself booked against him as I would have been if I was booked against just about anyone else. That's not to say that I didn't appreciate what Ox Baker had accomplished in the wrestling business. I didn't just dismiss him as worthless. I knew that he had drawn significant money in different places during his career, but at this juncture he was living off of his reputation, his size, and his legendary look, which consisted of his ugly face, his hulking frame, his bald head, and his thick, dark, handlebar mustache.

When I was in my early 20s, I was full of piss and vinegar, and raring to go. Ox was the type who was constantly trying to clamp down on me and say, "Slow down, kid. Just slow it down. This is *not* a race."

Ox's act might have been effective in other areas, but the Florida audience was a little more refined. Eddie had attuned the Florida crowds to become accustomed to the highest wrestling quality in the world. That usually involved a lot of movement, a lot of technique, and matches that went back and forth, with clearly told stories, and finishes that had been well thought out.

Other territories rarely had guys booking them that were nearly as intelligent or detail-oriented as Eddie was. The storylines were often weaker, or the wrestlers characters allowed them to work in ways that necessitated minimal effort being applied, and with minimal risk on the back end.

Ox was *still* a big man with a freaky look, and he was very boisterous in the ring. He had a deep voice and did a *lot* of yelling. He just never appealed to me, and I also wasn't intimidated by him no matter how scary his gimmick and appearance made him look to the naked eye.

Trying to give Ox Baker a nap

Even if Ox Baker wasn't a great worker, the fact that he was an attraction still gave him value to a promoter. You needed to put people in seats 52 times per year in the same cities, which meant you needed to continuously draw fans and keep things moving steadily forward. Also, wrestling fans generally weren't the rich people; they were usually middle class. They would cut back on their money when it came to entertainment, and that's what wrestling was regarded as by them.

Being a good hand *could* also mean you were an attraction, but Ox's matches were of very low quality. Once people saw Ox Baker in person, a lot of the fans who might have been attending the shows regularly for 30 years would write him off and say things like, "Oh man… if I have to see another Ox Baker match I'm gonna *throw up!*"

As a point of comparison, there were guys I worked with, like Jos Leduc, who were similar in appearance to Ox Baker in some ways, but who were also *far* more believable. Jos was intense in the ring; Ox was comparatively lazy. I'm sure if Ox Baker was telling the story of Steve Keirn, he would tell people that I was "a crowbar," or he'd say, "Steve potatoed me 100 times in a match." He might even go so far as to say, "Steve put the sleeper on me and almost put me to sleep for real."

That *might* be true, but that's because Ox wasn't the kind of guy you whipped into the ropes and backdropped a bunch of times, or who you body-slammed and arm-dragged repeatedly during a comeback. Ox would only let you knock him down once or twice, and he didn't get up like a limber, nimble wrestler either. He needed to roll over to one knee and grab a rope just to get back up.

Ox simply didn't want to do much in the ring, and he certainly wasn't a worker on the level of Buddy Roberts, who went out of his way to make me look good during the tag team matches that I was having against him. Ox was more like Buddy's partner in the Hollywood Blondes, Jerry Brown, who always resembled George Washington to me. Like Ox, Jerry always seemed like he was just passing time and getting by.

When it comes to the Hollywood Blondes, Buddy Roberts was undeniably the superior worker on that team. The only problem with him was that he always had a funny smell emanating from him. When you're working with a guy that doesn't wash his tights, there's simply no escaping it. That sort of a stench sits right there on top of you when you're in the ring, and it *clings* to you. Buddy wasn't trying to purposefully do things to make you uncomfortable, but you couldn't help but to end up with your nose in the vicinity of his tights periodically during a match, and you had to do your best to hold your breath.

Despite the excellent quality of his work, Buddy's poor hygiene was the talk of the babyface locker room. He would readily admit to you, "No, I don't ever wash my gear." When you're wrestling seven nights a week, you're sweating *a lot*, and when that gear just sits in a bag, it produces an *unreal* odor, like the foulest high school locker room you can imagine.

In terms of the action, Buddy called better spots, had better movement, and was more fluid than Jerry. He was also a guy who taught me a lot. No matter who you're working with, either they're teaching you, or you're teaching them. Either you're better than they are, or they're better than you.

When you call effective spots, it's not about randomly calling for movement spots where you string a bunch of moves together. You need to be working off of something or toward something. In the regionalized territories, almost all the basic moves were the same. Most of the spots being called were focused on wearing down a single body part over the course of a match. In contrast, Jerry didn't work nearly as hard as Buddy at calling an effective match, and when he got in with you, he preferred to just jerk you around.

If I was wrestling someone as a babyface, I would take their arm, I would work their arm over, and I would keep coming back to their arm. If someone shot me off the ropes, and we then did a dropdown, leapfrog, criss cross, or anything like that, I would still probably end up arm-dragging them, and then I would pounce right back on top of their arm and begin working it all over again. In other words, we had gone through a series of movements that made it look like the heel had successfully freed his arm from me, but I outsmarted him and regained control of their arm.

My job would be to continuously work that same body part for the duration of the bout. I wouldn't hop from an arm over to a leg, then start working their head, then scoot onto their back. The mission was to work one body part, per night, per match. The exception would be if you were wrestling for an hour in a world title match. That was the lone case where you might move to two or three body parts just to spread it out. A match that long might get split into four different mini-matches.

Buddy would call spots where I would get the arm back, or get the headlock back, and then take control again. That's how we'd build it. Then he would cut me off and start to get heat by beating on me, and also taking shortcuts like jabbing me with thumbs to the throat, or other underhanded tactics executed behind the referee's back.

Similar to Buddy Roberts, working against veterans like Ivan Koloff and Masa Saito was also easy. Everybody in that group was in tune with one another, knew what was going on, and had experience.

The first time you wrestle somebody, when all you know is how long the match is supposed to be, and the finish, you're in an awkward position, but you have to pick up and learn the speed and timing of the other person. You have to be cognizant of how they move and react to certain things. You know you're inevitably going to wrestle them multiple times, and the more times you work with them, the better it's going to get, and the easier it's going to get.

Masa Saito was always *really* sharp. He didn't speak much English, and he had some funny characteristics and mannerisms about him that made him someone I *loved* to mess around with. Saito was such a serious-looking guy with no neck, and eyes that shot off in two different directions. He had been to the Olympics as a wrestler, and you knew that meant he was a *serious* shooter.

I always asked myself a question about how I could get over with Saito: Should I just kiss his ass and do whatever he says, or should I throw a monkey wrench into the equation?

Well, being the way I am, I threw a monkey wrench into the equation with Saito. I wanted him to know I was having fun during our matches and wasn't taking everything too seriously. Saito didn't wear wrestling shoes during the early part of his career; he was barefoot. Coincidentally, I worked the leg *a lot* during my matches, but I intentionally took it to another level when I wrestled Saito. A lot of my opponents were bigger than me, so working a leg was always a smart way to communicate to the audience that I was trying to keep the larger men grounded by putting different holds on them.

Punching away on Masa Saito

When I would take Saito down, I would start working his leg, and then every once in a while I would bite his feet when the referee looked away, which the fans loved, and which drove Saito *crazy*. Then I would start tickling his feet, which would drive him absolutely *berzerk*. The reaction from tickling Saito was tremendous. For him to be such a legitimate killer, Saito was *unbelievably* ticklish. If I tickled him, he would respond to me by delivering the *stiffest* kicks trying to break out of the holds.

He'd be kicking the shit out of me while uttering in broken English, "No ticklish my *feet*!"

Of course, that was just an invitation for me to take him down once again, ensnare his foot, and tickle him yet again. Instead of murdering me, Saito actually laughed about it. He appreciated that I had the balls to try to tickle him repeatedly even though I had full knowledge that he *could* kill me whenever he felt like it. I was still spicy enough to keep messing with him.

With Masao Hattori

Some guys warned me and said, "Hey... I really wouldn't be tickling Saito's feet anymore. I think it's really starting to irritate him!"

"Okay, well... we'll see how it goes!" I said, and kept right on doing it.

Poor Masao Hattori. He was another Olympic-style wrestler from Japan who was a bantamweight shooter, and he also won a world championship in amateur-style wrestling. Hattori was simply standing there at ringside waving the flag for Saito and Mr. Sato when they teamed together, and during the beginning of every match, I targeted him and tried to leg dive him just to say I'd done it. It would be the *funniest* thing. Hattori would look one way to wave the flag, and I would shoot in on him and try to get his leg.

"Quit trying to leg dive Masao!" Mike scolded me.

The company would up booking us in matches together, and Hattori wound up stretching the shit out of me a few times over the course of those matches as payback for all of the times I made him nervous by attempting leg dives on him. I know Hattori didn't request those matches to get even with me, but I'm sure whoever was booking the territory and watching me do that to Hattori every night said, "Oh yeah? Okay... let's see what Steve can do with Hattori when he *isn't* distracted by a flag that he has to wave!"

I outweighed Hattori by a good 60 pounds, but none of that mattered. He could put me into whatever hold he wanted to put me in out there, and there was nothing I could do about it.

Six months after my return to Florida, I had to contend with an unexpected case of the past catching up with me. A highway patrolman showed up at my door. I was forced to surrender my driver's license to him because I'd come back to Florida and registered that I was living there. They responded by revoking my license because of the incident that had happened in Georgia with Ricky Gibson years prior when he handed my driver's license to them and told them he was Steve Keirn.

There was a state attorney down in Fort Lauderdale that liked me and who was a big wrestling fan, so I asked him if he would help me clear the matter up. He had me take fingerprints and a picture, and he sent it to that tiny Georgia town. He identified himself as the state attorney for the State of Florida, and he asked them if they could identify me. The town responded in a letter saying they couldn't identify me because they didn't have any photos of me, or any records with my fingerprints. They had to drop the charges because the guy they'd booked, fingerprinted and photographed as Steve Keirn had actually been Ricky Gibson. That kept me out of trouble.

During this successful run in Florida, I learned something no one had ever taught me during my training, and that's how important it is to get on good terms with the announcers. If there's *anyone* who should be sucked up to, it's them. As a main-eventer, whether I liked Gordon Solie or not, I learned that I needed to kiss his ass, because he's the guy who was talking about me to all the people at home and educating them as to how they should interpret what I was doing in the ring. Gordon couldn't have been any more at home around all of the cameras and microphones.

On the flipside, even as a main-event wrestler, I was still so nervous around the cameras that I looked like I thought I was about to be arrested for a DUI. I'd have gladly wrestled 10 times in a row if it meant I could avoid being subjected to a single TV interview. I was surrounded by tremendous interview guys, and that only added to my inadequacy. In Florida, I was having to get up and do interviews right after Dusty Rhodes, who was phenomenal on the microphone, and one of the all-time greatest. He was one of the rare wrestlers capable of delivering a compelling interview as a babyface.

In fairness, it wasn't essential to be dynamic on the microphone in order to be an attraction. Even an all-time great wrestler like Jack Brisco, who was idolized by myself and many other wrestlers, was very cut-and-dried and bland during his interview segments.

We'd do seven interviews for the towns the following week in between taping the show on Wednesday morning and then hitting the road for Miami. My interviews were usually pretty weak. I would often ramble and go off on some tangent, and I would be wondering what the hell I was talking about even when I was right in the middle of saying it. The worst part was the fact that we usually only did one-take interviews. This meant that whatever came out of our mouths made it onto our

The Fabulous Wrestling Life of Steve Keirn

programs no matter how badly we'd screwed it up. No one ever said, "Let's try that again."

As I climbed the rungs of the territory, I started to cut my head far more frequently by virtue of being in so many main-event matches. I carried my blade in my mouth between my cheek and my gums just as I'd rehearsed the very first time I cut a blade with Stan Hansen. Whenever the time was right, I would fall face-first onto the ground and spit the blade into my hand to identify where the sharpest part of the blade was, then I would hold it between my index finger and my thumb before jabbing the sharp end into my forehead.

Getting color against Bob Orton Jr.

One of the nights when color was requested of me was when Mike and I were working against Bob Orton Sr. and Bob Orton Jr. in Tampa at the National Guard Armory. The match had a specific spot where I was supposed to get color. As usual, I spat my blade into my hand and was preparing for the moment when I would slice myself. I grabbed Orton Jr. by the head and I went to smash his head into the turnbuckle pad. When I did that, Bob's head popped right back into my hand,

and I watched in horror as my blade went sailing out into the audience.

As I began to panic, I looked up toward the section of railing where Eddie Graham could normally be seen standing on the second floor of the Armory. He was staring right back at me, waiting to see color. I was supposed to be bleeding at this point in the match, but I couldn't simply go crawling through the audience to retrieve my lost blade.

I leaned over and whispered to Orton Jr., "I just lost my blade; bust me open *hardway*."

Bobby held me by the hair, straddled the top of me, and started punching me full blast in the head and trying to bust me open. He hit me *so* hard that I wound up with golf-ball-sized knots where he'd slugged me. Despite all that pain and effort, no blood flowed from my forehead.

"It's not workin'!" Orton said between punches.

"No shit! And you're *killin'* me, too!" I complained. "Do somethin' else! Run me into your dad's knee or somethin'!"

Orton obliged and grabbed me by the back of the head.

"Dad, put your knee up!" he commanded.

Bob Orton Sr. stuck his knee through the ropes, and as Orton Jr. propelled me toward his father's outstretched leg, I decided to throw myself into his knee as hard as I could, figuring that it would be a surefire way to bust my head open. Unfortunately, I hit Orton Sr.'s knee with so much force that I blew him clean off the ring apron and busted his *knee* open instead of my head. To my great frustration and physical discomfort, no matter what I did, nothing was sufficient to get any blood to spurt from my forehead.

Eddie saw me going the extra mile to sacrifice my personal safety and provide the bout with the blood he had requested. He could see how mashed and beaten my face was. That was one of the only times that I left a crucial piece out of a finish, and I'd done everything I could to try to give Eddie what he wanted. Meanwhile, back in the locker room, Orton Sr. flipped out at me because he's an older guy and I'd rammed his knee so hard with my head that I'd actually damaged his knee more than my face.

Eddie's finishes to tag matches would be *so* long. I could remember freaking out while standing on the ring apron one time when Backlund was trying to tag me. I knew the finish of the match was getting ready to start, but my mind went completely blank. I even kind of reluctantly held my arm out there for the tag because I didn't really want to be tagged in when I was so uncertain about what was supposed to occur. Once I got in the ring, I asked referee Sonny Myers how the finish was supposed to start. After he gave me just a piece of the finish, I was able to recall everything else, including the ending. At no point in my career did I ever encounter anyone else who took such great care to piece together match finishes as Eddie Graham.

Eddie was *such* a genius. Everyone involved in the wrestling business that I ever respected also respected Eddie and how gifted he was for creating great wrestling moments. Unfortunately, I began to see the first signs of deterioration in Eddie, and I'm sorry to say that I may have had a hand in bringing about his eventual downfall.

In prior years, Eddie had been a notorious alcoholic, but he had managed to forego the consumption of alcohol for 14 years by this point. He always talked about being a rehabilitated alcoholic who had spontaneously given up drinking for more than a decade. Well, that all changed one afternoon when Mike, Eddie and I were out on Eddie's 37-foot Striker yacht, along with Kevin Sullivan. It was a very expensive ship, with an all-aluminum hull. It was also extremely fast, and everything aboard it was first-class.

Mike, Kevin and I were at the back of the yacht chugging beer from cans. The process of "shooting" a beer had just been popularized, where we would take a can opener, open the bottom of the can, put it up to our lips, and pop the top. The instant the top pops on the beer can, the beer *rockets* down your throat in an instant. The first time you experience it, you wouldn't think anyone could drink a beer that fast, but all of the golden fluid would spontaneously disappear down the hatch and into your stomach.

Eddie saw how distracted the three of us were as we played around with the beer cans, so he wandered over to us at the back of the boat to see what we were up to.

"What are you guys doin'?" Eddie asked.

"We're just shooting beers, Dad," said Mike, before explaining the process to him.

Eddie was clearly intrigued by the physics involved in the beer-shooting process.

"Hey, let me try that!" said Eddie.

We couldn't say no to Eddie, so we obliged and handed over a can of beer. Eddie shot a beer, tossing aside 14 years of sobriety in the process.

"That's kind of a waste," said Eddie, clearly underwhelmed. "You're just chugging your beer and not really tasting it."

Mike, Kevin and I exchanged puzzled glances with one another, because it was a little startling that Eddie had so casually downed an entire beer can after so many years of abstaining from alcohol. Sure enough, Eddie resumed the regular consumption of beer and liquor almost immediately thereafter.

Not only did Eddie start drinking when he was home and away from the business, but he also started drinking in the office, *and* during wrestling events. Most alarmingly, Eddie would show up at the airport with a paper sack, and he would be tipping it up and drinking from it. Then he would climb into the pilot's seat of the plane while he was drunk, and the plane would be sliding all over the sky.

Eddie didn't only fly talent to the Bahamas; he would fly us to cities throughout Florida. He never charged us to ride with him in his plane, and he was honestly an excellent pilot when he was sober. My dad even flew with us once, and since my dad was a U.S. Air Force pilot and a veteran of multiple wars, we believed him when he said of Eddie's flying ability, "Yeah, he's a good pilot."

One evening we were flying back from Melbourne, and Eddie was blasting one of his eight-track country music cassettes over the plane's speakers. Beneath us, the sky erupted as the day-ending fireworks display began at Disney World. Eddie cocked his head to look at me sitting in the passenger's seat and barked, "This is what your old man did in Vietnam!"

Without any further hesitation, Eddie pushed the steering column forward and dive bombed us directly into the fireworks display at Disney World. I thought my life was over right then and there, as a drunken Eddie Graham had sent us plummeting straight toward Cinderella Castle. Eddie pulled us out of the dive, of course, but sent us sliding back and forth during his recovery.

After the dive-bombing stunt concluded, we found ourselves approaching Tampa, and I was still sweating with angst. I was sitting in the seat that faces forward at the very back of the plane, and I was staring down at the runway thinking, "Why isn't Eddie turning that stupid music off?" It was *blaring*. That's when I realized Eddie hadn't called anybody, and he was simply going to land without alerting the tower ahead of time.

"Hey, man," I said to Mike. "Your dad's not talkin' to the tower. He hasn't spoken to anyone on the radio yet."

"Eh. Don't worry about it," replied Mike dismissively. "He does it all the time."

As we touched down, there was a huge commercial plane touching down on the same landing strip, but approaching it from the opposite direction.

"Eddie! Eddie! Eddie!" I screamed. "There's a *plane*!"

Eddie sharply turned the controls and simply cut us across the grass, and also across a couple of runways, and we wound up at the private airport where he parked his plane. Again, Eddie had neglected to turn on his radio to contact the tower before making his landing, and at an *international airport* no less. In the process, he had caused quite a stir down below.

Soon the entire plane was surrounded by cars from the Federal Aviation Administration. Eddie's recklessness was something that simply wasn't tolerated from licensed pilots. I couldn't smell the alcohol on him at the time, but Eddie was clearly more than a few sheets to the wind. He'd already dive bombed Disney World, and now he had narrowly avoided a collision with a commercial plane while making an unauthorized landing.

"Don't worry about this, kid!" Eddie assured me. "I've got this!"

Eddie opened the rear door to the plane, and there were three steps that you could descend to get to the ground, but you had to physically reach down and push the steps because they didn't deploy automatically. Cops and FAA officials were standing there awaiting Eddie's exit. They all knew who he was, because the plane had "69-EG" on the side of it.

The officials who were all concerned by the fact that Eddie had not engaged with the tower on the radio had their concerns climb exponentially when Eddie stepped out of the plane without placing the steps down first. In the process, Eddie tumbled out of the plane and took a bump right on the runway. His pants split open at the seam when he landed.

"Eddie, are you okay?!" the officials asked him as they rushed to help him up.

"Where am I?" asked Eddie groggily as he held his head.

Eddie was clearly selling the tumble and working the guys who were assisting him.

"Where am I?" he said.

"You're in Tampa," they replied. "Are you okay?"

"How did I get here?" said Eddie.

"You just flew your plane from Melbourne all the way here!" they told him.

"Oh, man. The last thing I remember is being in the ring, and Killer Karl Kox hit me with a chair!" said Eddie.

Eddie managed to talk his way out of it, but I was horrified. I could tell that his alcoholism was progressively getting worse.

The Fabulous Wrestling Life of Steve Keirn

This was just one of many episodes that transpired during the gradual deterioration of a guy that I had idolized, and who had broken me into the wrestling business. Each time I watched Eddie stagger around drunk – let alone fly in a drunken state while putting the lives of myself and others at risk – it lowered his standing in my eyes by several notches.

On a subsequent trip, we were taking off from Tampa and flying over to Sarasota. Eddie pulled the plane up into the air and made a hard turn to the right, which was *not* in the direction we should have been traveling in, and then he looked back at me.

"Watch this, kid! Watch the *cars*!" said Eddie.

Eddie then proceeded to make two distinct dive-bombing swoops toward the cars on the bridges below. It was like he wanted to impress me by flying like my father would have flown during a military mission. All of it was just scary, stupid, and pointless.

On yet another occasion, Eddie managed to cause a stir at the airport before he ever boarded his plane. He drove right up to the fence of the private airport and just sat out in his car drinking. I could clearly see that it was him, so I went over to Mike and said, "Hey, Mike, your dad's drinkin' again."

"Yeah. He's lost control," said Mike sadly.

Eddie was angry because none of the airport personnel were coming to the fence, which sat on wheels and needed to be rolled in so that cars could pass through. Instead of getting out of his car to seek assistance, Eddie sat in his Lincoln and revved the engine impatiently hoping that it would summon someone to assist him. Out of the blue, Eddie threw the car into gear and plowed straight into the chainlink fence, in what appeared to be an intentional effort to ram it. Eddie then attempted to reverse his direction, and the tires spun, but the car remained locked in place, as it was now hooked to the fence. Airport personnel had to be summoned to detach Eddie's car from the fence.

All of these incidents made me very reluctant to fly with Eddie. It seemed like every time I would meet him at the airport, something terrifying or embarrassing would occur. The Funks even told me how they watched from the passenger section as Eddie flew clear over Tampa while listening to music. Terry had to unbuckle his seatbelt and shake Eddie to awaken him from his daydream and inform him that he'd missed Tampa and was now flying straight into the Gulf of Mexico. Eddie quickly turned the plane around and landed.

This incident was quite telling as to the extent of Eddie's distraction. When you get airborne in Florida, you can pretty much see from one side of the state to the other because it's only 130 miles wide, and all of the towns below are easy to identify based on the lights. There's also light all around the waters of St. Petersburg, Clearwater and Tampa. When you pass Tampa, you're in the Gulf of Mexico, and you cease to see any lights. In other words, Eddie had bypassed all of the lights and obliviously flown his plane directly into the darkness.

The effects of Eddie's drinking didn't only influence his flying abilities. Alcohol caused him to lose his edge, along with the overall shrewdness of a mind that had once made him such a potent booker and match planner. The alcohol had taken over, and I could see the man I'd respected slowly slipping away. Everyone else noticed it, too, as Dusty and all of the top other guys were still in Florida at the time. It wasn't as if the situation made Eddie the butt-end of a lot of jokes; everyone was just sad to watch his decline, and to see the way alcohol seemed to derail his whole life.

Moments like these caused me to take stock of my feelings for another man as well. I'd placed Eddie on a pedestal even above my own dad because he'd been such an influential part of my life, and then I came to the realization of who the true hero was between the two of them. It was *easily* my father. He may not have been a muscular, wealthy and famous professional wrestler, but he was an authentic war hero who showed far more toughness and discipline over the course of his life, and in his service to his family. I came to realize how foolish I had been to pedestalize Eddie and look upon him as a father figure, and I vowed to uphold my real dad in a proper place of admiration from that point on.

That isn't to say there weren't other people in the wrestling business that I looked to for mentoring. Dusty Rhodes wasn't my in-ring idol; I certainly did not *want* to wrestle like Dusty. Still, no matter what people thought about Dusty as far as his theatrical elbows, hip gyrations and other performance mannerisms were concerned, he was undeniably one of the greatest promo guys who I ever listened to in my whole career. He was also spontaneous, and just a lot of fun to be with. The two of us became really close friends in Florida.

Wearing my "Tuck Fexas" shirt with "Superstar" Billy Graham

I absolutely loved to pick at Dusty to get reactions out of him. I wore a t-shirt that I got from Bill Watts. It said, "Tuck Fexas" on it, above a longhorn cattle with broken horns.

Watts was from Oklahoma, and they always had a huge rivalry with Texas, and I'm sure he knew that shirt would rankle the American Dream. He was right; Dusty absolutely *despised* it.

"Take that damn t-shirt *off!*" said Dusty the first time he saw me wearing it.

"Oh, no! I like *this* t-shirt!" I laughed. After that I made it a point to wear it far more often, and I *still* have it to this day.

I traveled with a lot of people, but I always took it as a compliment whenever Dusty asked me to ride with him. He told several hilarious stories about himself and Dick Murdoch, which always kept me laughing, and he also gave me my first cowboy hat. I wore it everywhere just because Dusty had given it to me, and I wore it over the objections of people who would say, "You're not a cowboy! You're a *beach* bum!" And I would say, "Yeah, well I'm a cowboy *now!*"

Sporting the hat Dusty had bequeathed to me, I would stroll into shows like I was suddenly a cowboy and take pictures with fans while wearing the hat. The thing was, they weren't coming up to me asking me to take pictures with them. I was actually the one going up to them asking them to take pictures with me. In Fort Lauderdale, I even scored a photo with a dirty guy who wore an old straw hat and looked homeless. Despite his haggard appearance, he was allegedly a junk collector who had sold his junkyard for millions of dollars. I just liked to wander around and take as many photos as I could with fans that I thought were odd-looking. Dusty's cowboy hat made it into a lot of those photos.

I frequently wore my cowboy attire while hanging out with Dusty and riding up and down the road with him. I was usually the listener on the road trips, but I also had some interesting stuff to share with the guys. I wasn't the typical young kid without a past; guys actually wanted to hear stories about my dad as a POW, and what it was like being without him for all that time when he was stuck in Vietnam.

I think it benefitted me that I was humble and told stories about the absence of my father, and about how I didn't have someone around to guide me in critical ways. It made me sound a lot more humble than the guys that would tell stories – most of which were lies – about the number of guys they had beaten up in high school.

Dusty and I were speeding out of Orlando on a Sunday night after the speed limit had just been lowered from 70 miles per hour down to 55. Dusty still insisted on going about 90, and we flew past a highway patrolman.

With my Weimaraner Elton

As we got pulled over, I stared straight ahead and said, "Well… I could see *that* comin'."

Dusty just laughed.

"Hey, baby… there's not a highway patrolman, not a sheriff, and not a police officer in the state of Florida who would give the American Dream a ticket!" proclaimed Dusty. "Watch this!"

The highway patrolman came walking up to Dusty's new Lincoln Town Car, which was dove-gray on dove-gray with a moonroof. My Weimaraner dog Elton sat patiently in the back seat, as Dusty had requested that I bring the dog along because Elton's color matched his car.

Dusty raised his head to address the police officer. He still had a big, fresh piece of tape on his head because he had done a blade job earlier that night. He also had his shirt off and his jeans tucked into his boots.

"I need to see your driver's license and registration," said the patrolman when he arrived at the window.

"Yessir, officer. What's the problem?" asked Dusty.

"You were speedin'," replied the officer. "Can I ask you what your hurry is?"

"Oh, I had a rough night," said the Dream. "I was over at the Eddie Graham Sports Complex here in Orlando and had a tough rasslin' match."

"Okay, well you were speedin'," said the officer, sternly. "If you were having such a hard night, why didn't you let *that* guy drive?"

The officer pointed over at me when he said that, to which Dusty replied, "This is my brand new car! He ain't drivin' *my* car!"

Dusty was trying to be funny and cordial with the officer, but he was also going out of his way to be recognized. Well, this officer didn't watch wrestling. He studied Dusty's driver's license and then said, "Well, Mr. Runnels… you are Virgil Riley Runnels, right?"

"Yeah, I am, officer," said Dusty. "But I'm also 'The American Dream' Dusty Rhodes! The rassler!"

"Well I don't watch wrestlin'," said the officer dismissively.

"*What*?!" said Dusty.

When the officer returned to the window and handed Dusty a ticket, Dusty was in no mood to be friendly anymore.

"Officer, do you have a grandmama?" asked Dusty.

"Yeah, I've got a grandma," said the officer.

"Good. Well I'm gonna tell you somethin'," began Dusty. "You go home tonight, call your grandmama, and you tell your grandmama that you just gave 'The American Dream' Dusty Rhodes a ticket, and I guarantee you ain't eatin' Thanksgiving dinner in her house *this* year!"

With "The American Dream" Dusty Rhodes

With that, we took off with 75 miles still to cover on our way from Orlando to Tampa. For the entire hour that it took us, I kept repeating in Dusty's voice, "Ain't a highway patrolman, ain't a sheriff's deputy, ain't a police officer, and ain't a *Boy Scout* ever gonna give 'The American Dream' a ticket!"

It absolutely *killed* Dusty that I was there to witness that exchange.

It would be no understatement to say that Dusty was figuratively on fire in the 1970s. He was easily the hottest act on the Florida wrestling scene. That's why I studied Dusty to figure out what made him so appealing, and I think I pinpointed it. Part of it came down to the fact that he wasn't anything to be worried about from an audience standpoint, which is to say that he wasn't a threat to anything the audience held dear.

If you brought your wife or your girlfriend to the wrestling matches, they might tell you that they liked Dusty, but you excused it because Dusty wasn't this handsome, captivating sex symbol that women desired. That's in contrast to Jack Brisco, who was a *stud*. Your girlfriend or your wife might look at Jack and say, "Wow. I like him. I wish *you* looked like him." They *never* said that about Dusty, so he posed no threat to the egos of the men in attendance.

Dusty simply had a special magic to his presentation, and he won everyone's hearts. It didn't hurt that he was the most phenomenal promo guy I ever watched. We'd do all of our promos Wednesday morning after TV until 2:00 p.m. before we'd drive to Miami. We'd do the promos for every town in the state of Florida for the next week. Dusty would get out there and bang the promos out one right after the other. I'd sit there in awe with my mouth agape in amazement at some of the stuff he said.

I think Dusty took an initial liking to me out of respect for my father. He met my father, sat with him, spoke with him, and became friends with him. Dusty also seemed to respect where I'd gotten solely out of hard work and a lot of luck; I was nobody's relative in the wrestling business, and I didn't have an amazing sports background like Dusty, Wahoo, or some of the other guys. I had simply been in the right place at the right time, had gone out of my way to be as likable as I could, and took advantage of whatever opportunities presented themselves.

Unfortunately, Dusty was absolutely obsessed with country music, which is something I didn't give a rat's ass about. My favorite music was the music of the era: I listened to anything from Creedence Clearwater Revival to Led Zeppelin. However, when I drove with the Briscos, all I heard was country music. When I was with Dick Murdoch or Dusty Rhodes, it was *also* a whole lot of country music. It was the same thing with Terry Funk. It was *maddening*, but I adapted as best I could.

I hadn't even heard of Willie Nelson until I started hanging out with Dusty, and one night we listened to Willie Nelson all the way back to Tampa after our show. When we arrived home, we went to the Imperial Lounge, which was a bar we patronized all the time in Tampa. When we got inside the bar, I found some space on the wall in the back to lean against. I was listening to the guy on stage, and they introduced him as Boxcar Willie. He was singing all the Willie Nelson songs I'd just been listening to for hours while riding with Dusty in his car.

Dusty came over to me and asked me, "What are you doin'?"

"I'm listenin' to that guy you told me was so famous," I said, gesturing towards the stage. "If he's *so* famous, what the hell is he doin' in the Imperial Lounge?!"

Dusty was *furious*.

"That's not Willie Nelson you dumbass!" screamed Dusty. "That's *Boxcar* Willie! He's not even close to Willie Nelson!"

"But he sounds just like him!" I objected.

Dusty corrected me so many times on things like that, but he seemed to enjoy it. He knew I was sincerely trying to fit in with him and the rest of the cowboys working in the Florida territory. He certainly knew that I wouldn't have worn cowboy boots and cowboy hats and hung out in country bars unless I was accompanying him.

At heart, I truly was a beach bum from Florida who spearfished and did things around the water during his spare time. And whenever I had an opportunity, I brought other wrestlers into that world and made them as uncomfortable as I possibly could, with comedic intent.

At the broadcast table with **Gordon Solie** and **Dusty Rhodes**

NINE

I learned how to spearfish while I was growing up, and I took a strong and immediate liking to it. As a kid, I would always ride my bicycle with a banana seat and butterfly handlebars down to the docks, get in the water, and just swim away from the shore toward where the docks were and the boats were tied up. Then I would dive underwater with just a mask, fins, a spear gun and a weight belt that I had bought for myself.

It was quite simple to swim beneath the water's surface and shoot fish all day long. At other times, Mom would drop me off at the Gandy Bridge so that I could spend the day shooting fish, and then she would pick me up at a certain time in the afternoon.

I caught so many fish so fast that it forever killed the idea of traditional fishing for me. When my dad was around, he would take me out fishing, and we could sit in a boat all day long and not catch a single fish. Then Dad would fall asleep in the boat, and I'd be bored out of my skull. Spearfishing was far simpler. You go down there. There's a fish. You *shoot* it. You go home. If there's no fish, you would know right away if you were wasting your time in that spot, as opposed to floating on the surface for hours on end.

From snorkeling and spearfishing, I transitioned over to scuba diving. A lot of the wrestlers who came through Florida would eventually come to me for scuba lessons, and as the business started developing and I began making more friends, I spent increasingly longer periods of time with them around the water doing what I enjoyed.

When Terry Funk came down to Florida when I was a kid, not only did I meet him at the airport to drive him wherever he needed to go, but I also packed my scuba diving gear and brought it to the motel he was staying in to teach him how to scuba dive. Terry and I were friends for life after that simply because I'd taught him something that he had wanted to learn so badly. I was only 16 years old at the time and had no

The Fabulous Wrestling Life of Steve Keirn

idea that I was ever going to have a career in the wrestling business, let alone as a wrestler who would one day share the ring with Terry.

Early on there were no licenses required to go scuba diving, but then all of a sudden you needed one simply to buy the air to dive with. I went through the dive course with Jerry Brisco and Jos LeDuc, and on one of our certifying dives we had to go down under the water and swim away from the instructors, then swim around underwater with our tanks on and return to where we'd began.

Scuba trip with Bob Backlund, Gerald Brisco and Jimmy Garvin

Jerry was really excited about getting his scuba license. He was from Oklahoma and hadn't spent much time in the ocean like I had, so he wasn't nearly as comfortable down there as I was. Unfortunately for Jerry, I'd grown far more confident with my standing amongst the boys, and along with that came increased confidence in my ability to rib people and get away with it. I hovered above Jerry while he swam along the ocean floor beneath me, and then I descended upon him, reached out, and squeezed his air supply completely off. Then I innocently circled around to the other side of him when he started to suck on his regulator, and he noticed me and began pointing to his regulator.

I gestured back with a shrug, as if I had no clue what might be troubling him. Jerry started trying to grab my regulator out of my mouth, and I just slapped his hand away until he gave up and swam for the surface. I emerged right behind him.

"My air stopped workin'!" said Jerry. "I don't know what happened!"

"*I* do. I shut it off!" I laughed.

"*Bastard!*" said Jerry.

When Jerry would start telling that story to people years later, he would always exaggerate and say that I pulled the rib on him when we were at a depth of 30 feet; there's *no way* we were more than 15 feet beneath the surface. At no point was he in any type of danger.

Jerry Brisco with Bob Backlund as he pretends to get in the water

That wasn't the only time I messed with Jerry during a scuba excursion. Another time we were beneath the surface, and I made sure to come down on top of Jerry with all of my force and pin him to the ground beneath the water, like I was an amateur wrestler. Through the regulator I said, "Two points!"

The things I was doing with the guys that weren't comfortable in the water weren't too dangerous, but they were *extremely* funny to me.

Unlike Jerry Brisco, Bob Backlund wanted absolutely nothing to do with scuba diving, but I managed to get him to wear all of my gear. I got him to hop in the water so that I could take a picture of him, but he refused to remove his hands off of the boat the entire time.

When English wrestler Billy Robinson arrived in Florida, he said, "Can you please teach me how to scuba dive?"

"Sure. Just meet me over at Mike's house," I told him.

Mike had a house right on the water, with a dock in his backyard for easy access. I brought all my equipment over to Mike's house so that Billy could use it, and then I guided Billy through the process of donning all of the diving gear. Finally, Billy was fully attired in scuba gear and standing on Mike's dock.

Once Billy got the mask on with the regulator in it, I asked him, "Are you comfortable? Can you breathe?"

"Yes," said Billy.

"Good!" I said.

That was the moment when I shoved Billy Robinson clean off the dock and into the water below. When Billy hit the water, he tore the mask off, spit the regulator out, and started thrashing around in the water like a four-year-old.

"I'm gonna kill you!" he screamed. "I'm gonna *kill* you!"

"Billy… stand up," I ordered him. "It's only four feet of water!"

Billy stood up with a bewildered expression on his face.

"Some day…" Billy said, "I'm gonna get back at you for this."

Billy was a notoriously tough guy, so he was a particularly risky target for a rib. I was wagering my life that he would find my rib to be funny, and that he wouldn't beat me up afterwards. Fortunately, I never suffered any payback for that rib on Billy. I'd heard plenty of bad things about Billy Robinson getting angry in the ring and stretching guys, or otherwise being a bully. There was an aura of intimidation that surrounded him everywhere he went, like there was always the potential for spontaneous violence.

When I finally got around Billy, I wound up ribbing Billy so many times that he was more or less in awe and admiration of the fact that I'd actually had the guts to rib him at all, let alone with such frequency. I became *obsessed* with the idea of ribbing him; it was like poking a rattlesnake with a stick. You weren't quite sure if the stick was long enough, but you wanted to see if it would work, and then how far you could go in poking the rattlesnake in the face before the snake was finally able to reach past that stick and sink its fangs into your arm.

For one of my favorite ribs on Billy, I enlisted the help of Jimmy Garvin. He and I were driving back from Arcadia together in my Corvette, and we were cruising down the two-lane backroads of Florida. All of us had been communicating on our CB radios as usual, and Jimmy and I had gotten a jumpstart on many of the other guys. Ultimately, the two of us arrived at a T-road where one highway reached a dead end as it connected with another highway. In this instance, it was the highway coming out of Arcadia running smack into the 301 Highway that takes you to Tampa.

There was a small gas station that sat a little ways back from the intersection. Jimmy and I came up with a brilliant idea while we were on the way home and keeping Billy engaged on his CB radio. The two of us got to the corner and I turned into the gas station. Then I swung the car all the way back around and parked it in a way that enabled me to get an unobstructed view of the road.

"Hey, Billy… You're gonna come to a stop sign up here pretty soon," I spoke into the handheld CB radio speaker. "There's nobody coming either way, so you can just blow right on through it. There's no cops or nothin'. Keep goin' straight."

The thing was, Billy *couldn't* go straight; there was an orange grove on the other side of the highway. As we sat and watched, Billy Robinson's Cadillac charged right ahead at 80 miles per hour. He bottomed out coming off of that little highway onto the bigger highway. His Cadillac's muffler hit the ground, sparks flew everywhere, and Billy plowed straight into the orange grove. Dirt and orange debris exploded into the air as the orange trees were either mowed down, or shot off to either side of the Cadillac.

As this was happening, I got on the speaker and said, "Wait! I'm wrong! I'm wrong! You need to take a *right*! *Don't* go straight through!"

After a delay of a few seconds, Billy's voice came on the speaker.

"It's too late," he stated, dejectedly. "I already went straight. Now I know what the inside of an orange grove looks like. I need to back out of here."

Jimmy and I sat there roaring with laughter while Billy backed his Cadillac onto the highway and then continued onward toward Tampa. We never let him know that we'd set him up to crash into the orange grove, or that we'd watched the whole ordeal from the gas station's parking lot. In fact, even though we were now driving behind Billy, I continued to feed him false information that led him to believe we were still in front of him. I figured he was going so fast that he'd attract the attention of any police officers that might be lurking up ahead, and they would be occupied with Billy by the time we cruised by.

No matter how much I enjoyed making Billy the butt of the joke, I couldn't deny how polished he was in the ring. I was always trying to steal stuff from the best wrestlers back in those days, and Billy had a couple of really good moves that I could never quite figure out.

One time I saw Billy do a really cool counter move on the mat, and I was dying to ask him about it once he came back to the dressing room.

"How do you do that one reversal?" I asked him after he took a seat on the bench.

"I'll have to teach you out there sometime, kid," smiled Billy, seemingly pleased that I had taken an interest in his repertoire.

I felt similarly about Tony Charles. He had a lot of really slick moves that were still solid. They were flashy, but they looked like something a skilled combatant could actually utilize in a real fight. The company actually booked me in matches against Tony just so that he could teach me things out in the ring like special monkey flips and other things that you didn't really need to be an acrobat to pull off. Both Billy and Tony taught me some British-style movements that I could incorporate, and they were happy to do it.

When it came to the development of my style, I stole a little bit from Billy Robinson, Tony Charles, Jack Brisco, Harley Race and Mr. Wrestling #2. Once you mix stylistic components from so many people together, you can successfully turn it into your own offering. You also prevent yourself from becoming a carbon copy of any single guy. That was one of the things that always bothered me about my buddy Dick Slater; he went so over the top in his obsession with Terry Funk. Terry was certainly an ideal person to emulate in several respects, but Dickie seemed hell bent on becoming an *exact* replica of Terry. I always felt he could have avoided that if he had blended together more aspects of other people's styles.

In terms of competency in the water, Mike Graham was every bit as skilled and fearless as I was. When the film Jaws came out, Mike and I immediately got turned on by the idea of catching sharks. The two of us would go out and shark fish by the Skyway, which is a big bridge that extends out and over the mouth of Tampa Bay and into the city of Tampa. There are always huge sharks there because they feed off of the ships that are traveling in and out of the Bay. If Mike wasn't available, I'd take his son Stephen with me. Mike and I were so close at the time that he had named his own son after me. He may have stated publicly that it wasn't because of me, but that was bullshit; Mike didn't know *any* other Stephens.

During an average week, the two of us would typically go out shark fishing two or three times. Then we decided it wasn't exciting enough simply to fish for sharks, so we thought it would be a good idea for us to go underwater, chum up the sharks, and then see how many we could kill with bang sticks beneath the water.

Chumming up the water attracted the sharks like a charm and initiated a feeding frenzy. When I swam up to the first sharks with the bang sticks, hitting the first one on the head caused an explosion that blew my mask clean off of my face. I couldn't locate my mask underwater while I was in the midst of a full-blown feeding frenzy.

"I think we may have taken this a little too far," I told Mike after I'd surfaced.

"I think you might be right," he replied.

We backed things down a little bit from there, but that wouldn't be the last time I would make a hobby out of hunting dangerous animals.

Just because Mike and I were so close didn't mean he was immune to being on the receiving end of ribbing from me. We were in Daytona Beach, and Jimmy Garvin and I had gone out to an ABC liquor store that had a bar attached to it.

We were having a few beers, and the guy sitting beside me said, "Hey, aren't you Steve Keirn?"

"Yeah, that's me," I smiled.

"I thought so! I'm a Daytona Beach police officer," he said.

"Oh really? Where's your uniform at?" I asked.

"Well, I'm off-duty right now," he said.

The lightbulb promptly went off in my head that I had access to a cop. Mike Graham was back at the hotel with a girl, and these were the perfect ingredients to incorporate into a stellar rib.

Jimmy got involved in my conversation with the officer, and the three of us began to collaborate on a plan to rib Mike memorably. We decided that the best thing to do might be for the officer to pretend to raid the hotel in an anti-prostitution sting.

"Yeah! You want me to run home, grab my uniform and meet you at the hotel with my squad car?" the eager officer asked.

"Oh yeah!" Jimmy and I both said.

The cop came back with his uniform and car, and then Jimmy added something else into the mix.

"It will be more believable if one of us is handcuffed already when you knock on Mike's door, like we're in custody," said Jimmy.

"Yeah! You can handcuff *me*!" I said. "I'll do it! I'll just stand there in only my underwear!"

So that's exactly what we did. As I stood in that hallway with my arms handcuffed behind my back, the officer pounded on Mike's hotel room door.

"Open up!" said the cop. "Daytona Beach Police! Open up!"

It took Mike a while to get to the door. When he finally opened the door, he left it chained, but he cracked it just enough for him to be able to see me out there with my wrists cuffed, and that I was standing next to a uniformed policeman.

"Yes, sir," said Mike, as he attempted to clear his sleepy eyes. "What can I do for you?"

"Do you have an unregistered guest in your room?" asked the officer.

Mike's eyes opened up to the size of saucers when this question was asked. Yes, he had a girl in the room; she was drunk, *naked*, and unconscious on the bed.

Mike stammered and stuttered through his answer.

"Yeah, there's a girl in here, but she's just gettin' ready to leave!" Mike finally spat out.

"Well, can you open the door?" asked the officer.

Mike slowly began to unlatch and open the door, all while cussing me out. He figured that I'd done something stupid, gotten busted by the police, and then ratted him out afterwards.

"Awww, man, Keirn!" said Mike. "What the hell did you do?!"

When Mike finally got his door all the way open, the officer finally said, "I need to get into the room to talk to the girl."

At that point, Mike stepped out into the hallway to make room for the officer to enter his room, and that's when Jimmy Garvin snapped a photo of Mike with the camera he had been holding at the ready. Everyone who had been in on the rib burst into laughter, including the officer. Luckily, once he realized he wouldn't be carted off to jail, Mike started laughing, too.

I *loved* to get guys arrested. It was one of my favorite ribs to pull off because it terrified the victims so deeply. Arrest ribs work so well because it's hard for a guy to argue with an arresting officer who has the force of the law on his side. A guy can't laugh at the cop with any confidence, or presume that it's a rib, because if you laugh at a police officer who's serious, you run the risk of having additional charges piled on top of you. Those ribs are also very hard to top.

Another guy I hung out with a lot at the beach was Brian Blair. He was just getting started as a rookie wrestler in 1977. He had a deep passion for the business, and he took great joy in hanging out with all of the other wrestlers. He did everything the veterans asked of him, which was exactly what you should do if you want to get a good reputation. The negative side effect to being so young, green and impressionable is that it makes you especially susceptible to ribs.

Brian rode with me quite a bit during his first few months in the business, and he fell asleep in the back seat of the car on the way to West Palm prior to one of his earliest matches. This created a perfect opportunity to give him a classic initiation rib. I moved the clock on the car's radio up an hour so that when he woke up, I said, "Brian, we're an hour late! You've got to put your stuff on!"

Brian freaked *totally* out. We even pulled over on the turnpike so that Brian could get dressed. In reality, we were right on time! We sped to the front of the West Palm Coliseum, and Brian hopped out thinking his match was going to the ring right then and there. He bolted up to the building, and everyone on the top that was watching him come in was like, "Boy, Brian… you sure are excited about being here!"

At the very beginning, there were common ribs that were played on green guys. I was very fortunate to be liked by some key veterans like the Briscos, the Funks, Dick Murdoch and Dusty Rhodes, and the guys that would like to be locker room bullies when they pulled ribs. They used to push around on their necks in the dressing room or be warming up, and some young guy like Brian would be sitting there watching them. Brian was especially fun to get with ribs. *Everybody* got Brian.

"What are you doing?" the rookie wrestler would say.

"Keeping my neck big," the veteran would answer. "You've got to keep your neck big and strong. If you land on your head and break your neck, you're *done*."

This rib worked especially well if the show was at a school with a locker room in it. They'd get the rookie to back up to a locker if your show was at a school with a locker room in it. The veteran would stand in front of the rookie and put their hands up behind their neck and pry their head down a few times while the vet was trying to help the rookie work his neck, all while telling the rookie to resist. You'd get the rookies really trying to show off how strong they were, and if you timed it right, you could suddenly let go of their head and watch them bash their head into the locker and then fall to the ground.

Clearly, it was one of those ribs that was funny to everybody in the dressing room except for the guy having the rib done to him. I pulled a memorable rib on someone that fell into that category, and it might have had adverse consequences for both my career and my health if it hadn't been so well received.

Paul Orndorff and I were driving to West Palm Beach, and we had to traverse a long, two-lane stretch from Yeehaw Junction to Lake Wales. There are a lot of wild animals on that road, and one of my *favorite* things to do was to ensnare snakes, lizards, or whatever other critters I could find roaming the roadside along that route, and then stuff them in some of the boys' bags in the dressing room. I became notorious for that.

As the two of us reached the turnpike at Yeehaw Junction, we came to a patch of land where armadillos used to congregate and eat the grass along the edge of the road.

"Have you ever tried to catch an armadillo?" I asked Paul.

"No, man!" replied Paul. "There's *no way* you could catch one of those!"

"Watch this!" I said, accepting his challenge.

I pulled the car to a stop along the edge of the turnpike and collected my towel from my gear bag. Then I got out of the car, unfolded the towel, and walked behind the towel as if it was somehow going to conceal my approach as I snuck up on an unsuspecting armadillo.

Cars were racing past us along the turnpike, but I didn't let that distract me. I got between the high grass and the road, and then I cut off an armadillo and ran him down. I put my hand on him as I was running alongside him to restrict his movement, since armadillos like to hop around a bit and bounce back and forth like rabbits. As I pressed the armadillo down toward the ground, I threw my towel over the top of him, and then I dropped down, tackled him, and wrapped him up.

Orndorff couldn't believe his eyes.

"Holy shit!" he said.

Paul assisted me as I carried the armadillo over to the car, dropped it into a bag that ordinarily held tools, and placed it in the back of my car. When we arrived at West Palm, I brought the bag containing the armadillo into the dressing room, and that's when I spotted the gym bag of Prince Tonga.

Better known in the wrestling world as Haku or Meng, Prince Tonga was a fresh entrant in the wrestling business at that point. He may only have been 19 years old at the time. He was a humble, slender, young kid at the time, and very naive. I had no idea he would one day grow up and develop a reputation as the toughest individual in the entire wrestling industry.

Tonga's bag possessed a rounded top and handles, and featured a zipper that went clear across the top of it.

"Watch the door and let me know if Tonga is coming," I instructed Paul.

While Orndorff was watching the hallway, I took the armadillo, jammed it into Tonga's wrestling bag, and then zipped it shut. Orndorff and I sat down, and we were absolutely dying of anticipation waiting for Tonga to enter the dressing room and find an armadillo nesting in his bag. Paul was so plainly anxious that he almost gave the whole thing away simply through his erratic, jittery movements.

Finally, the unsuspecting Prince Tonga entered the room, sat on a chair, and reached down to unzip his bag. Just as soon as he tugged the zipper, the armadillo's head – which resembles that of a giant rat with its tiny ears and long nose – popped straight up and out of the fresh opening in the top of the bag. When the armadillo's head was unveiled, Tonga looked down at it and nearly lost his breath trying to scream. He was gasping heavily, but no sounds were being emitted from his mouth.

The armadillo worked his way free of the bag, and Tonga took off running for the door. When he reached it, he slammed right into it at full force. The only problem was that the door needed to be pulled intead of pushed in order for it to open, and the resulting impact shook the entire dressing room. Unable to escape that way, Tonga then ran over to the bathroom stall located in the room, and inadvertently tore it down in his haste to open its door. From there, he sprinted back to the entrance door, succeeded in pulling it open, and *bolted* through it. However, the armadillo was hot on his heels, and also followed him out into the empty arena.

With Florida Tag Team Championship partner Bob Backlund

    It's one of those ribs I pulled that was innocent, but it scared Tonga half to death. I didn't realize later on that it would become an eternal threat to my life knowing that I'd ribbed him, and what he might want to do to get his revenge. Whenever I see him, the first thing I do is apologize profusely once again for a rib from several decades ago.
    Fortunately for me, Haku still seems to think the rib was funny. To this day, if Haku sees me in person, the first thing he'll ask is, "Have you put any armadillos in people's bags lately?"
    The original idea behind putting me on a team with Bob Backlund was for me to assist with teaching him. Eddie wanted to groom Backlund a little bit because Bobby was a shooter from Minnesota, but he was very robotic. Despite being a great athlete in his actual sport, Bobby's body movements weren't fluid at all. Usually it was the bodybuilders and guys with a lot of muscles that had that problem; they

couldn't produce fluid motion, which prevented a lot of their actions and reactions from appearing natural.

The chemistry of our team wasn't the best, but that's my opinion based on the fact that Bob had some tough acts to follow as my tag team partner. I'd been teamed up with Mike, who was effortless in the ring and was an excellent wrestler. Mike's only downside was the fact that he was small, so I was the dominant force on our tag team.

To his credit, Mike liked to sell because his dad owned the territory, and he didn't want everyone to think he was getting everything handed to him on a silver platter. Mike may have sold a lot in the ring, but between the two of us, I was better at getting blood. When it came down to cutting your head, I bled far better than Mike, who usually only generated a tiny bit of blood.

I also began partnering a lot with Jimmy Garvin, who had completed the transition from manager to wrestler. He had grown up in the wrestling business, and his years as a manager had helped him to become quite familiar with the business and very fluid in the ring.

Not everyone was happy to see new guys advancing in the business. By that time, Wahoo McDaniel had become an outright bully. He was an older guy in the business who was aging rapidly, and he was very insecure about it. He literally spray painted the top of his head because he had a bald spot. Often, he'd ask other wrestlers to spray paint the top of his head for him if there were no mirrors around and he couldn't see what he was doing.

Wahoo had already climbed the ladder to get to the very top of the business, but that's the point when everyone becomes a target to get knocked off of that ladder. Wahoo was gradually sliding down the ladder, and he would get mad at me and angry at some of the younger guys who were starting to get more attention. He displayed his displeasure regularly by making smartass comments and snide remarks.

"I don't know why they like *you*," Wahoo said to me. "You don't look like you could whip your way out of a bag."

I didn't want to say anything to Wahoo, because he was definitely one of the guys who could have kicked my ass if it came down to it. He'd try to put you down to get himself over, but it didn't work with me. I just dismissed him as a bully. There weren't too many bullies in the wrestling business, but he was certainly one of them.

When Backlund and I won the Florida tag team championships from Bob Orton Sr. and Bob Roop, by then it was just another day at work. It wasn't very significant in the grand scheme of things. Winning the Rookie-of-the-Year award represented a moment in time that I would never forget, because it felt like my first moment of any real value. By the time I got to work with Backlund as my partner, winning the Florida tag belts with him simply represented another posed picture of myself wearing a title as far as I was concerned.

I don't want to make light of it; winning championships usually signaled that you were important to the company you were working for, but in the grand scheme of things, it wasn't *that* important. If you were anywhere near the main-event level in Florida, a championship would eventually find its way over to you. The titles in Florida changed hands quite a bit. They wouldn't simply hang a title on a guy and let him run with it for two to three years consecutively. We were wrestling eight times per week, and were in the same cities 52 times per year. Dropping a title one week and winning another title the next week didn't have a great deal of significance to it.

In the long run, it helped to not take the championships too seriously. You don't win the title; you're *told* you're going to get the title. You don't lose a title; you're *told* you're going to drop the title. No one *actually* won or lost *any* of the championships. Celebrating with a title in real life would be like an actor celebrating with a prop from a movie they just filmed. I would much rather have made more money and remained beltless than won every title under the sun and been broke.

As big a fan as I was of ribs, I had a decent number of them pulled on me. Sometimes the ribs are of the subtle variety, and you're being ribbed to an extent, but you're also being used as a tool in a rib against someone else. One of the reasons this can happen is because you're also riding in cars half the time, taking 200-mile, one-way trips and listening to guys you trust talking about other guys, the business, and their experiences with different people. You can build a wealth of knowledge simply through all of the conversations, and you can also form firm opinions about people you've never met before.

I was definitely guilty of being caught in situations where guys have worked me up on the way to matches, and Jack and Jerry Brisco were certified *experts* at working me up. They'd spend hours in my ear insisting that the guy I was getting in the ring with that night was going to go out there and hammer me, so by the time I got in the ring, I was ready to buzz the guy I was wrestling and run right over him well before he could do anything harmful to me. Jack and Jerry would be watching and laughing knowing that they were the culprits responsible for getting me so hyped up. Then, after I'd pulverized my opponent, I'd come back to the dressing room, and the two Briscos would laugh and admit to me that they'd made up every element of their story.

One day, the Briscos decided to get me worked up about Pat Patterson. Pat was gay, and it wasn't a big secret. It was common knowledge to all of the boys, and Pat made zero efforts to hide it. Well, I was booked to work with Pat, and I'd never worked with a gay guy other than Terry Garvin before, or at least not one that I'd known about in advance. That wasn't something that was common in my world when I was growing up. Still, after the trauma that Terry had inflicted upon me in Georgia, I was extraordinarily sensitive to the thought of a gay wrestler taking undue liberties with me in the ring.

So thanks to Terry Garvin I was already predisposed to being sensitive about that sort of situation, and now I was stuck riding in the backseat with these two wild Oklahoman Indians for four-and-a-half hours, and they're saying things to me like, "I'm tellin' you, Steve, if Pat gets you in position and gets control of your leg, he's gonna try to grab ahold of your *balls*, too!"

By the time I finally hit the ring with Pat Patterson in Miami and locked up with him, my only mission was not to allow him to feel me up or grab my balls. He had no idea that I was in the paranoid mindstate that I was. I was unbelievably defensive about the situation and what Pat might have intended to do to me, so much so that I actually wound up roughing Pat up and pulling his hair very frequently to regain control during the bout. Eventually, Pat just gave up, decided to get himself counted out of the ring, and then walked back to the dressing room just to spare himself from further abuse.

It's *not* a situation I'm proud of, but in my defense, I'd had a series of awkward encounters in Georgia where I'd been propositioned for gay sex, and then I found out after the fact that there had been a bounty on me to see if I would cave in and engage in homosexual acts in exchange for favoritism. With that in mind, I was probably more sensitive to looming threats of being felt up in the ring than most other wrestlers.

The constant threat of ribs made wrestling a profession where you had to have your guard up constantly, both inside and outside of the ring. Before my time in Florida came to a close, I was going to be keenly aware of just how inescapably detrimental an accident that transpired inside of the ring could have on your everyday life, just when you thought you had *everything* figured out.

TEN

One of the best benefits to wrestling in Florida was that we could take relatively short flights to Puerto Rico to make appearances for Carlos Colon's World Wrestling Council, which oversaw Puerto Rico as a standalone territory. During one of those trips, Paul Orndorff and Jimmy Garvin were staying in a hotel room right next to mine.

Despite being a true killer, Paul Orndorff was also a really naive guy. I had already pulled a *bunch* of ribs on him during our time together. On this night, I just casually picked up the phone at 1:00 a.m. and called the room of Paul and Jimmy. We'd all gone to bed kind of early after the show because there had been nothing to do in the town we were staying in.

When Orndorff answered I said, "Wake-up call! Time to get up!" and then I hung up the phone.

I went to the wall to listen for movement, but their room remained silent. I picked up the phone again after a few minutes and called again.

"*What?!*" Orndorff answered, angrily.

"Paul, what the hell are you guys doin'?" I asked. "We're *all* down in the lobby! Didn't you get your wake-up call?"

"What?!" Orndorff said. "What time is it?"

"They just told me they called your room!" I continued. "The cabs are here for us, man! You better hurry up or you're gonna be stuck here in Puerto Rico!"

The aftermath was *awesome*. I could hear a whirlwind of activity in the room, and plenty of shouting, as Paul and Jimmy scurried about to collect all of their belongings and exit their room.

"Man, I heard the phone ring!" I heard Jimmy yelling at Paul through the wall. "*Why* didn't you tell me it was a wake-up call?!"

"I thought it was a mistake!" said Paul. "I didn't think we slept *that* long!"

Neither one of those guys had a watch, and there were no clocks in the rooms.

The two of them raced out of their room, and when I heard their door open, I opened up my own door and stood propped in the doorway still in my underwear. I had my Pulsar watch on, which you could twist to cause it to light up. I twisted my wrist and displayed the time to them, which plainly indicated that it was only 1:20 a.m.

"Good morning!" I said with a grin, before slamming my door shut. It was *awesome*.

Both of them were fully dressed, with packed bags, standing in the middle of the hallway.

"What does he mean?" asked Paul. "What's goin' on?"

"Ugh! I can't believe it!" said Jimmy. "We gotta go back to bed! I *can't* go back to bed after all that!"

It was a simple rib, but it was highly effective.

Back in the U.S., Eddie Graham enjoyed a close relationship with Vince McMahon Sr., the owner of the World Wide Wrestling Federation, which operated in the Northeastern United States. The WWWF often controlled the national conversation about wrestling in the U.S., and this was largely for three major reasons.

The first of these reasons was because the territory contained so many cities and major population centers considered to be of global importance – including New York, Boston, Philadelphia, Pittsburgh and Washington – all within reasonable driving distance of one another. The second reason was because most of the major wrestling magazines were produced in New York City, which resulted in wrestling throughout the surrounding region being afforded preferential treatment whenever it was covered.

Finally, the WWWF had access to Madison Square Garden, which was the venue where so many major fights in boxing history took place, like the first two world heavyweight championship fights between Muhammad Ali and Joe Frazier. The venue was synonymous with fighting in its most sophisticated and elevated form of presentation.

Due to his popularity throughout the country, Dusty made semi-regular appearances for the WWWF in Madison Square Garden, and I was packaged alongside him for a few visits to New York City to wrestle for Vince Sr. The Championship Wrestling from Florida program with Gordon Solie was also being delivered to New York on a bicycle during that period. They called it a "bicycle" when you would take a tape and mail it to a television station. So our programming was accessible to fans in some locations within the New York market.

Reaching for a tag as Nikolai Volkoff clings to my arm

To be quite honest, I had no desire to subject myself to an extended stay in a Northeastern territory and a cold-weather climate that was centered around New York City. Still, I wanted to be able to say that I'd worked in Madison Square Garden at least once during my career, just like I wanted to be able to claim that I'd worked in the Boston Garden, the Philadelphia Spectrum, and all of those other famous arenas that the WWWF enjoyed exclusive access to. Luckily, I did wrestle on a card in Madison Square Garden during my earliest trips to the Northeast to wrestle for Vince.

The worst thing about the experience of wrestling in the WWWF's territory was the wrestling ring itself. The ropes ran 20 feet along each side, whereas every other territory I had ever wrestled in utilized ropes that were 18 feet in length. Aside from that, the ropes on the WWWF rings were also real ropes; most of the "ropes" on wrestling rings were actually steel cables covered with garden hose. The tension on the WWWF's ropes was reduced, and the recoil on them was significantly lower than what I had grown accustomed to. Last but not least, the ring's mat was constructed to be very hard, solid and stiff to accommodate all of the massive guys they had working in the territory at the time, like Gorilla Monsoon, Ernie Ladd, Bruiser Brody and Andre the Giant.

Kevin Sullivan had been kind enough to prepare me somewhat for what I could expect in a WWWF match.

"Stevie… when you go up North, they're not like *you*," he cautioned me. "You're gonna have to change a little bit."

"What do you mean by that?" I asked him.

"It's a lot more punchin' and kickin'," said Kevin. "Don't be tryin' to call no long, complicated high spots. They don't do those."

"So I have to change everything?" I asked. "So why are they bringin' me? I thought they were bringin' me because they wanted somethin' different!"

"Well, the *promoter* might, but the *boys* don't want nothin' different," said Kevin.

It turned out that Kevin was absolutely right.

When I did get to wrestle in Madison Square Garden against Larry Sharpe, I was thrilled to finally be scratching that accomplishment off of my career bucket list. I was also thrilled to be sharing the locker room with characters I had only seen photos of in magazines prior to that point, like Lou Albano and Mil Mascaras. Meeting Mascaras was a somewhat disappointing experience because he never took his mask off even in the dressing room, so my meeting with him didn't really feel as meaningful as it could have been.

I got a quick eduction on the subject of how vast the WWWF rings were the first time I wrestled in one. Larry Sharpe would shoot me into the ropes, and it felt like it took me forever to get there. When I'd hit them, it felt like there was nothing propelling me forward from them, so it really threw my timing off. The first time you wrestle someone, it probably won't be that good, but you'll learn. Well, I learned a lot from that match. The way they wrestled up in New York was not aggressive like the style in Florida. I tried to push the pace and get aggressive with Larry, and he kept trying to smother me and slow me right back down.

"Hey, kid… this ain't Florida!" Larry whispered to me in the ring. "This isn't real. You know it's a *work*, right?"

Half the time he was saying this to me while trying to restrain me with a hold, but other times he would say it if I was merely jerking him around to get him to actually do anything at all. I felt like we weren't moving enough, and like I wasn't showing the audience enough of what I could do. I'm sure from Larry's perspective, he had been sent out there to do a job for me, which didn't give him much incentive to make me look good in the first place. I also had to consider the fact that he was certainly no ally of mine, and he probably didn't see much of a point in bringing someone from Florida up there to simply beat him and then leave.

I was from an aggressive territory where everyone moved around and kept going. Larry was from a kick-and-punch territory where popularity was based on nationality and ethnicity far more than ability. Most of the stars in the WWWF were Italian, Puerto Rican, Polish, Irish, Black, or had some other ethnic identity that a specific enclave in New York would identify with and show up to support. When you had representatives of two competing philosophies of wrestling and paired us in the ring with one another, it was like trying to stick the working ends of two magnets together; we didn't really connect. It was a crappy match involving two styles that didn't mesh. I was excited to be there, but Larry was grumpy and pissed off because he was doing the job.

All of the circumstances of the actual event weren't great, but it still gave me some bragging rights to come back to Florida and say, "Yeah, I worked Madison Square Garden last Monday night! Hey, what were *you* guys doin'?"

During another of my WWWF matches, I made a big mistake by running to Dusty and saying, "Look! I've only been here one time and they already put me in the semi-main event!"

I was wrestling after the intermission and a couple matches up. Dusty looked at me like I was a real mark.

"What are you talkin' about?!" said Dusty.

"Look at the program!" I told him. "Look where *I'm* at!"

Dusty shook his head.

"You see this match right here with Bruno Sammartino right before the intermission?" said Dusty.

"Yeah?" I said.

"*That's* the main event, kid!" said Dusty. "They put the main event on before the intermission so that those guys can get outta this buildin'! *You're* in the jabroni match just flipped upside down!"

Dusty just busted my bubble, and he was right. When I came out for my match following the intermission, I could see that there were clearly fewer people in the building than had been there prior to the intermission. A whole lot of people left after they'd had a chance to see Bruno.

The thing is, I was never very impressed with Bruno Sammartino when I saw him wrestle. I'd watched Bruno when he came down and worked in Florida with his punch-and-kick style like he was already over with the fans, but his style wasn't a style that would automatically get you over in Florida. The only thing he had going for him was that he was on the covers of all the magazines, and most of those were based out of New York.

It's not like Florida's wrestlers were completely shut out of the magazines. In particular, Dusty got a lot of publicity in the wrestling magazines; the bulk of the coverage from Florida centered around him. Sometimes I was able to get some of the bleed off of Dusty's coverage and get my name in the magazines as well, and it certainly helped my career. The one drawback was that they frequently misspelled my name as K-I-E-R-N. However, the photos were always of me whether my name was spelled correctly or not, and it was better to have your name misspelled in the magazine than not to have it in there at all.

Still, we almost always wound up with someone on the cover of the magazine like Bruno Sammartino or "Superstar" Billy Graham – whoever was a big deal in the World Wide Wrestling Federation at the time. The magazines wouldn't tell you a whole lot about their styles, though; they usually just had an article in them that was intended to sell a magazine.

Bruno was very appealing in the Northeast where ethnic identity reigned. Bruno had Italians throughout the Northeast who showed up in droves to watch him beat up all the other ethnicities. Ivan Putski was the hero to the region's Polish population, while Pedro Morales appealed to the Puerto Ricans, and Bobo Brazil was often brought in to cater to the Black fans. However, when I finally watched Bruno wrestle in the Garden, I couldn't believe that *anyone* had bought a ticket to see him.

I remember Dusty and I stepped outside of Madison Square Garden in the New York's downtown area just to walk around. We stepped into a store, and I wound up buying a coat just to say I'd purchased one in New York. I *never* wore coats in Florida.

Apparently there were other motivations for bringing me to New York aside from simply having me accompany Dusty. Kevin Sullivan told me that at one point he was walking into the Sportatorium, and as he was coming up the steps, he heard Eddie arguing with Vince Sr. on the phone about how he would never get Backlund over because he was too green, too stiff, and couldn't work.

"*Keirn* is your guy!" is what Kevin told me Eddie said. "I'll bet you $50 you'll never get Backlund over!"

Kevin said he asked Eddie afterwards what that had been about, and Eddie said, "I was trying to sell Vince on Keirn, but now all of a sudden he changed his mind and wants Backlund."

According to the rumor, Vince was looking to deviate from his ethnic champions and thought that a classic White wrestler would make for a good change of pace. Eddie had been trying to sell Vince on the idea that I would be an ideal fit to be the WWWF Heavyweight Champion if they could mention my father's tenure as a POW, and run an angle similar to the one we did with Roop, except this time one of the Soviet bad guys in New York would be disparaging my father and denigrating his service record.

Vince supposedly preferred Backlund for the role because he had more raw material to build from due to his amateur wrestling background. Eddie and Vince supposedly had a $50 bet going that Vince would never get Backlund over. Personally, I liked Bobby a lot, and I was happy to see him get a break. He was used to living in the North, and I sure wasn't. If I didn't see a palm tree in a regionalized territory, I was miserable. Bobby wound up having a *great* run in the World Wide Wrestling Federation as their world champion.

Since I didn't get the nod as the champion in New York, Eddie and Dusty instead decided they were going to send me on a quest to make me into the unquestioned champion of Florida by hanging all of the belts on me. This meant I would have to go after the Brass Knuckles championship, and this also meant that I would have to endure several matches with "The Missouri Mauler" Larry Hamilton, who was a rather unorthodox combatant.

Mauler was a big, burly guy, and there weren't a whole lot of guys lining up to work with him because the matches weren't the typical Florida style. He was more of a stiff brawler who would club you in the ring. Dusty booked me to defeat Mauler for his Brass Knuckles title, but it was an unbelievably horrible match. The *whole* thing was fisticuffs. Mauler wouldn't even lock up with you; he rushed straight out with his fists pumping. We exchanged a bunch of potatoes with one another, and somehow I wound up with the victory.

Dusty made a big joke about it afterwards.

"You know you're stiff when the Mauler comes back to the dressing room and he isn't sure where he's at, baby!" said Dusty.

Working with Keirn must have been pretty rough that night. I'd love to take credit for it, but I'm pretty sure I was simply defending myself. In his own mind, Mauler may have thought he was working a match, but *I* was fighting for my life in there because of how stiff he was.

Mauler was a lot like Johnny Valentine in that respect. Valentine would lean you back over the ropes and hit you *so* hard. It was like he was trying to unscrew the lightbulb out of the ring light, because that's how high in the air his hand was, and then he would bring it down and waffle you with it. Valentine would also have this stupid grin on his face after he would whack you, like he knew he'd just gotten away with something on you.

Around that time, Mike had a girlfriend on the side who came to the Tampa airport to pick him up following one of my flying experiences with the drunken Eddie Graham. As we exited the plane and walked toward the parking lot, Mike's girlfriend greeted us and announced to me, "I want you to meet my sister, Terri!"

I walked over to the car, and staring up at me and smiling from the passenger seat was the most beautiful girl I'd ever seen.

"*This* is your sister?" I asked in disbelief. "Where have you been keeping *her*?"

"She had a boyfriend until not too long ago, but that's over with," she said.

"Well, she's got a new one *now*!" I said.

With that, I immediately leaned in and kissed Terri right on the lips.

From that moment on, Terri and I were inseparable, and I fell so hard in love with her.

With Terri, the love of my life

As an accomplished second-generation wrestler who was often wrestling right alongside his father, Bob Orton Jr. was one of those guys who was a perfectionist. If you messed up anything, whether it was a spot, or even something as simple as your reaction to a move, Bobby would get angry at you in the ring, and he'd let you know. This could be verbal, or he might physically jerk you around. He was one of those guys who would get a little pissed at you for simply not doing the right thing at the right time. Luckily for him, he was a heel, so the crowd couldn't differentiate between his anger at your subpar performance and typical bad-guy rage.

Even in the hands of a perfectionist like Bobby, the situation could still turn highly dangerous if communication wasn't clear. Mike Graham and I were wrestling Orton Jr. and Bob Roop in a small spot show in Dade City, just north of Tampa. Bobby draped me over the second rope and then told me something that I couldn't quite understand, and before I could clarify the message, Bobby just took off running in the opposite direction.

In retrospect, he must have told me not to move, because he bounced off the ropes that were on the opposite side of the ring from where I'd been draped and came storming back toward me. I turned myself back around to face him, only to find that he was already airborne, flying toward me full force, and holding his knee in his hand. Bobby rocketed his knee right *through* my face and didn't withhold any velocity from the impact.

When Orton's knee connected with my mouth, my whole face went numb. I heard Bobby cussing, but my attention was solely on my own predicament. I looked at Mike Graham, and Mike looked at me with really wide eyes, and simply said, "Tag!"

I looked back at Mike with wide eyes, and he emphasized his point by yelling, "Tag! Your *face* is messed up!"

I tried to say, "It's not time!" but then I realized that my bottom row of teeth wasn't where it was supposed to be on the inside of my mouth; it was sticking *through* my lips to the outside.

I tagged out of the match as panic shot through my mind. I was wondering how badly I had been injured, and whether or not I could even finish the match. Mike made the comeback on our behalf, and they hurriedly completed whatever impromptu finish they concocted to get us out of there. I went to the bathroom, assessed the situation, and decided that the only thing I could do was pull my bottom lip up and out so that my teeth would be back on the inside of my mouth. The instant I did that, my mouth began to spurt blood everywhere. I wrapped a towel around it, and Mike drove me 30 miles to the hospital in Tampa. The team in the emergency room assessed my lip, and the doctor said, "You *really* need a plastic surgeon. I can sew this up, but you're going to need a plastic surgeon for sure."

"Here I go," I thought to myself. "I'm going to go from pretty to ugly in a hurry."

I was a pretty-boy wrestler back then, and I was always worried about something like that happening. When I got my lip sewed back up, my lip was fat for a week, and I did whatever I could to protect it.

What Bobby did clearly hadn't been intentional. No one would deliberately try to bust my lip open while it was vulnerable. Bobby might have been speaking carny to me at the time of the accident, and I just didn't catch what he was saying. A lot of the times when guys were speaking carny to you in the ring, they were trying so hard to keep the audience from hearing what you were saying that they'd also end up keeping it from you in the process. I can't tell you how many times I had to say, "What's that?" or "What did you just say?" I wanted to be sure, because if you're not sure about the instruction you received, it always pays to get it straightened out before a disaster occurs.

    I never needed any additional reminders about the importance of in-ring communication. To this day, if you see me smile, you can see a bump on the left side of my lip that kind of folds over my teeth. That's all due to the knee of Bob Orton Jr. If I peel my lips open, you can also see a t-shaped scar. I *never* had a plastic surgeon fix it. The way I looked at it, when you got injured as a wrestler, it was going to mount up over time. Every time somebody said something needed to be fixed, I had to weigh the cost of getting it fixed against the time I would be forced to spend outside of the wrestling ring not earning a paycheck.

    I also had two dark teeth from being sucker punched as a kid. It killed the nerves in both teeth. People would always ask me why I didn't get my teeth fixed. I'd say, "Nah. I'm a wrestler. I'm waiting for somebody to knock them out before I put them back in right." It would be just my luck to fix something and have it made right only for it to get messed up even worse the very next night.

    I may have been nonchalant about some injuries, but there was one injury that was absolutely *disastrous* to my wrestling career. A critical turning point in my life occurred when I broke my leg while executing a baseball slide between the legs of "The Spoiler" Don Jardine. My foot got snagged in the mat, and the bone simply snapped. As bad as it sounds, it's all part of the business. It just so happened to occur on the very last move of that match. I'd hooked my toe in a fold in the mat cover. I later learned that what happened to me occurs frequently with running backs on the football field; they hook their toes in the turf, and the bones in their legs completely give out.

One half of the Florida Tag Team Champions

When I got to the back afterwards, I saw Wahoo McDaniel and I said, "I hurt my leg pretty bad."

Wahoo watched as I took my boot off, and he said, "You *broke* your leg, Steve. I can see it from here."

I didn't want to hear that, because whenever you break something, that means you're out of the picture completely. You immediately become unemployed, and you're not getting a paycheck or any sympathy payments from the office. There were no unemployment benefits in the wrestling business.

I went to the hospital in West Palm, and they confirmed exactly what Wahoo had suspected: I'd broken the bone on the outside of my leg, down in my ankle, and I needed to be seen by a surgeon. Jimmy Garvin drove me on a 200-mile, pain-drenched trip back home as I contemplated my future.

We were in Tampa the next night, which was a Tuesday. I entered the Sportatorium that day sporting a temporary cast, and with my movement aided by a pair of crutches.

"Do you think you can walk down the stairs in the Armory tonight?" asked Eddie Graham once he spotted me with the crutches. "We can get that cast cut off of your leg in the dressing room."

That was quite the demanding request on Eddie's part. I had a *shattered* ankle, and there were quite a few stairs from the second level where the dressing rooms were down to where the fans sat.

"No. I can't do it," I told him. "I can't put *any* weight on it."

"Well if you can't do that, what do you think about taking some pain medication to block the pain, and then when you get in the ring, Pak Song is going to attack you and break your leg!" said Eddie. "*Now* we've got an angle!"

Now I was pissed off.

"What are you talkin' about?!" I replied furiously. "I've got a *fractured* ankle! I *can't* walk! I need surgery!"

"If you can't do that, we'll do something where Pak Song breaks your leg on the way to the ring," continued Eddie.

Instead of shooting the angle Eddie wanted out of me, I went home. Soon after, Eddie took me to have my leg evaluated by the doctors of the Tampa Bay Buccaneers football team. One doctor suggested that we operate, while the other said, "Just put a cast on him and he'll be alright."

That's when promoter Milo Steinborn informed us of a surgeon over in Orlando that could aid me. In essence, he would cast the tie-breaking vote.

Once he evaluated me, the Orlando surgeon said, "I can't tell if you need a cast or an operation. What I'll do is put you under and prepare you for an operation. Then I'll give it an X-Ray. If I can pull your ankle out and twist it around, I'm going to operate. If I can't, I'll put a cast on it, and you'll know what happened when you wake up."

When I woke up, I discovered that my ankle was now being held in place with eight screws and a plate. Psychologically, it devastated me. I was put on the backburner from being the Florida Heavyweight Champion and holding a bunch of other titles to now being a guy with a broken leg who couldn't wrestle at all. I was out for four months. To top it off, I lost my position as the top guy in Florida. One misstep during the final move of a match had left me broke, unemployed and helpless, with zero income, and no insurance.

I didn't develop any animosity in that situation, at least not at the time. I just thought of it as bad luck. Any time you step in the ring, you're rolling the dice and handing your body to someone else while asking them to protect it. In this case, I didn't have anyone else to blame. Don Jardine didn't hurt me; he wasn't even touching me when I broke my own ankle.

Territorial wrestling was not an easy business to be involved in, and I discovered that there wasn't a whole lot of money to be made in it either if you were strictly a wrestler. I'd been making enough to take care of myself, pay for gas, and travel. Still, no matter what level I reached within the business, I discovered that if I made a little bit more money, I spent a little bit more money. I'd get a better car. I'd get a nicer apartment. There was always a reason why your money was never in a savings account. It was constantly going in and out of the bank, and being used to make your bills disappear.

When I started, a lot of the old timers would say to me, "Hey, kid… save your money. This ain't gonna last forever."

Even as late into my career as 1978, I remembered thinking, "Save *what* money?"

One injury had taken me from being on the top of the world to the depths of unemployment. All I could do was sit around while waiting for everything to heal up.

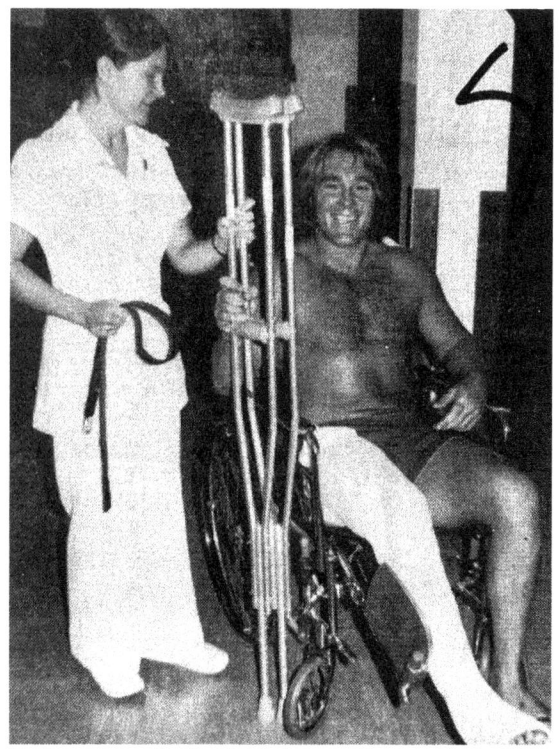

Going through physical therapy for my broken leg

I was also struggling financially. As nice as it was to be a main-event wrestler in Florida, you still didn't make enough money or save enough money that you could afford to live for four months without any resources coming in. I had to borrow money from my parents to survive. Eddie didn't sugarcoat *anything*. You could be a main-eventer one night, but if you got injured and found yourself lying in a hospital bed, there was no sense in even acknowledging your existence on television if it wasn't going to draw any money for the company.

The cover story Eddie used to explain my absence was that Pak Song had maliciously broken my leg at the Sportatorium while I was working out and training to wrestle Terry Funk for the world title. That was it. All payments stopped, and I was stuck in a cast from my ankle up to my hip.

To say that I regretted breaking my leg would be the understatement of the century. No one likes to break a bone, but this particular injury prevented me from working *and* caused me to lose all of the momentum I'd had.

Eddie and Dusty had me simultaneously holding the Florida Heavyweight Championship, the Brass Knuckles Championship, and half of the Florida Tag Team Championship at the time I was sidelined with the leg injury. I'd competed through broken fingers, broken ribs, a separated shoulder, and the flu, but the broken leg *totally* shut me down. The wrestling business had to keep moving without me, and in this business, if you stepped out of the line, you'd usually get moved to the *back* of the line.

Following the surgery that implanted all of the hardware in my leg, I sat home for four months and recovered while making no money. I was functionally unemployed and was also forced to pay for my own major surgery. From there, I was informed that I would need to have a separate surgery after the first four months elapsed to remove the screws. I truly did not want to have that follow-up surgery because I was under financial stress from being off for four months and being obliged to bear the burden of paying for the initial surgery on my own.

"I *can't* afford it!" I told the doctor. "What's the *worst* thing that could happen if I left the screws in?"

"I could do a lesser surgery that would be in-and-out," he said. "I'd only remove the single screw that's keeping your ankle immobile. You could leave the other screws in there with the plate."

To this day, if you looked at an x-ray of my ankle, you'd see a metal plate with seven screws in it. It kind of looks like an erector set. Luckily, keeping all of that metal embedded in my ankle never really hindered my movement later on.

It was only about two months after my initial meeting with Terri that I'd broken my ankle so badly. Terri had driven to Orlando where I was operated on, and she even slept on the floor of my room. She was seven years younger than me, but everything she did for me was *perfect*. She cooked amazing food for me, she had a wonderful disposition, and she was so easy to get along with. Terri waited on me hand and foot, and paid for our food and our rent as she helped me get back on my feet. I bought a hot tub and put it in the backyard, and spent the better part of four months stewing in the water and waiting to make a return to the ring.

Coming back from a broken leg after sitting out for four months wasn't easy. The injury put the fear in my mind that something similar could happen again at any time. To compensate for my feelings of inadequacy, I wrapped my ankle in gauze every night before taping it up. I maintained that pre-match ankle-wrapping routine until Harley Race came through Florida and observed me preparing for a match.

"What are you doing, kid?" Harley asked me.

"Just tapin' my ankle," I said. "I broke it a little while ago."

"Well why are you taping it?" he asked

"I'm tapin' it to secure it," I replied.

"Did they tell you it was okay to wrestle?" Harley prodded.

"Yeah, but I'm afraid about breakin' it again," I said.

"Throw that shit away," said Harley.

"Why?" I asked.

"What's gonna happen when you show up one night, and you don't have any tape, and no one else does either?" he asked. "Just walk away from the whole thing now and get it off of your mind."

I really respected Harley, so I listened to him and just dumped the whole strategy of taping my ankle. I still had a very hard time adjusting to simple movements like leapfrogs, where I would jump high into the air while someone else ran under me and through my legs.

I used to have no fear of doing a leapfrog, which is really just a simple jumping movement. I was never a super athlete, but I could do a leapfrog and jump pretty high. I even used to get a pop from the audience when I did leapfrogs because I would get higher up in the air than most people. Well, after the injury, I would favor my right side. I would go mostly on my left side, which looked a little awkward and conveyed to the crowd that something might be wrong with me. It would take close to a year before I felt like I could do that one simple movement safely and confidently again.

All of my functionality and confidence eventually came back, but I'd *definitely* lost my spot at the top of the company. Jimmy Garvin was now the Florida Heavyweight Champion, and the other belts got spread around amongst the other talent. I wasn't being factored into the plans for anything. It took me a while to bounce back, and when I did, I still had a chip on my shoulder.

Eddie and the rest of the people in charge had been more respectful to me prior to the injury, and had been far more excited about utilizing me. Now it seemed like they were suddenly withdrawing from me, and being very reluctant to use me. Instead of telling me what they'd like me to do, or talking about the opportunities they were going to give me, every sentence seemed to start with, "Well, do you *think* you can…"

There's no doubt that I developed a bad attitude toward the powers that be and the people in charge in Florida during this time. I also felt a bit of resentment toward Jimmy Garvin, not that any of it was his fault. In fact, he was the person who drove me to and from the hospital after I'd broken my leg. However, before my bad break, Jimmy wasn't even one of the top contenders; he was just a guy in the middle of the card. You always sized up the other people you were working with, and while Jimmy and I were about the same age, he was smaller than me, and he wasn't as aggressive as I was. He also hadn't done the things that I'd done. Now all of a sudden he was the Florida Heavyweight Champion, and I was admittedly jealous of him.

With Jimmy Garvin

     I was also more than a little annoyed that they hadn't put the belt on a heel, because then I could have been positioned to challenge for it. Realistically, the way the territories drew wasn't with all of the champions being babyfaces. Heels typically won the titles from the babyfaces, and then the babyfaces chased the heels through different types of matches in order to win the championships back. That was the reliable formula that sold tickets. The fans wanted to see their favorite babyfaces on a quest to win the titles back.

While my in-ring career felt like it had stalled, I turned my attention to making moves outside of the ring. Mike Graham wanted to diversify his investments, so he opened a bar called Graham's Lounge on Dale Mabry, which is the main strip through Tampa. It was open for only about two months before Mike came to me with a business proposition.

"Hey, do you want to invest in the bar?" he asked.

"Actually, yeah!" I said.

I figured it would be a great opportunity to make some extra money. At this point, I was considering getting married, so I was looking for investments that were separate from wrestling. I can't remember what the ownership percentage was that Mike offered me, but it was probably somewhere between 2.5 percent and 5 percent. I remember the amount I paid very well, because it was everything I had managed to borrow from my dad: $5,000.

"Well, there are three other partners," explained Mike as I handed over my money. "They're Italians. You know Tampa is a mafia city, and you've got to have an Italian or a Spanish guy on your liquor license if you're in the bar business."

Despite this revelation, I still handed the money over to Mike in exchange for my percentage of the bar's ownership. Everything seemed fine in the beginning, except that I never received *any* of the payments I had been promised in exchange for my $5,000 investment.

"Hey, Mike… when do we start making money on this bar?" I asked him.

"Shouldn't be too long now," Mike said.

Additional weeks would pass by, but Mike never handed over any income to me based on the bar's operations.

Mike always teed up a different answer to explain away why I wasn't getting paid. It was less than a month after I'd invested in the business that Mike abruptly said to me, "By the way, I *sold* the bar."

This revelation came out of nowhere. We were sitting in the car right in the middle of driving to one of the towns.

"*What?!*" I replied.
"Yeah, I had to sell the bar last night," he said.
"You did?!" I asked. "How come?"

Graham's Lounge

"We were having too many problems with it," Mike continued. "The bouncers were fighting all the time. We kept having to go to court over all the problems. It just wasn't worth the hassle."

"Well what about my $5,000?" I asked, knowing that I owed the money to my dad and I was flat broke.

"Oh *that's* gone," was Mike's matter-of-fact reply.

I *couldn't* believe it. Less than a month prior, Mike told me he was giving me a prime opportunity to buy into his bar. He had to have known even then that the bar was going under. He took my $5,000 that he'd known had been so difficult for me to make, and just allowed it to evaporate into thin air.

I never forgot that, and my relationship with Mike changed after that. I simply couldn't trust him any longer. I learned a valuable lesson from it, which was not to trust *anybody*. Don't trust the people in the car with you. Don't have loose lips, because they sink ships. Anything you say in the car after drinking one too many beers could result in you being screwed over or unemployed by the end of the week, and you'd never have any idea why you had been blindsided.

    I learned to be tighter mouthed and not to discuss business, not to talk about any other talent, and just generally not to divulge anything that someone might try to capitalize on. I'd mentioned being able to borrow $5,000 from my dad to Mike one day, he pounced on it, and then the money was gone. That was part of my education, but it was a very tough lesson to learn, and a painfully bitter pill to swallow. What made the lesson even sadder was that the person who betrayed me had been the closest thing I'd ever had to a brother.

    Little did I know, there were a few more lessons that would follow, and they would ultimately cause the permanent and unthinkable unraveling of a relationship that had taken a lifetime to cultivate.

ELEVEN

Most guys go through the business with their heads in the clouds, wanting to be superstars. I went through the business simply to learn it and study it, and some of the things I ultimately learned were things that I was never supposed to know.

Wedding day with Terri

Eddie Graham approached me one night after learning that I was marrying Terri, whose father was very wealthy from real estate.

"Hey, why don't you get your future father-in-law to give you 50 grand?" said Eddie. "Then you can own two-and-a-half percent of Championship Wrestling from Florida!"

I couldn't believe it. My ultimate goal in wrestling was to own a territory, because the owners, bookers and promoters were the primarily individuals involved in wrestling who appeared to have sustainable, comfortable livings. There were *very* few exceptions to this. The guys who exercised control over the industry were the only guys who were truly successful. By comparison, the wrestlers, referees, announcers, and anyone without a share in the ownership were all fly-by-night participants in one way or another.

Eddie had once told me, "Everybody in this business is a Chinese worker, and their work is like Chinese labor; they come here with big dreams, and then those dreams go away." His message was clear: Wrestlers would tour all of the territories where money was being made, and the main-eventers could make decent money for a while, but the *truly* big money was being made by the people who controlled those wrestling empires.

Seizing what seemed like a once-in-a-lifetime opportunity, I went to my soon-to-be father-in-law, and he actually gave me the $50,000 required to purchase 2.5 percent of CWF. I was thinking this would be another way for me to get ahead in life by owning part of the territory. After all, I couldn't be a wrestler for my entire life. Everybody involved in the Florida territory's ownership seemed to have a huge house and money to burn.

Two weeks later, some guy I had never seen before approached me bearing a paper sack in his hand.

"What's *this*?" I asked.

"This is from Tampa," he told me, as he handed me the bag.

I opened the sack, and it was full of cash.

"Cash? What's *this* for?" I asked.

"Just take it, kid," they told me.

Then I wrestled Miami the next night, and that show was *also* followed by the handing over of a paper sack full of cash. I don't recall the exact amount, but it was significant.

I also received a visitor after the subsequent Tampa show, and he arrived bearing yet another paper sack full of cash. The exact source of the cash was a mystery to me, and I didn't even know who I could ask about it. I was afraid that I might be inviting something unfortunate upon myself if I made inquiries with the wrong people. I was wary about saying anything about it to anyone.

"I don't know what to tell you, but this is what's going on," I began, and then I explained everything that I had seen and heard to my father-in-law.

"I don't know if I'd deal with that," he said. "You might be headed in the wrong direction. They're doing something in that business that they probably shouldn't be doing, and they're not explaining it to you. Regardless, you've become part of it now. That means they're going to tie you to it, and you'll never be able to bail yourself out of it."

Finally, I decided that I should ask some questions, and I went straight to what I assumed to be the top of the pyramid and asked Eddie what was up with the cash deliveries.

"Can you explain the cash that's being delivered to me in the bags?" I asked him.

In response to this direct question, Eddie became very red in the face.

"You need an *explanation*?!" he said.

Eddie lit into me for being stupid and asking questions about the source of the money, but he still somehow managed to beat around the bush with his answer. He hit me with quite a tongue lashing, but provided no relevant answers to any of my questions.

"I'll tell you what! If you're having such a problem with this, we'll just buy *your* percentage back!" said Eddie.

At the end of the next week, Eddie gave me the $50,000 back, and I handed it straight back to my future father-in-law. That's when everything started caving in around me in the territory. I deduced that the reason there was additional cash able to be dispersed amongst the ownership team every week is because they had all been skimming money off the top.

I did have one more moment of significance before the situation in Florida becamse totally untenable. Vince McMahon Sr. had just simplified the name of the WWWF into the World Wrestling Federation, and had attempted to work with Leroy McGuirk – who was in charge of the NWA World Junior Heavyweight Championship – to send somebody to New Japan Pro Wrestling to drop the championship to one of the wrestlers they were in the process of grooming for bigger things, Tatsumi Fujinami.

The NWA World Junior Heavyweight Champion

Vince had a deal in place with Antonio Inoki and NJPW that involved him switching out talent, and cycling some of the people from his WWWF roster in and out of the territory.

No matter what he did, Vince couldn't get Leroy to turn his belt loose, or to allow it to get dropped to a wrestler in

Japan. From what I understood, Leroy simply wasn't willing to trust Vince with his championship.

Vince got my phone number from Eddie and called me out of the blue.

"I watched you work when you were up here," said Vince. "I'm trying to shake hands with New Japan Pro Wrestling and Antonio Inoki. They've got a kid up there who's about your age and style. He's a really good worker, and I think you could really get over with him. If you'll do it, I'll send you a brand new belt, and I'd like you to take it over to Japan for a few weeks. They'll put you over at shows all across Japan, and then I want you to drop the belt to the guy they want to be the champion. I think they want the belt dropped to him in Sapporo."

"Yeah, sure!" I said.

"I'd also like to bring you up after that to start you in New York," he said. "You're pretty close to the end of your run down in Florida according to Eddie."

To hear from Vince that Eddie thought he was almost done with me in Florida was news to me. I went along with the program, though. I picked up the brand new NWA World Junior Heavyweight Championship belt that Vince had commissioined and shipped down to the office in Florida, and then I packed it up and traveled with it over to Japan.

To be clear, I didn't defeat *anyone* to win this world championship; it was mailed to me by Vince, and I simply carried it to Japan with me. It had the same name as Leroy McGuirk's championship, but it was *totally* different.

Throughout the New Japan tour, I wore a t-shirt that was once very popular in the U.S. It featured an image of the atomic bomb going off, along with the caption, "Made in America; Tested in Japan." My Japanese opponents seemed even stiffer in the ring with me than usual, and I couldn't quite put my finger on why.

"Man, I think I've taken every suplex that these guys know!" I said to Stan Hansen.

"It might be the sweatshirt, Steve," Stan said.

"I figured it would get heat with the audience," I replied.

"Well, you know your opponent's *also* Japanese, right?" said Stan. "I'd think about ditchin' that sweatshirt if I were you. You're gettin' heat with the *wrong* people!"

Being tagged into the match against Fujinami by Dynamite Kid

When you wrestled in the regionalized territories, the fans would jump through their asses for highspots and feuds. In Japan, you'd go through four or five serious moves and reversals and come out on top, and you'd get a golf clap like you just sank a putt to take a one-stroke lead over Arnold Palmer at The Masters.

Guys like Abdullah the Butcher, Stan Hansen and Bruiser Brody stomped out to the ring, threw Japanese people to the side, hurled chairs through the air, and generally freaked everybody out. They were the exceptions; there weren't many foreign wrestlers who worked like that in Japan. The majority of us were like myself, Bob Orton Jr. and Brian Blair, who could work technical matches with the Japanese guys without having to call complex spots.

The only thing I knew how to say in Japanese was "itai," which meant, "it hurts." I didn't even know how to order food in Japanese, but I said "itai" so much in Japanese wrestling rings that I wore that word out.

On the night of the scheduled title change in Sapporo, Eddie had flown to Japan so that he could be present the night I dropped the championship belt to Tatsumi Fujinami. Fujiinami was already the WWF Junior Heavyweight Champion, so this was intended to be a big title-for-title unification match.

There was a guy in the locker room that night who'd been on the tour with us who wrestled under a mask: Skip "Sweet Brown Sugar" Young. While we were in the back preparing for the show to get underway, the New Japan referee came over to give us the finishes to our matches, and I decided to have a little bit of fun with him. After the ref got done describing the finish of my match to me, I looked him in the eyes and shook my head.

"I'm not doin' that!" I said bluntly.

Skip had been within earshot, and when he heard that, he went and found Eddie Graham and said, "I knew it! I knew it! I knew he was gonna hold them up! *I* should've been the one you put the belt on! *I* should've been the one you sent over here as the champion!"

After receiving this report from Skip, Eddie went and found me, and actually said, "You've gotta pull a rib on Skip. He's too much!"

So between Eddie, Stan Hansen, myself, and a few other people, we came up with the idea that I was going to pretend to hold up New Japan Pro Wrestling for more money. We got word to the referee about the attempted rib, and he was actually delighted to help us out. When the referee returned to me with another idea for a finish, I vehemently rejected his suggestion.

"Get the hell outta here! I'm *not* doin' that!" I said, getting right in his face. "I'm not gonna drop that belt. How about *that*?! I'm takin' this belt and goin' back home with it unless you get me 200 grand *right now!*"

"No! You make deal!" complained the referee. "You make *deal!*"

"The hell with the deal!" I continued. "I want that $200,000 in cash before I hit the ring tonight, or I'm takin' this belt home with me!"

Posing in Japan with Sweet Brown Sugar and Dynamite Kid

The ref made a convincing show of throwing a fake fit, and then he walked off in a huff. About 30 minutes later, he came back with two small kitchen-sized garbage bags full of chopped up newspapers, but from the outside, the bags easily looked like they could have been full of cash.

"Okay!" the ref said, while holding the bags out toward me. "Your money!"

I turned to Hansen and said, "Come on, Stan! Watch my back while I count this money and make sure it's *all* there!"

As Sweet Brown Sugar stood there in wide-eyed disbelief, Stan and I disappeared behind a door and pretended to count the money, but in reality, we were laughing at the rib we were in the midst of pulling. After sufficient time had passed, I opened the door and exited like I was all business.

"Okay, it's all there! Let's go!" I said, as if I was anxious to get the title match underway. Then I grinned at Skip and stated, "Time to drop the belt!"

I *loved* working with Fujinami. He was so good in the ring and very easy to work with. We had some great matches prior to this, and our match that night was flawless. Still, the most memorable thing about that night was the rib we pulled on Sugar, who thought I'd spontaneously become filthy rich as a result of holding up Inoki and the New Japan executives.

When I got home, I thought I was going to be headed to New York. There'd been a suggestion that Vince was losing faith in Backlund as his champion, and was once again considering revisiting my patriotic storyline with Bob Roop on a bigger stage. However, when I returned from Japan, I was pulled into the office in the Sportatorium, and Eddie said,

"Vince changed his mind; he's going to keep Backlund as the champion."

At the time, I wasn't even upset. I hadn't really wanted to go to New York in the first place. I was intimidated by the sizes of the cities up there. It was one thing to work there as part of the undercard, but to be responsible for drawing money in major cities like New York, Boston, Philadelphia and Pittsburgh was quite the psychological burden. I also wouldn't have had any friends up there with me except for Backlund, and I would have had no confidence in him being nice to me if he felt that I'd bumped him out of his championship position.

With Terri and all of the Florida territory's tag team gold

The only guy who'd been even remotely nice to me when I went up there to work the first few times had been Mr. Fuji, and that was primarily because he was a huge fan of pulling ribs himself. Everyone else had been somewhat cold to me. I also hadn't been thrilled with the complaints I got from guys who didn't think my style was compatible with New York's. I would have been *way* out of my comfort zone.

Even though I wasn't going to be headed to New York, I could tell that I would still be needing to find a new home territory. I wasn't getting remotely the same respect in Florida that I'd received over the previous years.

I was supposed to wrestle Harley Race, who was the NWA World Heavyweight Champion at the time. Except for giving guys like Dusty Rhodes and Giant Baba short reigns here and there, Harley had been the NWA champion from 1977 right through 1980.

Mike Graham was running things that night, and he asked me to simply get beaten, cleanly, without putting up much of a fight or mounting much offense. I couldn't believe what I was hearing. Anytime before that, my matches with the world champion were always handled with care: Either we did a countout, a disqualification, or a 60-minute Broadway whenever I wrestled the world champion. Now all of a sudden, I was being told to wrestle for a few minutes and then Harley was simply going to *beat* me.

I had nothing against Harley, and I would ordinarily have done it with no problems. The issue was that I had an image in my mind of where I was rated in Florida, and I had an understanding of how they treated people who they saw a future in. When they told me to go out there and get crushed by the world champion, I felt like that was the Grahams' way of communicating to me that they were done with me in Florida.

"Ain't no way in hell I'm doin' that!" I told Mike.

"What do you mean?" said Mike.

"I ain't just gonna go out there and do a job," I said. "I have a future here in Florida, but I also have a past that supports where I thought I was going with my future. Because I had a broken leg and I've come back, I understand you guys don't know if I'm gonna be able to carry the ball, but in my mind, I can carry it, and I'm *not* gonna do easy jobs."

There was a bit of controversy there, because Harley and I were in separate dressing rooms, but I wound up not wrestling him that night. Mike got on the phone right away and called Eddie, and they arranged some sort of substitution.

The next day, I was asked to drive down to the Sportatorium and have a sit-down discussion with Eddie. I wasn't in the mood to talk to him; I'd just driven 200 miles home from West Palm that night. I had it in my mind that it was over, and I'd be moving on, and I'd already accepted it.

When I sat down and talked to Eddie, I said, "Here's the deal, Eddie: Whenever it's your son Mike, you guys always work out a deal where he doesn't look bad no matter what. All of a sudden, I'm a *job* guy. I understand Harley is the world champion, but we *always* used to do things where we got around it. It didn't hurt the world champion, but it didn't hurt me either. Now you're just wanting me to point blank go out there and accept the fact that I'm not a contender anymore."

Eddie started getting a little rough with me, but then he said, "Hey, maybe it's just time for you to move on!"

"I think it *is* time for me to move on!" I agreed.

I stood up to Mike and Eddie, and I knew that doing so was going to close the book on Florida for me, and probably permanently. I didn't really care, though. I was so pissed that I never wanted to come back. I felt the heat in the dressing room from that point on, and I knew I needed to call around to any territory I could successfully get booked, and then give the Grahams my notice.

The common practice back then was to give a two-week notice. That way you could do whatever you needed to do for everyone else in terms of putting other people over. They didn't really try to job me out when I left. I think they knew that I would probably just walk out if they tried to get too carried away with beating me. So they didn't beat me on TV. Instead, they just asked me directly if I minded putting certain people over as I made my exit in July of 1980.

"I don't mind at all," I replied. "I'm on my way out."

I got in touch with the Georgia office, where Ole Anderson was still in charge as the booker. I'd already wrestled him years prior with Tiger Conway Jr. as my partner, so Ole was familiar with me, and respected what I'd done in Florida enough to bring me in.

The Fabulous Wrestling Life of Steve Keirn

The wrestling business is a very tough profession to be married in. You leave every day to go to work, and every single night you're on the road. Your spouse has to accept quite a number of irregular rituals in order to accommodate your lifestyle.

From Terri's perspective, it was as simple as me coming home one day and telling her, "Okay, we have to rent a U-Haul; we're moving to Atlanta next week."

That was it. She had to be ready to pack up her whole life and move to another place, and to her credit, she did it. This is why wrestlers and their spouses have to totally get along, because you can't argue and fight and still expect your relationship to last. The two of us bought a house in Stone Mountain, Georgia, and Terri became pregnant shortly thereafter.

To Ole Anderson's credit, he threw me right into the thick of several championship pictures as soon as I arrived in Georgia. Ole almost immediately booked me to win the Georgia heavyweight title and the tag team titles with "Mr. Wrestling" Tim Woods as my partner. However, just a few months after I arrived in Georgia, I joined a tour of Japan that I'd already committed to participating in because Antonio Inoki wanted to book a return bout between myself and Tatsumi Fujinami.

This particular tour became infamous, and by the time it reached its conclusion, Jimmy Garvin, Paul Orndorff and I were supposedly banned from ever returning to wrestle for New Japan Pro Wrestling.

Included on the tour were myself, my buddy Terry Bollea who was now wrestling under the name "Hulk Hogan," Jimmy Garvin, Paul Orndorff, Chavo Guerrero and Ron Starr. Throughout the tour, Jimmy Garvin and I were relentless in our terrorizing of Freddie Blassie, and our tour acquired a reputation as being the number-one bad boy tour of young boys.

All of the wrestlers were driven from place to place while riding in these very ornate Rolls Royce coach buses. It was first-class transportation. Freddie Blassie would always tuck a towel into his bus seat before plopping himself down on top of that towel as it rested over his seat. It just started irritating me that he would take so much time to carefully tuck his towel in and lay it over the top of these beautiful seats.

Poster from New Japan's infamous "Bad Boy" tour

    Even more annoying than that was how Blassie would talk about how indisputably great he was all the way from the hotel we were staying in to whatever Japanese town we were appearing at that night.
    Our group of young guys all sat in the back of the bus, and we weren't at all interested in listening to Freddie Blassie's relentless boasting. We didn't really know about him since we

hadn't grown up in New York or Los Angeles where he had been a big name, and we weren't impressed with him. To us, he was just some old guy in his 60s.

"You know, the first time I got color in Japan, six people watching on TV *died* of fear!" Blassie bragged.

"Yeah, right!" I said.

"It's true!" Blassie insisted. "They were *traumatized*!"

Waiting to catch the bullet train with Umanosuke Ueda, Paul Orndorff, Jimmy Garvin, Hulk Hogan, and Ron Starr

The only one getting traumatized was me from having to listen to Blassie drone on about how incredible he used to be. I opted to target Blassie with ribs, and I decided to start off slowly with him and ramp things up over the course of our three-week tour. Every time we got on the bus, Orndorff, Garvin and I would sit in the back. Each time I'd walk by Blassie's seat, I'd pull his towel out from where it had been carefully tucked into the seat, and I would drop it to the floor in a crumpled heap.

When we reboarded the bus after our shows, Blassie would scoop up his towel, tuck it back into its prior place on the seat, and then cut a promo under his breath while talking about "piece-of-shit young guys."

I maintained this pattern of irritating Blassie, and he finally blew up after a solid one-week stretch of me yanking his towel out of its position. After the week of torment reached its conclusion, Freddie got aboard the bus and finally snapped.

"You little asshole young guys!" roared Blassie. "I'm gonna fix *you*!"

Freddie turned to the Japanese referee and snarled, "Peter, I'm not gettin' off the bus until the last guy gets off! Then when I leave, I want you to lock the bus door and don't let anybody back on until we come out!"

Blassie was Hogan's manager, which meant the two of them were in the last match of every show on the tour. Blassie's decree guaranteed that all of us would have to wait in the locker room all night until the show was completely over with.

I turned to Jimmy Garvin and said, "Go ahead and crack that window. Just pull it down a little bit."

Jimmy stealthily cracked our window to ensure that it couldn't be locked.

Once we were done working that evening, Jimmy and I snuck outside toward the bus, and Jimmy proceeded to crouch down while I climbed onto his back, slid the window all the way down, and climbed back inside of the bus through the window.

This time, I didn't just yank Freddie Blassie's towel out of its place; I *shredded* it. I tore it into about 100 pieces and stacked them in a pile on his seat. Then I hopped back outside, and completely shut the bus window. Jimmy and I nonchalantly walked back inside the building and acted as if we'd never left. We couldn't stop laughing the entire night at the thought of how Blassie was going to explode when he discovered the remnants of his towel after he'd enacted what he believed to have been a fool-proof plan to protect it.

At the end of the night, we all gathered outside of the locked bus and waited for the driver to let us back inside of it.

Blassie was the first person in line, and he boarded the bus as soon as its door opened. From the back of the line, while I was still standing out in the chilly air, I could clearly hear Blassie yelling, "Assholes!" and "Pieces of shit!"

While Blassie was freaking out, I stifled my laughter and boarded the bus sporting a poker face, acting totally oblivious as to what sort of scene Blassie had just discovered.

"What happened?" I asked. Then, when I was within viewing distance of Blassie holding up the shreds of his treasured towel, I let loose an equally insincere, "Oh no!"

Blassie turned to face us all, and he said, "I was ribbin' guys while you bastards were still in your dads' *nutsacks*!"

That was only the beginning. After that, I began to target Blassie even more intensely. One of my favorite ribs involved filling a hotel-room garbage can with water, opening the window, and monitoring the people below. After selecting a target, I would dump the water, watch as it drenched them, and then duck my head back inside of my room before they spotted me.

A few nights after the towel incident on the bus, we knew Freddie was headed to a special dinner event with a local sponsor. Jimmy and I sat by the window and waited for Freddie to make his return.

"That's Freddie! That's Freddie!" Jimmy yelled gleefully. "Look at his socks!"

Jimmy was correct. Freddie always wore silk socks, which made his legs easy to spot as he swung them to one side and lifted himself up and out of his cab. I had a full garbage bin full of water at the ready, and as soon as Freddie was within striking distance, I dumped the water out of our hotel room window on the 10th floor and absolutely *doused* "The Classy One." Somehow, despite 10 stories of separation from my victim, I'd timed the drop *perfectly*.

Freddie clearly knew it had to have been one or more of the disrespectful young punks that had been tormenting him. He took the elevator up to the 10th floor and cut a promo on all of us from the hallway.

It was a non-stop battle with Blassie, but the stunt that ultimately got me banned from Japan had nothing at all to do with Blassie. Instead, it involved my camera. I was one of the few wrestlers in my day to bring a camera along to document everything I did, and the camera I brought with me on this trip to Japan had a timer on it that enabled me to frame my shots and then jump in front of the lens before the photo was taken.

All of us went to one of the Japanese bath houses, which was a common pastime for the wrestlers to engage in. We would spend large chunks of our days inside of those bath houses, and especially in the saunas.

While we were all standing around naked, I said, "Let's get some pictures!"

Everybody was looking around and laughing and saying, "Yeah, right!"

"Come on! We're in Japan!" I said. "Nobody is *ever* going to see them, so who cares?"

That argument was adequate to get everyone to agree, and so we took a photo where we all bent over and mooned the camera. Then we took a full-frontal shot where we're all just standing there naked and facing the camera; it's still the *only* picture I've ever taken in my life where I was ever totally naked. When the photo of our rear ends was developed, we decided to take it and have it enlarged. Then we all signed it and sent it to Antonio Inoki.

That was a mistake. Japanese humor isn't like American humor, and our joke didn't translate well. Inoki looked at our naked asses mooning him inside of a bathhouse, and he became absolutely incensed. He wanted to know whose idea it had been, and who the owner of the camera was, and everyone pointed their fingers directly at me as the instigator of the stunt. Everyone was in the photo, and everyone signed their name to it, but *all* of the blame fell directly at my feet.

Thanks to my clever stunt with the photo, I was told I wouldn't be welcomed back to Japan once the tour concluded, which left me with absolutely nothing to lose in my aggravation of Blassie. That's when Orndorff came up with an idea to really land a knockout punch on Blassie with respect to our ribs.

Paul had Jimmy head down to the street market by the hotel where you could buy fish on a stick. Jimmy returned to our room in possession of a *bunch* of raw fish. Freddie Blassie had already explained to Peter the referee that he had arranged all of his suits on clothes hangers, that he would be wearing one suit to travel in, and that all the rest of his suits should be shipped straight to the airport. Well, on the last night of the tour, we got access to all of Freddie's suits that were awaiting shipment and stuffed all of the pockets with *raw* fish.

We would have never known Freddie's reaction to the rib if it hadn't been for the fact that Hogan was with Blassie in Madison Square Garden when the shipment of suits arrived. Blassie opened the bags containing his suits, and *blew his stack*. His suits were pretty expensive, and all of them were irreparably ruined.

I'll admit that it was a bit over the top, but Blassie had upset all of us so much that we decided to single him out. I was pegged as the gang leader for the entire thing, resulting in Freddie Blassie hating me until the day he died. It wasn't entirely my fault, but I was absolutely responsible for brainstorming a sizeable share of the mischief. We all sat around and tried to think of the funniest, most unpredictable ribs we could pull on Blassie, and we wanted to come up with stuff that people would be talking about for years. I just happened to be *better* at it than most people.

When I returned from Japan, I was almost immediately booked to defeat Masa Saito for the Georgia territory's National Television Championship. Saito was phenomenal in the ring, but he still didn't understand English very well. This was an instance where acquiring experience wrestling in Japan became beneficial to me.

You had to learn how to express to your opponent through your actions that you didn't want to take too much from him, and that you also wanted to ensure that the match would be a good match without forcing the issue. I'd make a move on Saito, and if I sensed that he didn't want me to continue with that move, I'd ease up so that he could easily reverse it or change it.

In the clutches of Masa Saito

I was never afraid of Saito because we were working, but if the combat had been real, I'd have been terrified of him. First of all, he had Jim Duggan eyes, where one eye went one way and the other eye went the other way. When you're getting ready to lockup with Saito and you're not sure he's looking at you, you're relieved when he actually locks up successfully with you. It's only at that point that you knew for sure he was even paying attention to you.

The other thing was that Saito had spent so much time in the United States by that point. He had adapted well and could work wonderfully. He also knew enough English to understand the basic wrestling movements if you called them out, but you couldn't have rattled off long high spots for him to follow because he would have gotten lost.

However, when you were working against Saito and any of the other great Japanese wrestlers like Fujinami, you could wrestle by feel. If they put you in a hammerlock, you could start to reverse it, and if they allowed you to do it, you knew you'd made the right move. If they didn't, they'd block you and direct you elsewhere. If I go stumbling toward a turnbuckle and I don't seem to be very surefooted, I'm tacitly feeding my opponent the suggestion to run up from behind me and drive my head into the turnbuckles. If they don't, I'm going to turn back around and make an offensive move instead of taking their moves.

It's a silent way of communicating the places where you want your opponent to lead the match. Alternatively, I might *really* start selling my leg and start limping, and that would be my way of letting my opponent know that they should keep attacking my leg.

There were a few places in Georgia where heels and babyfaces were able to dress together and simply emerge through different doors. One of those places was in Augusta. Thanks to that arrangement, I got to know the Fabulous Freebirds a little bit outside of simply working with them in the ring. The Freebirds were a great team because they were colorful, added variety to everything they did, and they had a lot of character and charisma. The fact that there were three of them didn't hurt either, as that was very rare to see in our business.

Terry Gordy and Buddy Roberts were the two Freebirds that you hoped you wound up in the ring wrestling against. Michael Hayes was the colorful guy of the group, and the one with all of the charisma on the microphone, but he was clumsy and unorthodox, and he wasn't a great worker in the ring. He was more interested in moonwalking than actually having a technically sound wrestling match.

No matter how lousy Haytes was in the ring, Buddy Roberts' wrestling gear continued to smell so atrocious that you'd still often prefer to work with Michael Hayes simply so that you wouldn't have to contend with the stench emanating from his tights. You could *even* smell him coming to the ring. If he tried to headscissor you, the match would turn into an actual shoot as you fought to keep your head – and especially your nose – from having to go between his legs.

Terry Gordy was a big guy who could *really* move. He had tremendous balance and control of his body, and he was a total joy to work with. The challenge of wrestling the Freebirds was the fact that you never knew what you were going to get out of them on a nightly basis. You could never count on being able to rein in Michael Hayes, and if you were rotating through different partners while regularly facing them, you had to constantly strategize about how you were going to tackle that challenge. You also didn't want to raise any concerns or ruffle any feathers, because they were usually being pushed heavily as a unit.

I'm not sure that anyone ever told Michael Hayes at the time that he was the weak link in the Freebirds as far as the in-ring work went. Usually you expressed your opinions privately. Terry Taylor would have been the type of person who would have gone up to Michael and told him to his face that he sucked. The rest of us would usually just try to avoid wrestling Michael altogether. When Michael would tag in, *we* would tag out. That became a joke in and of itself.

It was rare to tell a bad worker that you thought they were lousy. When guys weren't very good and they were still getting utilized, it was often because they had a friend somewhere in the territory, like a booker, an owner, or whomever. You knew that if you went so far as to publicly state the truth about someone who wasn't very good, but who was valued and protected, you'd be gone quickly. Somewhere or another, *everyone* usually had at least one connection to someone of significance in the pro wrestling profession.

To his own credit, Terry Taylor actually was a very good wrestler, and a great technician in the ring. He'd emerged from Florida like I had. That's not to suggest that he went through his training there, because he didn't, but he grew up there while watching Jack Brisco, Harley Race, Terry Funk, and the other greats of the business. Later on, Terry would tell people that he stole the flying forearm from me because I'm the one that got that move over in Florida. It's nothing that I held against him; you're *supposed* to take the things that work from other guys.

Terry's biggest problem at that time was actually his blunt honesty. He would express exactly what he was feeling when he would have been better served keeping his mouth shut. He'd open his mouth in the dressing room and tell people things like, "You need to go back to wrestling school because you don't know what you're doing," or he would talk to a promoter or a booker and be frank with them to the point of pissing them off. You had to work the workers if you wanted to have a low-stress life in the wrestling business, but Terry wasn't like that.

One guy who was *quite* vocal about his disdain for the antics of the Freebirds at that time was Harley Race. There's no denying the fact that Harley was a very serious man who protected the wrestling business at all costs. If someone went out to the ring and clowned around, he'd cut a promo on them the second they returned to the dressing room.

"So I guess I have to go out there and follow *that*, huh?" Harley would ask. "You might want to think twice about doing that again the next time you see *my* name on the card!"

Harley would put the fear of God in you.

Well, the Fabulous Freebirds had a well-earned reputation for doing all types of stupid shit back when they were together. One time they were all chasing each other around in the dressing room in Augusta with their hands gripped tightly around their wieners. They were trying to restrict the flow of their urine to build up sufficient force so that they could squirt someone with piss from a long distance.

Harley Race and Johnny "Mr. Wrestling #2" Walker took offense to the Freebirds running around the dressing room like children and trying to piss on one another, and Harley ultimately screamed at Michael Hayes. The promo Harley cut on Michael included about 100 F-bombs, and it can be summarized in a single sentence from Harley's tirade: "If one drop of piss touches me, my bag, my clothes, or anything I own, I'm going to kill *all three* of you little pricks."

Johnny Walker was a badass in his own right. He stood up at that moment and added, "And who he has problems with, I'll make sure *I* kill 'em, too!"

Ted Dibiase was in Georgia with me at the time, and the two of us were very close friends who often rode together. I even worked against Ted a few times, and when I did, I would call highspots where I kept him going back to my arm over and over again. From there, I'd call a series of moves that required him to do a wide range of things, and then I'd double cross him right in the middle of the move series just to see how he'd react to it.

During one bout, I called for him to fall to the mat so that I could leapfrog over him, only to then drop onto his back and yell, "Two points!" like it was an amateur wrestling match. Ted started laughing at me and wasn't quite sure what he should do to follow that up.

"Sorry; I just had to do that *one* time," I expressed to Ted after letting him up.

We continued the match, and I called the next spot. Ted shot me into the ropes, leapfrogged me, and then dropped down to monkey flip me on the other side. Instead of taking the monkey flip, I decided to drop down next to Ted and hooked him.

"Now that's *three* points!" I shouted.

Then I hopped up and patted myself on the back, and Ted did his best to keep from laughing once again.

"I'm not letting you call the match anymore!" said Ted.

Georgia was also the first place I ever worked with Bobby Eaton. He was one of the smoothest workers of all time, and definitely would make my list of the five greatest in-ring workers ever by the time his career was over with. Every time I ever worked with Bobby, it was an easy match. On top of being smooth and effortless, he was also a very generous opponent. He would try to give you as much of the match as he could give you. At that point in his career, Bobby was merely being used in an enhancement role to put me over and have me dominate the matches.

Georgia had proven to be a necessary sanctuary for me to revitalize my career outside of Florida. However, the most invaluable takeaway from my stop in the Georgia territory would be the advice that I received while I was there. Heeding that advice would be the first step in turning Steve Keirn into something "Fabulous."

TWELVE

Fortunately, I hadn't been required to start over at the bottom in Georgia. Instead, I began as a guy positioned somewhere between the middle and upper tier of the card, and I was trying to create enough space for myself to eventually reach for the top. Aside from traveling with Ted Dibiase, I spent the bulk of my time driving with Kevin Sullivan, even while we were working against one another in matches.

Kevin had leaned out considerably since the earliest stages of his career. He was now incredibly lean, but this also made him really light compared with most guys I wrestled. Everything we did in the ring seemed to hurt him more than it hurt other people because there was no non-essential meat on his body to pad his landings.

When I slammed people, I slammed the *shit* out of them. Kevin was my only friend who called me "Stevie," and when I would slam him, he would cry out, "Stevie, you're *killin'* me!" Or, when I'd punch him, he would shove his head down into his shoulders to keep me from hitting him in the neck where I usually would.

I got around to referring to Kevin Sullivan as "The Cringer."

"I'm working with Kevin 'The Cringer' Sullivan tonight," I would say within earshot of him just to get a rise out of him.

"Have *you* ever been hit by you?! Do I owe you money or somethin'? You're *really* hittin' me, Stevie!" complained Kevin.

"Yeah, but those people are excited to see it, ain't they?" I laughed. "I have to give them what they wanna see!"

It was as a result of the time I spent traveling with Sullivan and talking to him that I started to make major changes in my own physique. I was honestly quite jealous of Kevin. I *loved* the way he looked. He transformed himself from short and squat with an unimpressive body into a lean, mean, fighting machine.

Kevin had started competing in Atlanta in bodybuilding contests. Being a longtime friend of Kevin's, the change in his physique was one of the first things I noticed about him when I arrived in Georgia, and when we started riding together I told him how noticeable the results of all his hard work were to those of us who knew him prior.

"I *really* love the way you look!" I admitted. "For some reason – maybe it's my genetics or something – I can't get myself to look like that."

Fit and trim thanks to Kevin Sullivan's advice

I was taught that it was good to be as big as possible in the wrestling business, and that body fat didn't matter. Most wrestlers were barrel-chested and barrel-bellied; all you needed was a good pair of legs to carry you through the night. I had never had anyone influence me in a way that made me want to be a bodybuilding type. That included ripped guys like Billy Graham and Paul Ellering, who had both come down to Florida. However, Graham and Ellering both proved the point, because they sucked in the ring, and didn't offer anything at all, aside from having ripped, muscular bodies, so I didn't think they were worth patterning myself after.

Kevin changed my perception on body types, because he could *definitely* work, and now he stood out physically on top of everything else. He forced me to reevaluate my position on getting lean. If this was going to be a new phase in wrestling, I wanted to be part of it.

"So what do I do to get a body like yours?" I asked Kevin.

"First of all, it's mostly about your diet," answered Kevin. "It's all about what you eat. So what are you eating?"

"Pretty much everything," I admitted. "I don't pay any special attention to my food."

"Well you need to eat a *lot* of protein, and you should start counting your carbohydrates and keep them low," replied Kevin. "You should also stop drinking beer if you're drinking it. You can have some wine, but beer will keep you fat."

From that point on, I followed Kevin's instructions. On the way home from the matches, we'd go to the liquor store and get a big bottle of Chablis wine, along with some ice and some cups. We'd fill the cups with ice, pour the wine into it, and sip on that all the way home after the matches, but beer was now completely cut out of my diet.

"Every time you pick something up to put it in your mouth, ask yourself if you should really be eating it or not," advised Kevin. "If you shouldn't eat it, don't."

Kevin also had me cut milk and dairy products out of my diet. By the time he was finished, my diet was pretty much down to meat, melba toast, and cups of post-match wine. He had me *laser*-focused.

In a relatively short period of time, I went from wearing butcher tights that covered up my gut and my obliques to wearing shorter tights. By incorporating all of Kevin's advice, I changed my workouts and went in a totally different direction. I shrank from 225 pounds down to around 210.

After I'd strap my boots on in the dressing room, I started lying on a table in the back of the building and cranking out leg raises. I'd put my hands under my butt to make sure I could raise my lower body to a position that was higher than parallel, and then I'd start doing five sets of 25 raises. The sets escalated in their volume and intensity each night, and I worked my way up to 1,000 leg raises each night, non-stop. Then I would get up and do free squats, and then I'd lie back down and do another 500 to 1,000 leg raises, or as many as I could before it would be time to hit the ring for a match.

At home, I had an end table that was as solid as a rock. I'd sit on that, hook my feet in dumbbells on the floor, and do crunches. All of this work caused my core to strengthen *dramatically*.

Tony Atlas was in the Georgia territory at the time, and when he'd see me doing leg raises, he'd give me crap about them.

"Aw, man! You're waistin' your time!" Tony ridiculed me. "You ain't gonna get *nothin'* outta leg raises!"

Obviously, there was a *world* of difference in genetics and physical makeup between myself and Tony Atlas, who was a world-class bodybuilder. He could get away with only doing crunches and still develop a tremendous midsection. Still, I let him show me how to do crunches the way he did them even though I continued to do my leg raises. I enjoyed the total abdominal stretch I achieved from that exercise.

All I had ever done up until that point was heavy weightlifting. I had *never* done any sort of bodybuilding. All I'd done before were squats, deadlifts, bench presses, behind the neck shoulder presses, and some curls. I never went after giant arms like Austin Idol or Hulk Hogan. I just wanted to have decent arms. Now my system of training changed completely, and I soon resembled a totally different guy.

Changing my physique became my foremost mission during my second pass through Georgia. The average physique in wrestling had changed since I'd started. The typical look had started with big, barrel-chested men who I'd fit in perfectly with, and it had progressed toward something that more closely resembled a bodybuilding look.

That's not to say that what I was doing would have provided me with a true bodybuilding look, or even that a pure bodybuilding training style was desirable to a wrestler who wanted to remain conditioned for ring work. Bodybuilders were very mechanical in the ring, and tended not to be able to move fluidly. They were constantly flexing, very rigid, and frustratingly hard to work with. I didn't want my in-ring functionality to devolve as I improved my appearance.

I'm not sure if it had to do with the fact that I was turning 30, but I believed I needed to do something to ensure that I would continue to appeal to crowds, and I thought improving my physical attractiveness might help to elevate my position on the cards.

Jody "The Masked Assassin" Hamilton set up a life-changing angle between Kevin and I. The angle aired on TBS – the cable station Georgia Championship Wrestling that broadcasted the GCW program all over the United States. This meant that whatever we did in Georgia for the main program could be seen nationwide, which was a big deal from a self-promotional standpoint.

To set up the angle, Gordon Solie introduced Kevin and I and informed the audience that they were going to see a very technical match that night between Kevin Sullivan and Steve Keirn for the TV title. Having two babyfaces wrestling one another is a common way to set the table for a heel turn. It's the type of match where neither wrestler is trying to take advantage of the other one, so it goes back and forth with a lot of moves, countermoves and reversals.

In a match like that, everything works like clockwork, and you don't even have to call spots. You can simply wrestle based on feel and a basic understanding of what should logically come next after each move is made. Kevin was fluid and easy to work with. If anything, *I* was the problem in the matches between us. I was always a little stiff, which sometimes helped with the acceptance of the matches, because if my opponent acts like he believes I can hurt him, then the people in the audience will believe it as well.

Promoting my upcoming upcoming match against Kevin Sullivan

Kevin and I worked in one spot where he went out to the floor, and I sat on the second rope, pushed the top rope upwards, and invited him to climb back into the ring. It was a real babyface, ass-kissing type of move. Kevin climbed back in, acknowledged my gesture of sportsmanship, shook my hand,

and we continued with the match. After another exchange of moves, I was the one who fell out to the floor, and this time Kevin reciprocated my gesture of sportsmanship by sitting on the middle rope and inviting me back into the ring.

Just as I stepped through the ropes, Kevin sucker punched me, then hooked my legs and successfully covered me for the three count. Kevin then scooted out of the ring and departed, leaving all of the fans in the building completely speechless.

Clearly, Kevin had double-crossed me turned heel on me, and I responded to it by delivering one of those crappy babyface interviews about how I never would have thought Kevin Sullivan would have double-crossed me like that.

Despite now being bitter on-screen rivals, Kevin and I *still* rode together. He was living in a hotel close to the airport called the Falcon's Rest, which is where a lot of guys stayed when they passed through Atlanta. One night when I was dropping Kevin off after a show, a colossal possum emerged from the garbage cans outside of the Falcon's Rest and scampered onto the street.

"Watch *this*!" I told Kevin.

I grabbed one of the empty garbage cans, and I chased the possum for three full city blocks. The possum darted in and out of the street and sought shelter behind everything within its line of sight. I finally managed to run him down, and then I dropped the open end of the garbage can over the top of him and scooped him up.

When I came back, Kevin was still sitting by the car where I'd left him.

"Stevie! I thought you were never coming back!" he said.

"I got the possum!" I said triumphantly. "I want to go show it to Dennis Condrey!"

I entered the Falcon's Rest holding the garbage can which now housed a live possum. I didn't even know Dennis that well, but that didn't mean I didn't want to get a rise out of whichever of the boys was available.

I knocked on the door of Dennis' room, and he opened the door a few seconds later.

"Hey, what's up?" Dennis said while standing just inside the entrance to his room.

"I've got somethin' for ya!" I told him.

I made a sudden scooping motion with the lidless garbage can, and the possum flew through the air and into Dennis' room like it had been fired out of a cannon. When Dennis turned his head to follow the motion of the possum sailing through the air toward his bed, I reached in and pulled the door to the room shut.

Dennis chased that possum around his room and finally got rid of it, but I'm sure he didn't take too kindly to having that sort of furry visitor so unexpectedly hurled into his room.

In the aftermath of our television angle, Kevin and I were booked to wrestle one another in the Omni in Atlanta, which was the major venue we would wrestle in when we worked in Georgia.

By the time Kevin and I began working in the ring together, I was nearly as shredded as he was. It was the first time in my wrestling career that my waist was so tapered and my tights fit so well that I wasn't constantly pulling them up over my obliques. Working in Georgia was the first time in my life that I ever had noticeable abs. I had no idea there had been abs lurking underneath my body fat the entire time. The transformation was remarkable.

Even though I was lean, I never incorporated any form of cardiovascular training into my routine, nor would I ever. My mentor on cardio was Jack Brisco. I studied Jack Brisco, and when he became the NWA World Heavyweight Champion, I watched him very closely to see what he did to prepare. All he did was stand in the hallway with a cigarette in his mouth, do five or six jumping jacks, and then go out in the ring and wrestle for an hour straight against somebody who was in really great shape like Mr. Wrestling #2.

"Jack, do you have a stationary bike or do you run or do anything to exercise?" I asked him.

"Never," Jack laughed. "Wrestling *is* my workout."

Jack was right. I never needed to do any cardiovascular exercise to support my wrestling conditioning. My daily cardio routine was seven days a week, in an 18-foot-long wrestling ring, from rope to rope. You *had* to be in unbelievable shape, because we were wrestling for an average of 15 to 20 minutes every night.

Over in the Memphis territory, Jerry Jarrett had taken Tommy Rich away from Jim Barnett's Georgia promotion, possibly because Barnett had grown tired of booking Tommy for four straight years. Prior to that, Tommy had a long run in Georgia, and he was one of the top babyfaces during the Georgia territory's initial foray onto national television. He was a good worker who had a lot of fire, and was a very believable babyface. He also had a Southern accent, which didn't hurt his ability to appeal to wrestling fans in the Southern states.

Even though Jarrett had taken Tommy off of Barnett's hands while Tommy was a popular national figure, Tommy had difficulty getting over with the wrestling audiences in the Tennessee territory. Tommy was a fish out of water there, as the wrestling styles of the guys he was working with in Tennessee were dramatically different from what he had been used to in Georgia.

Tommy hadn't lived up to Jarrett's lofty expectations, so Jarrett made a subsequent deal with Barnett that involved Jarrett traveling to the show at the Omni, scouting the show, and then making a trade to exchange Tommy back to Georgia for someone of value. Their needs coincided perfectly, because Barnett actually wanted Tommy back desperately at that point, and Jarrett didn't want him at all.

As fate would have it, Kevin and I arrived at the Omni fresh off of shooting our national television double-cross angle, and we designed a match that would capitalize on the buzz we had generated. The two of us had worked together for a long time in multiple territories, and we both knew that wrestling audiences loved it when you fought through the crowd.

Since the two of us were booked in a no-disqualification match, we were at zero risk of being counted out of the ring, so we entered the stands and brawled our way through the crowd until we were nearly at the very top level of the Omni. Once we reached the top level, Kevin took a bump and rolled all the way down the stairs. We did plenty of *stupid* stuff that night, but it impressed the crowd because it was vastly different from anything else that had been presented on that night's wrestling card.

The biggest compliment you can get as a wrestler is when you walk back into the dressing room after wrestling for an hour with a guy like Harley Race, and guys stand up and clap for you, then tell you your match was awesome and give you credit for the hard work you did. Kevin and I both enjoyed those sorts of compliments, so when we walked back through the curtain to a round of applause and a chorus of that-was-awesome compliments, it was music to our ears.

Barnett walked over to Kevin and I soon after we got back to the dressing room, and he said, "I need you boys to come in here *right now* and talk to Jerry Jarrett."

Kevin and I walked into one of the offices at the Omni and sat down in front of Jarrett to listen to whatever it was that he wanted to tell us.

"I have a wrestling territory based in Memphis," said Jarrett, which was a silly way for him to open the discussion because *everyone* in the wrestling business knew that about him. "I'd really like you two guys to come over to Memphis. Jim wants Tommy Rich back, and I'd like to trade him for the two of you."

I looked over at Kevin and then back at Jerry. I didn't mind that Kevin and I were being traded for Tommy Rich at a two-for-one exchange rate, but there was something else that was concerning to me.

"The thing I've always heard about Tennessee is that no one can ever make any money there because no one can get past Jerry Lawler or Bill Dundee," I stated plainly.

That was the recurring complaint I'd heard from anyone that had ever worked in Tennessee at any point in the prior seven years. If you wrestled in Tennessee, you would always find your path to the main events blocked by the same two-headed monster: Jerry Lawler and Bill Dundee. The story was that no one could ever supplant them as the top draws in the area, nor would anyone ever get put in a position where they might even become a threat to do so.

Between the two of them, Lawler and Dundee *ruled* the territory with an iron fist. Dundee booked there for a long time, and when he stopped booking, Lawler picked it up and started booking the territory himself. The other talent simply accepted the fact that they were locked in at a certain level, and that they would never get into the big money as long as Lawler and Dundee maintained their influence, either politically, or through control over the booking.

I never asked how much more a wrestler made from booking the talent, because by no means would I have *ever* wanted to be the booker. The only thing that was discussed in the cars and dressing rooms along those lines was whether or not the booker was a wrestler with an ego, and if it was clear that they were booking themself on top all of the time.

The most common and effective ploy was for a booker to craft an angle involving talent that was far hotter and more popular than him, but then to put his match in the main-event slot. While the semi-main event had undeniably drawn the crowd, the booker would create the impression that his match was the *true* attraction, and then he would reward himself with main-event pay.

Since Jarrett had openly expressed that he wanted me, I felt like I was in a position where I could state my concerns to him directly, and then hopefully barter with him over how Kevin and I could be put in a position to actually make decent money in Memphis.

"I don't believe that," said Jarrett, shaking his head. "I believe there's always the potential for someone to get over and get a main-event spot."

I didn't believe him, and I'm pretty sure Jarrett didn't even believe himself, but Kevin and I ultimately agreed to leave Georgia behind and transfer our feud over to Tennessee.

In the background of all these career transitions, my wife Terri was now *very* pregnant. Having a pregnant wife while I was wrestling added a lot of stress to life's equation.

I never knew precisely when Terri was going to give birth, and I still had to make it to all of the shows and hope that somehow I wouldn't miss the delivery. If at all possible, I wanted to be available to drive her to the hospital.

One night after a show, Ted Dibiase dropped me off in the parking lot where my car was, and I drove home only to discover that Terri wasn't around. You can only imagine the scope of my panic when my pregnant wife had seemingly disappeared in the middle of the night. I drove down the road toward the grocery store, and that's when I spotted Terri's Toyota Tercel teetering over the edge of a low roadside cliff, hanging by a single wheel.

Terri had taken our Weimaraner named Elton with her, and after she pulled into the grocery store parking lot and got out of the car, Elton knocked the car out of gear. The car rolled down a hill, jumped the curb, and it was hanging from the cliff by its left rear wheel. When I pulled into the parking lot, I could tell it was my car hanging off of the edge. Several people were gathered around the car, and fortunately Terri was among them.

"Terri, are you *okay*?!" I asked her as I ran up to her. "Are you all right?!"

"I wasn't in the car!" Terri assured me. "Elton knocked the car out of gear, so he was the one in the car when it went over the edge! He's okay, too!"

I called Ted Dibiase and Steve Olsinowski who both lived nearby.

"You're not gonna believe this, but I need your help," I told them. "My car is hangin' over a cliff."

There was a guy standing nearby who said, "I think I can pull this car back over the edge for you, but it will probably tear up the bottom. It will cost $250 to set up a crane and pull the car back over."

Our Toyota Tercel was a tiny car, and I was actually thinking it wouldn't be too difficult to lower it the rest of the way off of the ledge, and then hoist it back over.

Teddy and Steve arrived, and they both started laughing when they saw the state of my car. The nose of the Tercel was stuck in the ground, so it couldn't have continued to slide any further down the hill. There were also trees that would have prevented it from sliding much further, but it was still hanging from that lone wheel.

"Come on!" I said. "I figure we can get to the front of the car and press it over our heads!"

That's *exactly* what we did. Working together, the three of us managed to guide the car back onto the road and saved me $250 in the process.

Finally, on the night of April 21st, I walked through the door of our home to find that Terri's contractions had started.

"I'm going into labor, Steve!" she announced.

The fad at the time was the Lamaze method of natural childbirth, and the two of us had been attending Lamaze courses to prepare ourselves. The only problem was that we had to take a blanket and a pillow to the classes, and since I was constantly exhausted from living the pro wrestling lifestyle of non-stop training, traveling and working, I always fell asleep during class right on top of the pillow and blanket.

When it actually came time for the birth of our baby, Terri changed her mind and decided we would be better off going to a hospital. I didn't argue with her. We hopped in the car and drove straight to Peach Tree Hospital.

Ted Dibiase also arrived at the hospital and sat in the waiting room with my mother and mother-in-law. Terri was in quite a bit of pain, and I stayed right beside her, watching TV in the delivery room until I fell asleep. We remained there for several hours before it was time for the delivery, but when the moment of truth arrived, I presented a special request to the doctor.

"Listen, I don't know what to do," I told him. "I've got no clue. I wasn't paying attention at all during our Lamaze classes. Now she has an epidural, and this is totally different, but I still want to be involved. What do you think about me doing the delivery?"

"What?!" the doctor asked me. "Are you serious?"

"Yeah, well I was a pre-med student in college," I lied.

"Really? *You* were a pre-med student?" he asked, stunned.

"Yeah!" I told him.

"Well, we've never done this before, but if you want to stand down there and bring your baby in, I'll watch from over your shoulder and make sure everything is going okay," the doctor offered. "If anything goes wrong, I'll push you out of the way and take over."

"Good idea," I told him.

The doctor gave me a pair of rubber gloves; I immediately went over to Terri, put my hand on her shoulder and leaned over to kiss her.

"Get him another pair of rubber gloves," the doctor told the nurse.

They gave me another pair of gloves. That's when I went to sit down by Terri's feet, and I grabbed the stool to pull it closer.

"Get him *another* pair of rubber gloves," the doctor ordered again.

Once I had donned a third pair of rubber gloves, the doctor admonished me, "That is our *last* pair of extra large gloves. You really need to *not* touch anything else except for that baby."

I sat right there and touched nothing else until my daughter's head began to pop out. I followed along with the instructions the doctor was telling me, like balancing her head.

Before too long, my daughter Heidi was out. She was *beautiful*.

"It's a girl!" I announced proudly.

One of the nurses gave me a set of clippers and advised me where to clip to free my newborn daughter from the umbilical cord.

"Take your daughter and walk over there. We'll clean her up," the nurse told me.

With baby Heidi

I walked her over and proclaimed, "That was amazing!"

As much as I've tried to take credit for everything connected to the birth process because of how involved I'd made myself, I knew my wife had done all of the work.

I'd always wanted a child, and I was thrilled. I'd also always heard the phrases "mama's boy" and "daddy's girl," so I was thrilled that we'd had a girl.

When I saw Ted Dibiase afterwards, after he had endured the rigors of keeping my mother and mother-in-law entertained in the waiting area for *18* consecutive hours, he grinned and said, "I now know *everything* about you!"

Ted hung in there with me for the entire birth experience, and I'll *never* forget it.

Then again, the exchange was somewhat even. Ted had been living in Atlanta by the airport when we first arrived in Georgia, and I said to him, "Why don't you come move out to Stone Mountain by us?" Well, Ted wound up meeting his wife Mel in Stone Mountain, so he always tells people that if it hadn't been for me he never would have met his wife. The two of us have *quite* a tie to one another.

Heidi's birth overlapped perfectly with the arrangements Kevin and I had made to begin working for Jerry Jarrett in Memphis. I took a bit of a working vacation to take Heidi down to Florida and show her off while we stayed at my father-in-law's beach house. I also worked a few dates for Eddie while we were down there, and didn't have any issues with him despite not departing from Florida under the best of circumstances. Even though I was on a vacation of sorts, I still needed to work. I hadn't earned enough to have a true savings account, and I still owed my dad some money thanks to the investment debacle with Graham's Lounge.

One month later, in June of 1981, I was inside of a U-Haul office with my wife and baby Heidi, and I rented a U-Haul to move all three of us to Memphis so that I could wrestle for Jarrett. In the meantime, Kevin Sullivan had already made his debut on Memphis television, and he was telling all the people how happy he was to be rid of Steve Keirn. The instant I showed up, we continued our angle.

It was probably the very first tie-in angle between two wrestling organizations where a feud had shifted locations by design, although in this case it transferred from national cable to local Tennessee television. Our feud from Georgia Championship Wrestling was cited directly, as Kevin stood at the commentary desk and said, "The only reason I'm here in Tennessee is to try to stay away from Steve Keirn."

That was my cue to show up the next week as the guy who was so hell-bent on getting revenge on Kevin Sullivan that I would uproot my family and follow him across state lines in order to seek retribution and make him suffer. The arrangement might have seemed like a good idea at the time, but the angle didn't turn out to be as hot as Jarrett had anticipated. He seemed to think the fans in Mid-America would love having an angle that had just occurred on national television showing up in the middle of Memphis, but Kevin and I weren't characters in the vein of what the Memphis territory's fans were accustomed to watching, and it quickly fizzled out.

I couldn't help but notice that most of the wrestlers working in the Memphis territory weren't taking their matches nearly as seriously as the wrestlers did in the territories I'd worked in before. Most of them seemed to be locking up with all the aggression of two feeble old ladies and simply going through the motions. More often than not, the stipulations of the matches took precedence over the actual wrestling. Some of the stipulations would be as silly as forcing the loser of a match to consume a can of dog food.

It was a dramatic change for me, as I had arrived there with a stiff Floridian wrestling style that elevated the action as close to a shoot as the fans could tolerate. In fact, I liked my matches to resemble legitimate fights so much that a lot of the workers in Tennessee mistakenly thought I was a legitimate shooter when I arrived there.

All of the wrestlers there certainly knew I wasn't a shooter on the level of Masa Saito, Bob Roop, Jack Brisco, or anyone else with a background in authentic wrestling. All the same, because everyone knew I broke into the business down in Florida, there was an instant respect for me, because they knew I'd been repeatedly stretched and battered for months on end, and that I'd kept coming back for more. Due to this, the innate toughness of Florida-spawned wrestlers was presumed to be present in all cases, and we were all given the benefit of the doubt.

Wrestlers that got trained in Florida might not all have been shooters in the sense that the term was commonly used, but it was assumed that we would all stand up to a challenge and hold our own if someone stirred up a conflict with us. It was common to hear people in the dressing rooms say things like, "You broke in with Eddie Graham down in Florida? Oh, man! You guys are *crazy* down there!"

People who broke into the business in Calgary received a similar level of respect, but that was due to the Dungeon of Stu Hart. Stu had an industry-wide reputation for being a sadistic son of a bitch like Hiro Matsuda. Stu liked to inflict punishment on his trainees, and I liked Stu, but torturing trainees had nothing to do with actually teaching them how to be efficient wrestlers.

Once things in Memphis got underway, the regulars of the Tennessee territory like Wayne Ferris would talk to me after our first matches together and say things like, "Do I owe you money or somethin'? You're too *stiff* out there! You know this is a work, right?!"

They tried to make light of it and make fun of me for taking things so seriously and making the action look realistic, but it was a dramatic change for both of us.

Jerry Jarrett recommended that Terri and I should move to Hendersonville, Tennessee, which is about 16 miles north of Nashville. That's exactly what we did, and we quickly found an apartment there. Plenty of people involved with the business lived in Hendersonville, including Bill Dundee, and Jerry Jarrett himself, who lived in a small house on a lake.

Not much changed in my day-to-day life despite the fact that I had a newborn baby. Pro wrestling remained a fast-paced lifestyle where I was wrestling in front of a different audience every night, and in a different town every night. I was on the road constantly; home life became secondary for me out of necessity. I wouldn't get home until really late at night, and everyone would already be asleep. Then I wouldn't get up until very late in the morning or early in the afternoon because I hadn't gotten home until 3:00 a.m. the night before after driving 250 miles, and everyone else in the household had been up for at least four hours by then.

After that, my foremost priority was getting to the gym, so we would put the baby in a carrier, drive to the gym, check the baby into the nursery, work out, get the baby, go get something to eat, and then I would be back on the road and headed off to the next town. It's not as simple as saying you'll be gone for the evening. I may have been off wrestling at night, but I'd left home at 2:00 p.m. to get to the venue by 7:00 p.m., and then I wouldn't get home until 3:00 a.m. My time with baby Heidi during the day was very limited even during the periods when I was physically home at some point each day.

Terri was the star of our parental arrangement because she did everything with Heidi while I was off wrestling at night, and she also took care of the necessities in the household. Fortunately, I earned enough of an income that Terri wasn't also required to work, and we didn't have to put Heidi in daycare. It was a win-win. Heidi received special attention and had constant supervision.

In my earliest days wrestling in Tennessee, I rode to shows with Eddie Marlin, who was Jerry Jarrett's father-in-law. He opened up the territory to me by regaling me with its history. He explained who people were, which guys mattered the most, and how significant wrestlers like Jackie Fargo, Bill Dundee and Jerry Lawler were to wrestling fans in the area.

I appreciated the knowledge, but to me going to Memphis was like going back in time in terms of both the wrestling style and the bodies of the wrestlers. Everyone was *fat*. Everyone was out of shape. Nobody went to the gym. I'd emerged on the scene with my strict training regimen and disciplined nutrition plan, and it became very challenging to fit in.

I *wanted* to fit in, but I certainly had no interest in looking like the rest of those guys. Jerry Lawler was the biggest star in the territory, and he wore a singlet because he was chubby and was attempting to cover himself up.

NWA Mid-America Champion in Memphis

It was so backwards compared with what I was accustomed to. In the wrestling business, you earned a certain amount of respect in the dressing room simply by taking care of yourself. There were a number of guys who didn't do dick with respect to self-maintenance. They never went to the gym, they were never in any kind of shape, and they ate and drank beer far too often. Then they went out to the ring and worked in a manner that never required them to be physically fit.

Adrian Adonis was like that. He was just a fat guy. Bobby Jaggers was also like that. Both of those guys could work very well, but they never did anything to suggest that they took any sort of pride in their appearance. If you took Jack Brisco and stood him next to a guy like Adrian Adonis, you would *always* respect Brisco more based solely on his appearance. That's the natural inclination. The guys who trained outside of the ring simply looked more like credible athletes than the guys who didn't. The best thing you might have said about a guy like Adonis is that he moved well "for a guy of his size," but he always would have been better off in the long run if he'd gotten himself in better shape.

That was the one thing I definitely had going for me when I went to Tennessee: I was a *stud*. The wrestlers reacted to me like they'd never seen anybody in Tennessee with abs before. Every night that I would go to the ring with Norvel Austin, he would make it a point to gesture toward my stomach and say, "Oh my God! He's got *abs*! Hey, ref… look! He's got abs!"

It was the biggest challenge of my career. For all of the cultural differences and the elevated level of stiffness involved with working in a company like New Japan, even *that* style was more similar to wrestling in a traditional NWA style than working in Tennessee. I was the proverbial square peg being jammed into the round hole. I quickly came to the conclusion that I needed to get out of Tennessee and go somewhere else.

It's a very good thing for me that I defied my own instincts and stuck around in the Memphis territory for just a short while longer. If I'd left, I would have missed out on the career-defining events that were just around the corner.

THIRTEEN

Every night in Memphis was like a new experience to me even after I'd accepted the differences in the match styles. One of the first shocks to me came in Tupelo, Mississippi. The building we wrestled in there was a roller skating rink. They had a shower in the back for us, but it was really just a fiberglass stall.

Everyone used it, and the drain at the bottom of the shower filled with hair so quickly that it would rapidly clog up. Guys would stop showering in it after the third match because it would be so full of water. If your match was any later in the show, you had to go outside and rinse yourself off with a garden hose.

"What kind of a territory is *this*?" I thought to myself. "I have to wash off outside with a hose and then dry off and wear sweatpants to Memphis to go do TV the next day?"

To say the Tennessee territory was a family operation would be a gross understatement. The northern part of the territory was controlled by Jerry Jarrett's mom, Teeny Jarrett. I couldn't take it seriously that the mother of the owner was running a piece of the territory. Similarly, the southernmost part of the territory was run by Jerry's father-in-law, Eddie.

A major transformation in my understanding of what professional wrestling could be occurred in Memphis. I had grown accustomed to NWA strongholds where most people were attempting to emulate the Harley Race style of wrestling. Tennessee was a place where even the ordinary matches would incorporate a bunch of midget highspots. Everything was entertainment based, which was a concept I hadn't been introduced to in prior environments.

Kevin Sullivan drifted away and left Memphis, and suddenly I was stuck in Tennessee by myself. I didn't have any personal friends there, or anyone that I had any real performance experience with. I began riding and teaming with Bill Dundee primarily because we lived in the same town.

Bill was a fun guy to team with, but I still couldn't help but to notice how it just seemed like Dundee and Lawler were fighting over who got to be the Elvis of the territory, and I mean that in a sense that is more literal than figurative. I enjoyed Elvis' music, but I wasn't interested in *being* Elvis in the wrestling ring like they seemed to strive for. Dundee even wore Elvis-style jumpsuits. I thought the whole concept was goofy, but I kept my opinion to myself.

With "Superstar" Bill Dundee

Dundee also had a bit of a short-man's complex. He reminded me of Mike Graham in that way. He was a good worker, and was kind of comical, but he legitimately had a great fan following.

"I'm just cute. That's what it is," is how Bill chose to explain away his popularity.

It was frustrating to be in a strange territory without any direction. In my opinion, Jerry Jarrett didn't understand how to utilize me best, but I could still tell that he liked me. Part of that was probably owed to how I dealt with him. Kevin Sullivan taught me to kiss somebody's ass every once in a while to see if it worked, and once I was in Tennessee, I *seriously* kissed Jerry Jarrett's ass.

I had stopped being so defiant. That defiant edge hadn't made me any money. Being defiant only worked to get over with guys in the dressing room. Defiance earned me the respect of my peers, but *they* weren't the ones paying me. The light went on in my head that the object of this whole game was to get over, have people like you, make the booker and promoter like you, and maximize your earning potential.

Eventually I was booked to win the tag titles with Bill Dundee, as Jarrett tried to test me out in different roles to see if anything would stick. Despite being one half of the tag team champions, I continued to feel like I was drifting aimlessly. It was during one of those rides with Dundee that the respected Tennessee veteran laid things out for me in plain terms.

"Brother, you've got to change," said Bill.

"Change?" Change *what*?" I asked.

"Your style in the ring, man," said Bill. "You're *way* too serious."

"What are you talkin' about?" I asked, growing annoyed. "I'm not changin'!"

I was pretty confident in my abilities since my presentation had worked well enough everywhere else that I'd been during the prior seven years.

"When in Rome, Steve," said Bill. "You've got to do what you would do in Rome if you were a Roman. You're too realistic, man. You've got to get looser in the ring. You've got to get crazy. Don't be afraid to be silly. First make the people laugh, and *then* make 'em cry."

Heeding Dundee's words, I began to adapt my in-ring presentation to match the expectations of a Tennessee audience. There was no benefit to me insisting on being the lone outlier in the territory. Something had to change; either I had to modify my act, or I needed to somehow convince the audience that *they* were the ones who were wrong. Well, it's a lot easier for a single person to make an adjustment than it is to change the entertainment tastes of thousands of people at once.

I now started to monitor Bill Dundee's work very closely when I partnered with him to see if it would provide me with any guidance as to how I should modify my style. Frankly, Dundee did a *whole lot* of goofy shit, but the people were all eating it up. I made the decision right then and there that I couldn't force the fans to go along with what I wanted to do, so I would have to do my best to blend in with everyone else.

I began to change slowly. Every once in a while I would attempt something silly, and the people would pop for it. Feeling encouraged by the improved reactions I was getting, I got progressively goofier until I eventually became one of the goofiest guys in the entire territory. Honestly, I was more than a little embarrassed to be doing those types of spots in my matches, and I prayed to God that Eddie Graham wasn't sitting somewhere watching footage of what my presentation had devolved into, or he would have flipped out.

Despite my early obstinance, the whole thing was a tremendous learning experience. I'd never thought of looking out at the people in the audience to connect with them before. I'd always been the serious athlete who'd been focused on his opponent. I'd never smiled at, waved to, or conversed with any fans during matches in prior territories, but now I was doing whatever I could to make people laugh, and intentionally clowning around in the ring for the first time in my career.

Before, everything in the ring had been strictly business. Now I was grabbing headlocks on guys, and if they shot me into the ropes, we'd do this silly spot where they'd drop down so that I'd leap over them, and then they'd spring up and prepare to punch me as I rebounded off the other set of ropes. Instead of continuing toward them, I would grab the ropes to bring myself to a halt, turn and strut away from them, and then shake my ass in their direction while they acted incensed. That sort of spot had *never* been in my repertoire until I got to Tennessee. Only someone like Dusty Rhodes could have gotten away with something like that outside of Memphis.

Similarly, if I did a test of strength, rather than making it look completely legitimate all the way through, I would put my opponent's hands on the mat and then jump up and stomp on them. Then we'd do the same spot except that my opponent would gain the upper hand and set my hands down on the mat, but when he leaped up to stomp on my hands, I would pull them away so that his feet landed harmlessly on the mat, and then I would slug him in the face. I was eliminating some of the seriousness from my bouts and replacing it with comedy, and somehow it was working.

Giving credit where it's due, almost every tactic I was using had been something that I'd seen midgets use in their matches. The midgets were always fun, and funny, and no one ever stole their spots in Florida. In Tennessee, all of those spots were *gold*. I'd get thrown out to the floor, sneak around and come up on the other side of the ring while my opponent was looking over at the place where I went out. I'd come up behind him and tap him on the shoulder, and he would say, "Go away, ref!" and shrug me off. Then I'd tap him on the shoulder again while holding a finger to my lips to tell the audience to shush. When my opponent finally turned around, I would pop him with my right hand and the match would continue. That was a *pure* midget comedy spot that I borrowed from start to finish.

As much as I had been encouraged to change, there were at least a couple of occasions where the wrestlers in Memphis appreciated having a "shooter" from Tampa on their roster. One of those times was in Blytheville, Arkansas, which provided us with a really crappy building and horrendous dressing rooms.

The Fabulous Wrestling Life of Steve Keirn

That night in Blytheville, guys were coming back into the dressing room after working their matches and saying, "There's a mark out there that keeps pickin' on the boys!"

Plowboy Frazier approached me while I was putting my boots on to personally voice his concerns.

"Steve, there's a guy pickin' on everybody," he said. "When I walked by, he tried to pick a fight with me goin' to the ring. On the way back he called me names, and he still wanted to pick a fight."

Please keep in mind that Plowboy Frazier was a big, rotund monster of a man who was nearly as big as Andre the Giant, but who possessed a very childish brain. Plowboy seemed to have gotten the impression that I was a shooter from Florida, and because I was in such good shape, I needed to be the one to go out into the crowd and put the mark in his place. For some odd reason, despite being larger than 99.9 percent of people on earth, Plowboy wanted *me* to be the one to handle this fan on his behalf.

"Okay…" I said. "Open the door and show me."

Plowboy and I walked over to the dressing room door, and he held it open.

"Where is he?" I asked.

"That guy over there leanin' against the wall," said Frazier.

I looked out into the crowd, and I couldn't believe my eyes. The fan who was causing such a stir was nowhere near the size of Plowboy. He was just a stout, raw-boned country guy from Blytheville.

I took note of where the annoying mark was situated in the building and filed it away for when I would be headed out for my match. That night I was scheduled to wrestle Atsushi Onita, a Japanese guy who was being mentored by Tojo Yamamoto. On the way to the ring, I walked by the pernicious mark, and as I looked him up and down, I carefully sized him up. He was wearing a cowboy hat, and was leaning back against the wall. He also had a sizable gut that protruded in front of him.

I decided to pull the stunt of cutting a wrestling promo on the guy assuming that he would back down and leave. I stopped on my way to the ring, took my index finger, and jabbed it into the guy's chest.

"I hear you're lookin' to fight a wrestler," I told him, as I pressed hard into his sternum.

"I *am*!" the man responded, without hesitation.

"Well *I'm* a wrestler," I continued. "I'm goin' to the ring, and if you wanna fight somebody, come follow my ass up there!"

With that, I turned and walked away, assuming that the mark's hasty answer had been motivated by adrenaline, and that he wasn't really interested in climbing into the ring and fighting me publicly.

Paul Morton, the father of Ricky Morton of the Rock 'n' Roll Express, was the referee that night. He and I climbed into the ring, and the instant that I turned around, I spotted the problematic fan casually strolling down the aisle and up to the ring.

"Holy shit," I thought to myself as the fan grew ever nearer. "I'm really *not* a shooter. What did I just get myself into?!"

I could take care of myself well enough as a result of what I'd been taught, but picking a fight with someone in the audience that you've never seen before was a great way to get your ass whipped. It's *never* a wise move.

The man stepped into the ring, and my mind was racing through a thousand different ideas for how I could get out of this situation. I quickly decided that this country boy would probably be a little too risky to fight head-on. The fan stood there and looked me up and down. At the same time, he suddenly seemed taken aback by the fact that he was now standing in a wrestling ring, and now he was contemplating if there were any official rules he needed to abide by now that he had stepped between the ropes.

"Ummm…. Do I need to take my hat off?" he asked.

"Yeah, you might wanna take your hat off," Morton answered him.

The large fan looked back over at me, and then down at my feet. Then he looked down at his boots. After examining his own choice of footwear, the man leaned toward me and asked, "Do I need to take my boots off?"

"You're not gonna be here that long!" I told him.

To my great relief, this mark honestly thought this was going to be a fair fight. As soon as he leaned down, I took that opportunity to sucker punch him in the face as hard as I could. The punch sent him backpedaling, and I rapidly followed up with several additional swings. A few of my punches landed solidly, and the man crashed to the ground.

Now that the fan was down on the mat and vulnerable, I didn't have a clue what I was supposed to do with him. I couldn't think of a hold to apply to him to make him submit or incapacitate him, even though a sleeper should have been my logical choice. Instead, I just repeatedly kicked him over and over again until he rolled underneath the bottom rope and out onto the floor. I'd kicked him in the head, back, and every other piece of his anatomy that my feet could reach.

When the guy's body reached the floor, my biggest fear was that he was going to collect himself, climb back into the ring, and kick my ass. That's why I followed him out onto the floor and continued kicking him until he rolled completely beneath the wrestling ring to protect himself. After absorbing so many blows, he wasn't moving nearly competently as he had been before the assault. I knew I'd done a debilitating amount of damage to him.

Out came Sonny King from our dressing room, and he sprinted to the ring. When Sonny reached me, he grabbed me by both shoulders.

"Steve! Stop!" yelled Sonny. "You're gonna kill him!"

I rolled beneath the bottom rope and back into the ring, and I could see Sonny looking down and examining the mark. Then Sonny simply turned and walked back toward the dressing room as if the presence of a badly beaten fan lying in front of the ring was no big deal. As that was happening, out came Tojo Yamamoto with Atsushi Onita, who I was supposed to wrestle. They'd been peeking out of the dressing room doors the entire time and decided the coast was now clear.

    As the two made their approach, Tojo held his hands out and kept saying to me, "Calm down! Calm down!"

    Meanwhile, I was pacing back and forth in the ring like a caged lion watching the bottom rope in case the fan recovered and climbed back in. I quickly snatched a headlock on Onita. He was trying to communicate with me, but I wasn't interested in having a match of any quality at that point. I was watching for the mark to see what he was going to do in response to getting beaten up.

    I held Onita and grounded him at the beginning of the match so that I could stare out in the direction where the mark had been left lying on the ground. There were no signs of life at first, but all of a sudden the fan's hand emerged from below the ring and into my line of sight. His hand stretched up and grasped the bottom rope, and then his head slowly rose into view. The mark's face was bleeding and swollen from the pounding I'd dished out to him. After an intense struggle with his equilibrium, the man pulled himself completely upright, and began to stagger around. The people in the front row all held their hands out to protect themselves as he wobbled over toward them and nearly collapsed on top of them.

    Instead of heading toward the ring, the mark staggered in the direction of the dressing rooms, and then I watched him walk straight through the back door and out of the building. Now I had a *completely* different sort of fear rushing through my mind. I was convinced this guy was making a beeline straight for his pickup truck to load a gun so that he could walk back inside and shoot me. Onita and I worked our match and executed a very quick finish where I got the win, got the bout over with, and got both of us out of there.

    During my walk back to the dressing room, I mentally prepared myself for a confrontation with a gun-toting fan in the hallway, but it never materialized. Once I reached my destination, everyone started coming up to me and congratulating me for sticking up for them. In my mind, I hadn't done anything worthy of a compliment. All I'd done was sucker punch a guy and then kick him while he was down and practically defenseless. Just about any one of them could have done *that*. I'd simply taken the fan out swiftly, and by any means necessary. It's not like we had dueled in a fair fight and I'd bested him with my superior skills.

I sat in the dressing room for a while, then took my shower and got dressed. A full 30 minutes after I'd returned from my bout, we heard hard pounding on the dressing room door. When Bill Dundee opened it, there was a tall, Black sheriff's deputy standing there in his uniform.

"Did any of you guys get into a little scuffle with a guy in the audience here?" he asked.

Everyone in the dressing room turned and looked *right* at me. It was the ultimate stooging-out of a fellow wrestler. In that moment, I couldn't have talked my way out of handcuffs if I'd tried.

"Could you step outside, please?" the deputy asked.

I stepped forward and out through the door into the hallway, readying my wrists to have cuffs slapped on them. Awaiting me in the hallway were four other deputies.

"So what happened?" they asked me.

I told them the full story of how the mark had tried to pick a fight, how I'd invited him into the ring, and how I'd beaten him down.

"Well he's in the hospital," the Black deputy informed me. "He might have a concussion. Luckily, he ain't gonna die."

In my mind, this was clearly leading toward an arrest for a violent assault.

"Anyway, we all came down here to *shake your hand*!" grinned the deputy.

"What?!" I responded.

"We wanted to shake your hand!" One of the other deputies chimed in. "That guy has been the biggest *dick* in

Blytheville. He's a bully. He always beats people up. He gets in trouble constantly for fightin' in the bars. Now that he's gotten his ass handed to him, we wanted to come meet the guy who did it!"

One by one I shook their hands and received their congratulatory pats on the back before walking back into the dressing room and yelling at everybody for stooging me out to the authorities so quickly.

The events of that night had provided me with a shot in the arm, but now I had also been saddled with a reputation that I didn't particularly want as the guy that the wrestlers could come to whenever someone in the audience was taunting them. Sooner or later, I knew that wouldn't work out in my favor.

I was concerned over nothing, though. The only other time someone asked me to commit an act of violence occurred when we were in Jonesboro, Arkansas. Jerry Lawler asked me to break Chick Donovan's leg during our match, and it was all over one of the girls coming to the shows. Chick had hit on a girl that Lawler had his eye on, and Lawler got jealous about it.

"Ain't no way I'm gonna break one of the boys' legs," I told Lawler.

Anybody in our business could do that to their opponent because we have to give up our bodies and place our trust in one another. I could have easily figured out a way to do it, but it would be something I'd have gnawing at me from the back of my mind going forward. That would have destroyed my reputation with the rest of the boys, and no one would have ever trusted me again. If you hurt someone, they're going to tell everyone they ever work with about it for the rest of their career. If you're malicious to the boys in this business, it will *kill* your career prospects.

Jimmy Hart was a witness to the entire thing, and when he saw that I'd declined to do Lawler's dirty work for him, Jimmy loved me ever since. Jimmy was a good guy to have on my side, because he was the foremost manager in the region, and a very influential guy. His First Family stable usually contained all of the top heel wrestlers in Memphis within its lineup.

During one of the few bouts I worked in Memphis against Stan Lane, he hit me with an arm drag that drove me into the mat. The landing separated my shoulder so badly that I couldn't raise my left arm enough to do a lockup. I was forced to sit out for a while to recover from it.

This wasn't even close to the first time I'd been in the ring with Stan. The first time was in Florida when he was working for the CWF. He had a partner named Brian St. John, and the two of them were facing Mike Graham and I as the seasoned team.

Stan spoke to me for the very first time in the ring and said, "Would you mind calling the match?"

My first thought was, "Uh oh. These guys must be *really* green."

Usually the heels called the matches, but I didn't mind getting the ball rolling. I called a few simple things at the beginning of the bout just to get a sense of what sort of experience levels Stan and Brian were bringing to the table.

One of the simple spots I called involved a lock up, and then I quickly pushed Stan into the ropes. From there, he pushed me back, and I said, "One, two." That's a *simple* spot where the heel punches you when you break, and then the babyface punches the heel right back.

Well when Stan backed away from me, he punched me *twice* and said, "One, two!" In response to that, I said, "Okay… *three* then!" and I whalloped him in the chin.

My separated shoulder wasn't the only physical impairment I was dealing with in Tennessee. I was in the dressing room one night, bouncing a rubber ball against the wall and catching it on the rebound. In the midst of my one-man game of catch, I noticed that my right arm was incapable of straightening itself. No matter what I did, my arm simply would not allow itself to be extended completely. During my subsequent trips to the gym, I'd try different things, like going to the preacher curl station, dangling my arms from the pad with a barbell in my hands, and seeing if I could get my right arm to fully straighten itself out. *Nothing* seemed to work.

Hoping to get my arm fixed, I made an appointment in Nashville to meet an orthopedic surgeon. He took x-rays of my elbow and explained to me that bone fragments had been chipped away from my elbow, and those chips had become lodged in my elbow joint. Whenever I attempted to straighten my arm, I had chips in the way that would block its progress. It turned out that years of using the flying forearm as a finisher had resulted in a sea of bone chips getting lodged in my elbow joint that prevented it from fully opening.

"I can clean this out, but I'll have to operate on you. You won't be able to wrestle for at least three weeks," the surgeon told me.

It wasn't giving me arthritis or anything like that, but I started noticing from looking at wrestling magazines how many of the older wrestlers appeared incapable of opening or closing their arms. I'd always thought it was stiffness from years of working out, but I soon learned that in most cases it was from an accumulation of damage to the elbow joint from dropping elbows to the mat and other things.

"I need to get this fixed," I told Jarrett.

Shortly thereafter, I had an operation at Vanderbilt Hospital where they cleaned out my elbow and put my arm in a cast.

To explain my absence, we worked an injury angle in Memphis with Bobby Eaton and Koko Ware – long before the WWF inserted a "B" initial into the middle of his name. I hooked my arm between the top rope and the middle rope so that I was dangling from the ring solely by my trapped right arm. Bobby Eaton smashed my defenseless arm with a steel chair, and that was intended to be how we explained my injury to the fans while I endured my elbow surgery and sat at home recovering from it.

The only problem was that Eaton was bashing my arm so convincingly with the chair that one fan actually hopped over the barricade and invaded the ringside area to try to assist me. From where I was positioned, I had a clear view of the guy running down the aisle toward us.

"Hey, you've got a mark coming at you!" I told Bobby.

In response, Koko snagged Jimmy Hart's cane and tried to swat the mark with it, but the guy avoided Koko's swipes with the stick and still hopped onto the ring apron to try to protect me. The guy swung on Bobby, but Bobby stuck his left arm out and grabbed the mark by the throat. Then Bobby deftly turned the mark's head so that none of the guy's punches could reach Bobby's face. Now that his own face was safe from harm, Bobby measured the mark and cracked him with a *big* right hand that knocked him completely off the ring apron and left him lying like a crumpled shirt on the ringside floor.

I was so impressed that I even forgot to sell the damage to my arm for a few seconds. I hadn't thought of Bobby Eaton as a particularly tough guy until that instant, but he gave an incredible accounting of himself in that situation.

While I was away recovering from my elbow surgery, I managed to grow a full beard, which wasn't a difficult thing for me to do; it only took three weeks of laziness for me to accomplish it. I assumed I would be shaving it off before I made my full-time return to the ring. That's when Jerry Jarrett approached me in the dressing room with a sparkle in his eye.

"I've got an idea. I'm thinking about putting you and Stan Lane together," said Jarrett. "You guys are the same height and pretty much the same size. Stan is also letting his beard grow out. In this area for years, the Fabulous Fargos were the deal. I'd like to call you and Stan 'The Fabulous Ones!'"

"The *Fabulous* Ones?" I asked. "Holy crap. Do you know how hard that will be to say to people when they ask us who we are? So you're going to switch my name?"

"No. You'll *still* be Steve Keirn," Jarrett assured me. "Stan will still be Stan Lane. You're just going to be the Fabulous Ones as a tag team."

"I'm not sure I like this idea," I told him.

"Well, I can offer it to Terry Taylor," said Jarrett. "He could possibly do it."

When Jarrett said that, I immediately realized that it would be asinine of me to reject an opportunity that the owner of a wrestling territory was so passionate about.

"Hmmm… Fabulous Ones… Sounds like a good name to me!" I finally said.

"Great!" said Jarrett. "So we're going to wipe the slate clean on who you and Stan are. We're going to take him off TV for a while, too. Then we're going to tell people that Jackie Fargo put the Fabulous Ones together and endorses you two. Then he's going to manage you guys for a bit and give it his stamp of approval."

The Fabulous Fargos were a favorite wrestling unit composed of Jackie Fargo, Donnie Fargo, and Sonny "Roughhouse" Fargo. The trio had been put together back in the 1950s with Jackie and Donnie as the pair that would usually handle the wrestling, while Roughhouse was the nutcase of the trio. He'd usually just hop into the ring and do goofy, stupid shit to make all the fans laugh.

The Fargos were kind of like an early version of the Fabulous Freebirds as a three-man unit, except they were local to the Tennessee territory. They wore bowties and top hats, and they were flamboyant and outspoken. I had never heard of Jackie Fargo in my life until I moved to Tennessee, but he was *insanely* over with the fans.

When you have someone with a reputation as strong as Jackie Fargo's endorsing your team in that territory, it takes you into a transcendent dimension of popularity. Suddenly, all of the old Fargo fans began to turn out at the shows midway through 1982. It was almost like Jackie Fargo had two illegitimate boys and taught them to wrestle. He went through the motions of coaching us and having us perform all of the Fabulous Fargos' classic stunts, including his famous strut.

Both Stan and I had worn short tights for most of our careers, but we started wearing long tights with lightning bolt emblems on the sides once we got together as a team.

Everything was identical, from the boots to the tights and the outfits, whether we were wearing sequin tuxedos, top hats, or sets of suspenders. From a distance, Stan and I could even switch places in the ring fairly easily without the crowd telling who was who.

Stan and Steve – The Fabulous Ones

The main reason behind the switch to long tights was because the knee pads in that era weren't great. You had to search long and hard to find knee pads that fit properly and functioned like they were supposed to. You couldn't simply substitute basketball knee pads. If you didn't have a good knee pad, it would slip down, and then you'd need to adjust it during the match, which only created distractions that would keep you from focusing on your opponent. Having long tights eliminated that from the equation. Once I was wearing long tights and had no obliques, I was all set in that respect. All I had to do was focus on getting my match over and not getting beaten up.

The Fabulous Ones as U.S. Tag Team Champions

As the Fabulous Ones, Stan and I quickly became major sticklers for presentation. The two of us would always coordinate our outfits ahead of time. On a typical afternoon, I would place a quick call to Stan to confirm the specific colors of the suspenders, bow ties, top hats and jackets we would be wearing out to the ring that evening. On other nights when I wanted to *really* cause a scene, Stan would call me and ask, "What are we bringing tonight?" and I would laugh and say, "Bring it all!"

The influence of Jackie Fargo notwithstanding, the thing that set Stan and I apart from the crowd and helped to make us unbelievably captivating to the audience was the fact that the Fabulous Ones debuted around the time MTV was in its earliest days of generating popularity through music videos. To the Tennessee viewing audience, the Fabulous Ones became the embodiment of MTV coming to life inside of a wrestling ring. From the very beginning, the Fabs were associated with pop music tastes.

The first song associated with the Fabulous Ones was "Everybody Wants You" by Billy Squier. A videographer came to film with us for hours to put a video together, but he only used little pieces of his supplementary filming shots for the finished video product. We wore our sequin tuxedos, and had a little strobe light going off around us. This video producer combined those clips with in-ring action shots, and footage of us interacting with the crowds. We then debuted an MTV-caliber music video starring the Fabulous Ones on Tennessee's wrestling program.

As simple as it seems in retrospect, the whole thing lit our gimmick and the entire Tennessee wrestling territory ablaze. I could have beaten 1,000 enhancement guys and not gotten over as incredibly as this video gimmick got Stan and I over in the Tennessee territory. It was a combination of Jackie Fargo's name and reputation – combined with the production people who put those videos together – that turned the Fabs into an instant box office attraction in the region.

The Fabulous Ones would come to the ring to the sound of one song for a couple of weeks, and then we would switch things up and start coming out to a different popular song supported by yet another video that appeared on television. We'd use everything from ZZ Top's "Sharp Dressed Man" to "Beat It" by Michael Jackson. Whatever the most popular song was during that week, we would use it to ingratiate ourselves with the fans who watched the wrestling program airing out of Memphis.

Stan and I did our best to mirror our wrestling gimmick in real life. The "Sharp Dressed Man" music video had an old car in it, so I went out and bought an old truck to match the aesthetic of the video. I wasn't all that creative, but Stan Lane added a lot of *great* creative input to the Fabulous Ones. Alongside Stan, Jerry Jarrett and Jerry Lawler also got involved in brainstorming ideas for the Fabs. Once our gimmick started drawing fans, and once interest in the wrestling product surged, *everybody* wanted to be involved in it.

It made sense; when the territory drew more fans, the owners, promoters and bookers all made more money, so they wanted to feed the goose that was laying the golden eggs. That also meant more teams wanted to work with us, because we were frequently booked in the main events, and they could also get their hands on some of that money.

My wife Terri was actually in one of the videos we shot. She didn't particularly like all of the changes her husband underwent, like growing his beard, bleaching his hair, or doing photo shoots in his underwear. I couldn't exactly blame her. If I'd married her, and she suddenly had to present herself in public as if she was a stripper of sorts because she wanted to earn some extra income for us, I certainly would've had a problem with it. It wasn't fair to her, but at the same time, there's nothing fair about the wrestling business, or life in general. Fortunately, Terri knew in her heart that I was doing all of it for my family.

Things got off to a tremendous start for the Fabs, and they were only getting better. We were emulating the Fabulous Fargos inside of the ring with their blessing, but I soon learned that there was another side to the Fargos that was even more fun to replicate outside of the ring.

FOURTEEN

Working with Jackie Fargo was a blast. He was just a really cool older guy. He was from a generation before mine – essentially the same era as Eddie Graham – but he built his reputation in the redneck territory of Tennessee. Given the vast differences between the nature of the wrestling business in Tennessee and Florida, Jackie and Eddie might as well have been wrestling on two totally different planets.

In the NWA territories of Florida, Georgia and the Carolinas, there was no goofiness allowed. In Tennessee, it was the polar opposite. Everything was goofy by comparison. You'd make the fans laugh because they were so happy, and then you jerked the carpet out from underneath them and made them upset because they were no longer laughing. That was the psychology in Memphis.

Roughhouse Fargo had been a referee in the Carolinas while I was there, and he came in for one or two shots once Stan and I got cooking in Tennessee as a team. Roughhouse would still be working the same gimmick that he had in the 1960s, which was to come into the wrestling ring and act like he was nuts. From my vantage point, he was sinking to depths in his presentation that I wasn't all that excited about having associated with the Fabs.

Roughhouse approached Stan and I one night and said, "Okay, boys… I'ma go like I'm gonna take my pants off, and you boys try'n stop me! Referee is gonna check me to see if I have anythin' in my pants, so I'm gonna make like I'm gonna pull my pants down!"

I looked at Stan, and Stan could immediately tell what I was going to do once we were all together in the ring. Roughhouse started to take his pants off, and he whispered to Stan and I, "Come on; stop me!"

"Pull 'em *off*!" I yelled.

Then I looked to the audience and waved my arms around in an effort to convince them to chant, "Take 'em off! Take 'em off!"

Roughhouse got *really* upset with me for that.

The Fabulous Ones with Roughhouse Fargo and Jackie Fargo

The earliest stories I'd heard about Jackie Fargo came from the many car rides I took with Bill Dundee. The tales of the ribs he pulled were *epic*. Just listening to the stories of Jackie's ribs taught me to think about the bigger picture whenever I ribbed guys, and how to utilize everything around me in order to make it more realistic, innovative and memorable.

The all-time greatest Jackie Fargo rib involved a trip when all three Fargos were driving from Memphis to Nashville, and the trio picked up a Black hitchhiker along the interstate.

During the trip, Jackie and Don got into an argument. Unbeknownst to the Black guy in the back seat, Don slipped his 22-caliber pistol full of blanks to Jackie, who was driving the car. Jackie started arguing back and forth with Don, and the hostility level slowly increased as time progressed, and the Fargos' language toward one another similarly worsened.

Finally, Jackie let out a yell of, "You no-good son of a bitch!" and fired in Don's direction twice. Donnie keeled over in the passenger seat, and then Jackie pulled the car over to the side of the road, got out, walked around, and opened the door. Then he unbuckled his brother's body, and hauled it out of the front seat and onto the pavement.

"I shoulda done this years ago!" said Jackie, as he dragged the "corpse" of Don Fargo away from the vehicle. "I've been sick of takin' care of your ass my entire life!"

After unceremoniously dropping Don's body onto the grass, Jackie looked back toward the car and said, "Hey, Roughhouse... get in the front seat, boy!"

As Roughhouse climbed out and took his very recently departed brother's place in the front of the car, Jackie looked at the horrified hitchhiker in the back of the car and said, "Don't you move!"

"I ain't goin' nowhere!" said the man.

They continued down the road, and Roughhouse justifiably decided he had an issue with the way Jackie had dealt with their sibling.

"Jackie, you shouldn't have shot our brother like that!" said Roughhouse. "You just left him dead on the side of the road! What are we gonna tell *mama*?! Oh, Jackie!"

Just in case the gentleman in the back seat didn't know exactly who they were – which he *did* – the Fargos took great pains to use their stage names.

This argument continued to simmer for another 10 miles of travel time until it finally bubbled over.

"You had no right to kill our brother, Jackie!" yelled Roughhouse.

"Shut up, dumb ass! I'll kill *your* ass, too!" responded Jackie.

With that, Jackie fired off two rounds toward Roughhouse at point-blank range. Like his brother before him, Roughhouse immediately slumped over in his seat, in a state of feigned unconsciousness. Once again, Jackie pulled the car over to the side of the road, removed Roughhouse's limp carcass from the car, and then turned to his sole remaining passenger, who was now trembling with fear in the car's back seat.

"Get your ass in the front seat!" ordered Jackie, as he used his pistol to wave the man forward.

The terrified man climbed out of the back seat and sat down in the very seat where he had just watched two men seemingly get murdered. Jackie then sat back in the driver's seat, placed the pistol on the dashboard where only he could reach it, and began to speed down the highway once again.

When Jackie told me the story, he said, "This guy next to me was shakin' like a leaf. He said to me, 'Mr. Fargo, *please* don't kill me! I know I'm the only witness, but please, Mr. Fargo! Don't kill me! I got a wife and children!'"

In response to the man, Jackie said, "If you don't shut up, I'll shoot your ass *right now!*"

As the man continued to whimper and cry, Jackie began to insult his murdered brothers, explaining to the petrified hitchhiker how worthless they had been, how they had pissed him off for the final time, and how Jackie would now be infinitely better off without the duo handicapping his life.

Just before they arrived in Nashville, Jackie looked at the man and said, "Listen! I've got an idea!"

Jackie then pulled the car off to the side of the road, and the passenger burst into tears once again.

"Get outta the car!" ordered Jackie.

The man rapidly opened the door, but before he could unbuckle his seatbelt, Jackie had some additional instructions to provide him with.

"I'm gonna give you 'til the count of *five*!" said Jackie. "I mean to give ya a fair chance, cuz you ain't did nothin'. But you *did* see me shoot my brothers, and you *will* testify against me in court!"

"No, no, no, Mr. Fargo!" whimpered the man. "I would *never* do that!"

"Shut up!" yelled Jackie. "I'm gonna give you until the count of five to get outta range, and then I'm gonna start firin'!"

The man unbuckled his seatbelt and bolted off into the pitch-black woods like a rocket.

"One…. two…." Jackie began his count slowly, before rapidly ramping up the speed as soon as the man hit the treeline. "Three, four, five!"

Jackie fired off his remaining blanks into the air as the man continued to flee.

A few hours later, Jackie was seated at his customary Nashville bar with most of the other wrestlers from that evening's event, along with Donnie and Roughhouse who were both very much alive. Both of the Fargo brothers who had been presumably executed had been picked up along the road by other wrestlers who were traveling in the same direction.

Out of the blue, several officers from the Nashville Police Department burst into the bar with their guns drawn.

"Jackie Fargo…" began one of the officers. "You're under arrest for killin' your two brothers!"

"Killin' my brothers?!" laughed Jackie. "Why… they're sittin' right *there*!"

The officers looked over to see the other two Fargo brothers waving at them, and then they holstered their weapons.

"Man… we just had a Black guy down at the station tellin' us this crazy story," said the officer. "He said you shot 'em both and dragged 'em out of the car, and then you threatened to shoot him! He was cryin' so bad, we figured it *had* to be true!"

It's incredible that Jackie's rib had gotten that far, and when he told me the story and I imagined the rib happening, I realized I needed to be able to pull off stuff like that one day. Jackie went the extra mile to make his ribs special. That was the caliber of ribbing I always aspired to match, and it remains the gold standard.

Aside from being excellent ribbers, all of the Fargos were also heavy drinkers, and they used to drink like fish while they were on the road driving to and from their shows. They would go to towns and do such stupid shit, like the one time they drove through a small town on the way to a show, and Donnie Fargo hopped out of the car naked and streaked the entire way through the town. Every story Jackie told me about these things made me laugh, and I realized how important it was just to make people smile and laugh at the end of the ribs. I made it a point that no one should ever get physically hurt by any of the ribs I pulled.

Another set of ribs that the Fargos were excellent at pulling involved their CB radios. By this time, I was already an expert at stirring up trouble on CB radios, so Jackie simply inspired me to take my mischief-making to the next level. Taking a cue from Jackie and some of the other guys in the territory, I extended my reach beyond simply messing with the wrestlers and now went out of my way to harass the truckers and other civilians that were always chatting on their CB radios.

I owned a Cadillac that didn't have the antenna on the back of the trunk. Instead, it went straight down with my radio, so people looking from the outside couldn't even tell I had a CB radio in my car because the antenna was hidden. I took advantage of my anonymity and stirred shit up on those radios all the time.

It was toward the end of the night, and Stan and I were driving back from Evansville, and there was an accident on the interstate going in the opposite direction. The traffic was backed up for miles, and I was bored.

I picked up the radio, and before I could even say anything, this other guy got on the radio and he kept rambling on and on.

"Well, it looks like we're gonna be stuck in traffic here for quite a while," he said. "They got us backed up all the way. Me and my wife up here in our RV want you to know if you got kids, or if your wife needs to use the restroom, y'all are more than welcome to come up here and use the restroom in our RV."

This was one of the *kindest* offers I'd ever heard expressed by someone over CB radio. He was simply a nice man.

Stan could see the smirk on my face, and he could see my hand holding the microphone at the ready. Knowing me as well as he did, he knew I was preparing to say something outlandishly rude and heelish to this kind gentleman.

"No," Stan said, shaking his head. "No. Steve... *no. Absolutely* not. Don't do it."

"Hey, that's mighty kind of you to offer that to all of us," I said into the microphone. "You sure are a decent guy. That was such a kind offer you made to us all, and the world would be a much better place if there were more folks like you livin' in it. But I gotta tell ya, I don't really need to use the restroom, but I was wonderin' with you bein' so nice, do you think your wife could have *sex* with me if I was to come up there?"

Stan started trying to snatch the microphone right out of my hand before I'd even finished my sentence once he knew where my monologue was headed, and once I'd uttered the last syllable, Stan started trying to pull the CB radio right out of my dashboard.

When Stan finally got his hand off of the button on the microphone to stop it from transmitting, you could hear all these guys saying things like, "Who the hell said that?!" and "Where is that son of a bitch?! I'll *kill* him!"

"We're dead," said Stan matter of factly, as if he'd already accepted death as his fate. "It's over. We're dead. We're *dead!*"

The Fabulous Ones with the World Championship trophy

"They don't even know where we're at, man!" I laughed. "*Relax!*"

I did stop transmitting on the radio, but the truckers were still angrily ranting about me right up until the time we got out of the standstill traffic about half an hour later.

Terry Taylor didn't have a CB radio in his gold Cadillac, which made him a perfect target for Stan and I. We were a few car lengths behind Terry, and we saw him roll right up behind an 18-wheeler.

I decided to hop on the radio to address the driver of the 18-wheeler directly.

"Can't you see me behind you in this gold Cadillac?!" I yelled over the radio. "Move your ass out of my way!"

Up ahead, we watched and cackled as the driver of the 18-wheeler intentionally locked up his brakes in front of Terry, and poor Terry had no idea what was happening. He had no clue that the reason the 18-wheeler was suddenly swerving to block his progress was because his friends had instigated it from several car lengths behind him.

Everyone in the Memphis area was obsessed with country music. I was far more into the music of J. Geils, Creedence Clearwater Revival and Bob Seger. It's not like I hadn't been forced to give country music a fair hearing. Much to my chagrin, half the roster in Florida, including the Briscos and Dusty Rhodes, had taken turns driving me insane with country music. In fact, I'd been completely forbidden to play anything on Dusty's radio that *wasn't* country music.

Plenty of country stars lived extremely close to us. Johnny Cash lived in Hendersonville, and Heidi even got to be friends with Conway Twitty's granddaughter. He had a swimming pool, and we would take Heidi to swim over at his house.

At the height of our popularity in Tennessee, there were country-western companies in Nashville that even had Stan and I doing some modeling so that they could use the photos for their catalogs.

My next door neighbor was Bobby Randall from the Sawyer Brown Band. Stan and I sponsored a little league baseball team called The Fabulous Ones, and they played against Conway Twitty's team, and teams sponsored by several other country singers.

The Fabs attained a lot of opportunities because of our popularity and due to our proximity to Nashville. Kenny Rogers even asked us to escort him to the stage during a concert there. I wasn't a Kenny Rogers fan by any stretch, but it was a cool thing to do.

The Fabulous Ones with Kenny Rogers

We didn't have to talk to Kenny for very long while we were at the concert. All we had to do was walk him to the stage, turn around, and walk away. Then we collected our money and sat to watch the concert. When we met up with Kenny, we walked into his dressing room and said hello, and then, we took a couple of photos together.

"I'm a *big* fan of you guys!" he said.

I wasn't sure if that was true or not, but I also told him I was a huge fan of his, and that *definitely* wasn't true.

That opportunity came when Jerry Jarrett was contacted directly by Kenny Rogers' agent. He knew Jerry Jarrett owned the wrestling company and lived in a huge house that Stan and I had essentially built for him through the success of our tag team run. When Stan and I first moved there, Jerry lived in a small house on a lake. By the time we'd been performing as the Fabulous Ones for a while, Jerry had moved into a *mansion* on top of a hill so that he could look down on all of the acreage he owned, which included the lake.

All of those arrangements were made through Jerry Jarrett. Everything had to go through the main office, because you didn't exactly want people being able to reach you at home or knowing where you lived.

Luckily for me, being paired with Stan Lane meant that I got a break from country music whenever I rode around with him. Stan was primarily into music from the 1960s as well as crooning music, and he had a disc-jockey-caliber voice that enabled him to sing everything well. He also had a collection for 45 RPM records, and most of the people living in Tennessee didn't even know what a 45 was.

One time we were both at the airport in Memphis on a Saturday after a TV taping, and Stan and I were standing in line to catch a flight.

This guy suddenly came up behind me and said, "Hey, are you leavin' town?"

I turned around, looked at him, and said, "What the hell is it to *you*?"

I stepped forward to get in the man's face, but Stan quickly intervened.

"No, Steve! *Stop!*" yelled Stan. "That's Michael Love of The Beach Boys!"

"Man, I just watched you guys on the TV!" said Love. "I really like what you guys do in there! You guys are *great!*"

It's a good thing Stan had intervened before I belted Michael Love. Stan knew every song in the Beach Boys' catalog, and I never would have lived it down if I'd slugged a music legend. It would have been difficult to remain a babyface after that.

While Michael Love was complimenting us, a young kid walked up to our group with a pen extended.

"Hey, can I get your autograph?" the kid asked.

"Sure!" said Love, as he reached for the kid's pen.

"Not *yours*!" the kid protested. "I want the autographs of the Fabulous Ones!"

I looked at the kid and said, "Well, your mom might want *this* guy's autograph."

The Fabulous Ones with Michael Love of The Beach Boys

Love looked bewildered that the autographs of the Fabulous Ones had taken priority over the signature of a Beach Boy in that setting.

It was a total transformation for me from before I had the elbow surgery to afterward. I had gone from a near-shooter to an entertainer that catered to the reactions of the audience and involved them in the action. I also reestablished my character within the Fabulous Ones as someone who was easygoing, but who you didn't want to make angry.

The New York Dolls – Rick McGraw and the Dream Machine – were a team that Stan and I got to beat as part of the beginning of our major push. They were a fine team, but for us they were simply one of our initial stepping stones.

Next up were The Nightmares, which were Danny Davis, and Buddy Wayne's son, Ken. They were an additional rung on the ladder for us as a team that was simply lined up for us to beat without any real angle behind it.

Whatever popularity I may have had with the people who lived in Memphis early on, once the Fabulous Ones became the hottest tag team in the territory, my popularity at least *quintupled*. I'd been popular in Florida for several reasons, including the Bob Roop angle, the length of time I'd been there, and all of the television time and interview time I'd received there. Being one half of the Fabulous Ones blew *all* of that out of the water in a *month*.

If you were out and about in Tennessee during that era, Stan and I were easy to spot. You'd never see two bleach-blonde guys with beards who were both about 220 pounds and in shape walking into a restaurant together, or going anywhere together without having it clearly connected with something serious in the world of entertainment. We stuck out.

The fact that our hair was nearly white wasn't purely for show; it had a practical use during matches. Having white hair created great visuals when it was time for us to bleed. If you get color during a match and you have bleach-blond hair, it shows up so well that anyone in the building can see how much you're bleeding even if they're sitting high up in the balcony. Even if you were only bleeding a bit, once the blood mixed with the bleach-blond hair, it would look like your hair had been dyed pink.

Outside of the ring, the bleach-blond hair in that era also helped everyday people who spotted us on the street to recognize that we didn't emerge from an ordinary walk of life. Someone with bleach-blond hair and muscles couldn't have been a doctor, lawyer or banker. It was an identity thing. Also, because there were no professional football teams in that part of the country at the time, no one would have made the leap to assume that the Fabulous Ones were simply a pair of professional football players.

A lot of weeks, Jarrett was devoting 15 to 20 minutes of a one-hour television broadcast to Fabulous Ones content, which was a *ton* of time. Memphis also had tremendous television announcers like Lance Russell and Dave Brown. If you have a great announcer on your television show, they can build you up and make you look and sound larger than life. To me, Gordon Solie was the best ever, but Lance and Dave were a tremendous team who could talk someone up and make them sound 10 times better than they truly were.

I'd learned to be close to the people who were putting me over during broadcasts. I bought Gordon a bottle of his favorite liquor every once in a while because I knew what he liked, and whenever I got an opportunity, I would make sure I mentioned how great Lance and Dave were at their jobs while I was being interviewed.

It was true; I legitimately liked them all, but there was also an element of working the workers to it. You worked them so that they would work for you. After all, it would be very easy for an announcer who didn't like you to negatively influence the fans' impressions of you. It's not like the announcers would necessarily be making you sound inadequate or incapable, but you wanted them to be working as hard as they could to make you sound better than you really were.

Through the combination of working out, getting abs, changing my hair, growing a beard, and now being 30 years old with 10 full years of in-ring experience, not to mention the wild wave of popularity I was now enjoying, I understood that I was in my prime, and this would be my best opportunity to make some decent money in pro wrestling. In the back of my mind, the clock was definitely ticking, and if I had any hope of saving some money before I got too old, *this* was the time.

I didn't want to be the wrestler who couldn't work well because he couldn't hear and couldn't see, and who wasn't able to take any bumps because he would never be able to get back up if he fell down, like Ox Baker. Even so, I still wasn't convinced that any major, life-changing money could be made in professional wrestling by the guys who were performing inside of the wrestling ring. I still hadn't seen *any* evidence of it.

When Stan and I popped loose in Memphis, almost everyone tried to emulate what we were doing to a certain degree. I was taught to protect my gimmick, my character, my style, or anything that was intended to be associated exclusively with me. If I was using the forearm as a finisher in a territory, no one else could use it. The same was true if I was using the sleeper as a finisher.

If I was a top guy, the last I wanted to do was walk into a building and watch a match where a guy caught his opponent in a sleeper and almost put him to sleep. That meant he was stepping on me, because that was *my* deal; you don't get to use *my* move as a false finish in your match. You knew better than to use another wrestler's finish for a high spot, a nearfall, or anything. If Mike Graham or Eddie Graham was using the figure four, no one else in Florida could use it for any reason.

When we started the Fabulous Ones, I had just come off of elbow surgery. I was feeling pretty solid with respect to my standing in the company, but I wasn't fully cognizant of just how solid I was yet, nor was I feeling totally secure about my position on the card. We were at a Memphis TV taping, and all of a sudden Koko Ware came out in a tuxedo coat and a cane as "Stagger Lee." He started strutting around in the audience doing an imitation of the Fabulous Ones gimmick right down to where he was shaking hands with the crowd.

I was *incensed*. Stan and I regularly wore bowties, tuxedo coats, white gloves and top hats, and we also entered through the crowd when we made our way to the ring. No one else had been doing those things prior to us, and there was no other way to interpret Koko's actions aside from them being a blatant ripoff of our presentation. That absolutely struck a nerve with me.

We had 200 miles between Memphis and Nashville that we had to cover on our way to that night's show, and I spent the entire time getting myself revved up to confront Koko. When you've been taught that you should protect your gimmick and at all costs, you can only imagine how I felt after watching Koko rip us off in almost every respect. He was copying our entire package just to get himself over.

When we got to Nashville that evening, Stan and I changed our clothes to prepare for the show. As soon as Stan and I finished dressing, I quickly said, "I'm gonna call Koko out when I see him tonight."

Stan immediately knew that this could turn physical, so he offered an alternative option.

"Maybe *I* should do it," suggested Stan. "You just had that elbow surgery."

"No, I've got it," I said. "I'm the one who has a problem with it. I'll handle it."

When we'd arrived at the building, Ricky Morton, Bill Dundee and Dutch Mantel were all already present in the dressing room, as was Koko.

"I need to talk to you for a second," I said to Koko sternly. "Come with me."

Koko followed me into the shower area, and when we got there, I absolutely lit into him.

"What the *hell* do you think you're doin' stealin' our gimmick?!" I started. "You're wearin' a sequin tuxedo and walkin' in through the damn crowd like me and Stan all of a sudden? Who the *hell* do you think you are?!"

"Whoa, man!" said Koko, holding his arms up. "I got *permission* to do it! I asked Lawler if it was okay, and *he* said I should do it!"

Receiving the revelation that Lawler had been the person in authority who had given Koko permission to act like he was an offshoot of the Fabulous Ones just pissed me off even more.

"That's bullshit!" I continued. "You want to get over, you need to come up with your own shit instead of stealin' from me and Stan!"

I was certainly screaming at Koko, but I was also searching for my best opportunity to sucker punch him, because that had been my intention the entire time. He was standing right in front of the fiberglass shower stall, but I made the mistake of backing myself into it to try to get away from the rest of the guys so that they wouldn't hear everything that we were saying. By this point, none of that mattered, because all of my ranting and raving had attracted an audience.

Seizing upon what I thought was an opening, I reared back to finally throw my punch. Bill Dundee saw the whole thing, and even though the punch connected, he said it looked like I was throwing a working punch instead of a shoot punch. My arm wasn't fully healed, so it couldn't move as freely and effectively as it needed to in order to be the truly effective shot that I'd hoped it would be.

Koko didn't fall, so I tried to duck down to take his legs out from under him. Koko swiftly snatched me in a front facelock and tried to pull my eye out. I could feel his finger grabbing at my eye, so I pulled his finger into my mouth and bit down on it. I considered biting Koko's finger off for a moment, but I just didn't have it in myself to bite a human being's finger off. That was *too much*. However, I did chomp down just hard enough to keep him from pulling my eyeball out.

The fight was quickly broken up after that, but we were both still raring to beat one another up.

"I ain't afraid of you, man!" said Koko. "I ain't afraid of you! Let's go!"

"Well let's do it then!" I responded. "Let's finish this!"

Dutch Mantel and other people got in between us and separated us, and nothing got going between Koko and I afterwards. The whole scuffle had lasted a maximum of 30 seconds. Koko had a mouse over his left eye where I hit him, and I had no damage done to me, but we never really resolved the issue between us in a physical sense.

Meanwhile, Ricky Morton was running around the dressing room screaming and crying like a little girl. He couldn't believe what was going on. He was just a kid at the time.

I will readily admit that it wasn't right of me to start a fight with Koko like that. My pride had taken over.

In the aftermath, Koko kept mouthing off about how he was going to get me back. It created a thick air of tension in the locker room for a time that was sufficient enough for Lawler to think it was wise to summon us both into his office. The King sat us down for a frank discussion. Lawler had been very influential in getting Koko into the business in the first place, so he was one of the few people that could reliably calm Koko down.

"I wouldn't keep pushing Steve," Lawler said to Koko. "He's already gone after you one time."

"Yeah, well, I kicked his *ass* when he did!" said Koko.

That remark really pissed me off because hardly anything had even happened. I never claimed to have beaten Koko up, but the idea that he'd kicked my ass was equally ludicrous. One punch was thrown by each of us, mine landed and his didn't, he got me in a front facelock that he let go of once I'd bitten his finger, and then people got in between us. That had been the *entire* scrum.

I definitely should have handled the situation differently, but you have a choice of how you're going to carry yourself. If you push someone too far, they're likely to come back after you. I chose the latter approach. I wasn't a tough guy by the standards of the wrestling business, but I thought Koko was taking advantage of us, and that I needed to stand up for myself, Stan, and our gimmick. There's a price you have to be prepared to pay if you're going to blatantly rip off another wrestler.

The animosity between Koko and I only grew even more intense, but then Stan and I started working against Koko while he teamed with Bobby Eaton. For some reason, once we started working against one another in the ring, all the heat between Koko and I just dissipated and subsided. It probably had something to do with the money he was earning while working against the Fabs. Regardless of the reason for the heat's disappearance, I was happy it was over with.

Stan and I usually rode to shows by ourselves whenever it was possible, but during one trip to Owensboro, Kentucky, we had Jacques Rougeau and Terry Taylor riding in the back seat. The two of them were talking incessantly the entire time, bickering like two little girls, and arguing about the stupidest shit. Jacques was honestly hard to ride with under normal circumstances. Being a French-Canadian, his humor was just very different from what Stan and I were accustomed to.

I kept turning the radio up louder and louder to drown them out because they were so insufferable. Stan repeatedly glanced over at me and gave me a look as if to say, "How the hell did we get stuck with *both* of these guys in here at the same time?"

We reached Owensboro, completed a show in which all the matches went off without a hitch, and then we got dressed and prepared to drive home. The instant we stepped out of the building, Terry and Jacques started up with one another again. Seriously, they were acting like children before we'd even reached the car. I don't remember what it was all about, but by the time they'd spent another 40 minutes needling each other persistently in the back of the car as we were cruising along on the interstate, I was ready to *kill them both*.

I issued several unheeded commands of "Shut up!" and "Quit fightin'!" from the driver's seat, along with more than one passive-aggressive announcement of "I can't stand listening to you two guys!" It was like I was the dad shuttling two little brats around. Eventually, I reached my breaking point.

"I gotta piss," I remarked to Stan, but I made sure to say it loudly and clearly enough to be heard in the back seat of the car.

I carefully eased the car off of the interstate and onto the shoulder of the road.

"I might as well piss while we're stopped!" said Terry.

"Yeah, I'll piss, too!" said Jacques.

As the two of them opened their doors, I reached out and grabbed Stan's left forearm.

"What?" asked Stan.

"Don't get out," I whispered.

Jacques and Terry closed the doors behind them and hustled over to the roadside shrubbery to relieve themselves. It was one of those classic nights out in the middle of the Tennessee mountains. It wasn't cold, but it was a nice, crisp night. The stars were out.

"Say goodbye to them two guys," I said.

Stan chuckled like he thought I was kidding, but I was dead serious. I locked the gas pedal down on that Town Car, and dirt flew into the air as the tires spun. We peeled straight out of there, and as I glanced in the rearview mirror, I could see Terry and Jacques were both laughing at the thought that I would even *pretend* to leave them stranded on the side of the road. They didn't even follow after us at all.

After I'd driven about half a mile down the road, the smirk fell from Stan's face, and he looked over at me.

"You *are* going back for them, *right?*" asked Stan.

"Well, I thought about it, but now I'm wonderin' if anyone else actually ever left somebody and just didn't go back," I said. "If someone is gonna tell the story about me, it might as well be a good one! Nah, I'm not goin' back!"

When we reached the parking lot where everyone had initially met up, I parked the car, grabbed the bags of Jacques and Terry from the trunk, and put them on the roofs of their respective vehicles.

Poor Stan. He was just an innocent bystander to a lot of the things I did. He was in total disbelief for the first hour after we'd left Terry and Jacques in the dust, but after he'd sipped a few beers, he was laughing about it and was happy they were gone by the time we got to Hendersonville.

Jacques and Terry didn't think there was any way that I'd permanently deserted them. At worst, they thought I'd make them walk for a little while, and then I'd be awaiting them. They continued walking along that long, empty highway until Ricky Morton's dad passed them while hauling the ring truck. He had torn the ring down in Owensboro, and he was

The Fabulous Wrestling Life of Steve Keirn

the last train home. He just happened to see them walking along the side of the road.

"Yeah, I seen them two boys walkin' 'long the side 'o the road!" he told me later. "I said 'Why them look like a couple 'o the boys that work for *us*!'"

Mr. Morton pulled over and scooped them up. Neither one of them would talk to me for a while, but they were aware that I'd been pissed off at them beforehand, and with good reason.

Stan bought a house in Hendersonville and moved there so that the two of us could elevate the convenience of our travels together. As we drove together through the territory, I kept reinforcing my belief that we should already have been planning our exits from professional wrestling.

"This ain't gonna last forever," I told him. "All the real money in this business is with the people who aren't doing the wrestling. I wanna start a wrestling school and start teachin' people!"

"I can help you out with that!" offered Stan.

I approached Jerry Jarrett and asked him, "Can I use a little spot in the program every night to advertise a wrestling school with classes taught by the Fabulous Ones?"

Jerry agreed, and we put advertisements in the event programs for wrestling prospects to send us their photos, along with their names, ages, heights, weights, and written statements elaborating as to why they wished to become professional wrestlers.

The responses to our ads became a *major* source of entertainment for the two of us on the road whenever we were bored. We'd go to the post office box, and we received some downright hilarious reading material courtesy of people who wanted to be trained to wrestle by the Fabs. While one of us drove the car, the other would read the messages left by these would-be wrestling trainees.

"I'm not going to show you the picture right away," Stan said. "I'm going to withhold that until after I'm done reading this to you."

"Okay…" I answered.

"Here's what one guy wrote us," began Stan. "'I four-foot-twelve. I one-two-zero. I want to be a wrestler.'"

That was this guy's way of telling us that he was five feet tall and weighed 120 pounds. I was already laughing, but then Stan showed me the picture included with the message. It wasn't a picture; it was a driver's license. Not a driver's license photo; it was the man's *actual* driver's license!

At the bottom of the letter, the man wrote: "Please send my license back."

It was endless. We got letters from people ages eight to 80, blind, crippled or crazy. As far as I could tell, no one had ever operated a wrestling school in that part of Tennessee before, and far too many people were chafing at the bit to learn to become pro wrestlers.

On Sundays, Jarrett allowed us to use the wrestling ring at the Nashville Fairgrounds to teach our classes. That's where Stan and I began to instruct our first wave of students, and things got off to a promising start because our very first student was Tracy Smothers.

Having Stan there to help me with Tracy's training was a blessing, because with two of us involved, one of us could teach him and wrestle with him, and the other one could watch.

We didn't operate the school the way wrestling training was conducted in Florida. We didn't go in there with a plan to smack people around, stretch them or beat them up. We honestly got in the ring with people on day one and attempted to teach them what we knew about wrestling.

I quickly learned that it was a terrible idea to be hands-on with wrestling students, even though it seemed like a good idea at first. In my experience, the only way to learn the fancy moves displayed by guys like Billy Robinson and Tony Charles had been to wrestle with them. I hadn't realized just how risky it was to hand your body over to a wrestling student who had no earthly idea how to convincingly wrestle *and* protect an opponent while he was doing it. I was getting hurt left and right, and all the trainees could really say to me in response to my pain was, "I'm sorry."

On top of that, I couldn't see what it was that they were doing wrong if I was on the receiving end of all the moves. That's how I realized it was a bad idea to even let the trainees *touch* me; trainees should only ever attempt their moves on one another. There was no sense in putting *my* career in jeopardy just to train someone else. A professional football coach doesn't get down on the line and sacrifice his own body to teach his players how to block. You're way better off standing back, watching and critiquing.

It didn't take very long before Stan and I both lost interest in carrying on with our poorly planned wrestling school. It simply wasn't working out nearly as well as we thought it would. We'd worked our way through five or six sets of guys, and Tracy Smothers was the only trainee who ever showed up that demonstrated any real potential or affinity for pro wrestling. Not only were we not breaking in new talent or making serious money, but we were also sacrificing one of our only days off in the process.

Sadly, we had also screwed up our pricing model. Stan and I were charging roughly $1,000 per student to teach them how to wrestle, but we made the mistake of not imposing a time limit on the instruction. That meant students could come for infinite wrestling classes until they finally started wrestling. That put far too much pressure on us as trainers, because some of the guys who showed up to be trained were so bad that they could have attended daily training sessions for the rest of their lives and they *still* would never have been prepared to grace a wrestling ring in a professional capacity.

It was just as well that the Fabs' teaching gig fell by the wayside. Between personal attacks, political hits, low-level swindling, and in-ring barbarity, there were so many other threats to contend with in Memphis that I hadn't initially noted. Stan and I needed to have our attention squarely focused on all of the potential adversaries that loomed around us if we were going to continue to flourish as the hottest attraction in Middle America.

FIFTEEN

The most blatant cases of skimming off the top that I ever personally observed occurred when I went to Tennessee. Stan and I knew we had been breaking attendance records. Despite this, we'd receive unsatisfactory responses at the small venues in Kentucky, Tennessee, Mississippi, Arkansas and Missouri when we'd walk in there and ask, "How's the house?"

The promoters would say, "Oh, well it's down a little bit from last week."

Yet, we would walk out later on for the main event of the show, and there would be *no* empty seats left in the venue. There would be no way in hell the house could have been down from the prior week. It was *impossible*.

I'd walk straight back into the dressing room and start complaining, "How is this down? We're getting ripped off!"

Your pay scale was based on the house, and promoters would *always* use the excuse that the house was down to justify not paying you what you were owed. My experience with paper sacks in Florida taught me that this is a business where people are coming to the matches, and they're spending $1.50 to $3.50 for tickets, all in cash. Who's checking on the people handling the cash? *Nobody*. So they could record whatever sales figures they wanted while telling the talent something else entirely. It didn't take a rocket scientist to figure out what was happening. I knew what the deal was. It was the very nature of the wrestling business.

I knew what I'd signed up for, so I figured I might as well shut my mouth and accept it, because I couldn't bail out now. In Tennessee, I bought a little clicker to count the people with, where you pressed the button, and it would register a single person as being included in the audience. I would walk out into the crowd and start counting by rows and people. At the end of the night, I would ask the promoter running the town, "So how many people did we have here tonight?" He'd usually give me a number that would be about 300 off from mine.

I went to Jerry Jarrett and I told him, "You'd better watch the guys running your towns. These guys are skimmin' money off the top, and you'd never know it because you don't go to those towns. I counted everyone in the crowd, and I've seen it personally."

I got a weird feeling from Jarrett at that moment that I shouldn't have been bringing it up like that. It's one thing to casually say it in the dressing room, but it's another thing to get a precise count of the crowd size and to tell the promoter that you personally counted the audience yourself. You had to be careful of how you handled yourself, because you didn't want to get singled out as someone who was meddlesome.

It all tied back to the paranoia generated through my experience in Florida as a wrestler who had opportunities to do business with the owner and the owner's son on two occasions. On both occasions, I either got screwed or realized that something wasn't entirely on the level. Even worse, I learned you couldn't even count on people you'd once considered to be like members of your family to take care of you when it came to business.

Speaking of families, the Poffo family – led by Angelo Poffo, along with his sons Lanny Poffo and Randy Savage – was running shows in opposition to us at the time as an "outlaw" organization. To operate an outlaw organization meant that you were holding shows without the blessing or cooperation of the National Wrestling Alliance, and usually in a wrestling territory that had already been allocated to an authorized NWA territory.

The opposition area was centered around parts of Kentucky, Illinois and Indiana. I hadn't realized that it had reached as far as Memphis, and I wasn't aware of the problems it was creating.

Bill Dundee was having a particularly contentious issue with Randy Savage. We all trained at a place called the American Fitness Center right outside of Hendersonville on the interstate. One morning, several of us were working out, and Randy stormed into the gym looking for Bill. Nothing of note happened inside the building, but somehow Randy snuck up on Bill in the parking lot while the rest of us were in the gym training. Randy punched Bill in the temple so hard that it broke Bill's orbital bone, and Bill responded by grabbing a gun out of the trunk of his car and backing Randy off with it.

Until that moment, I hadn't known the extent of the opposition in the territory, and before then, I'd never even heard of "Macho Man" Randy Savage.

Bill came running back inside from the parking lot looking for me since I'd accidentally developed the reputation as the dedicated shooter of the territory, but fortunately Randy had already left. I would *not* have wanted to fight an irate Randy Savage.

Later on, the Jarretts pushed the Poffos out of the region, and Randy began to get incorporated into the booking of the approved Memphis territory. Randy was permitted to promote shows in a small town in Missouri, and he booked Lawler, the Fabs, and half the card from Memphis in his town. The show was on an odd night, and when Stan and I arrived, we discovered that we were the only two wrestlers booked for that event who actually showed up. Lawler no-showed, Dundee no-showed, and several other guys also no-showed.

I'm sure Lawler and Dundee were still harboring resentment toward the Poffos, and the drive out to Missouri was so long that they weren't interested in driving that far to support a family they'd suffered through a bitter promotional war with. Meanwhile, Stan and I lived in Hendersonville, which was already halfway to Missouri anyway, so we had no issues making it that night. We had no clue that the other wrestlers had been conspiring to stiff the Poffos. If there had been a larger plan in the works to no-show the event as a group, Stan and I were totally unaware of it.

"Of all the people to show up, it was the *best* two!" declared Randy.

From then on, the Poffos treated Stan and I like we were members of their family because we were the only guys respectful enough to make it there for them. That included everyone from Randy and his wife Elizabeth to Lanny and Angelo, and even Angelo's wife, Judy. All of that goodwill was created simply by the fact that the Fabs showed up to make an appearance for them on a night when everyone else blew them off.

There were a lot of guys who you knew were going to be meaningless in your life, but Randy was so colorful that I assumed once he got the right break somewhere, he was going to do unbelievably well, and if he did, I had the potential to walk right in there with his endorsement.

The thing was, you *never* knew who was going to be the boss in the next territory you worked in, or who was going to be liked by the booker in the next company you were trapped in. If you screw somebody over, have bad matches, or talk badly about another wrestler, you might find yourself in a territory where the guy you shafted is now the booker, and good luck getting a push in that situation. You're better off contacting U-Haul and moving to your next territory, because you've already made an enemy who isn't going away, and who is probably going to do everything they can to bury you and ensure that you won't draw a dime while you're there.

It wasn't until Stan and I met up with the Moondogs – Larry Booker and Randy Colley – that we got into a well-established angle with a significant set of opponents. To put it in no uncertain terms, the Fabulous Ones were *on fire*. A lot of guys in this business will say that they were on fire during their primes, but nine times out of 10 it wasn't a full-blown fire; it might have been more like a lit match. The Moondogs saw the impact Stan and I were having in that area at that time. The peak popularity of the Fabulous Ones was a *five-alarm* fire, and the Moondogs wanted to get on the train.

Working with the Moondogs wasn't without its problems. Larry Booker was challenging to work with because he thought he was a badass. To me, he was simply a short, fat guy with a beard. I wasn't impressed with him. He clearly tried to eat up Stan and I a few times during our earliest matches together to show his domination. Of the two Moondogs, I would have said that Randy Colley was the true badass of the team. He was a stout, barrel-chested country boy with muscles. He still had a belly, but he looked like he could give someone a *much* harder time in a real confrontation than Larry Booker could.

Punching Larry Booker's bloody forehead

I would make it a point to throw stiff kicks and punches whenever I had to go toe-to-toe with Larry Booker, and that would be when the matches would start to get out of hand. The Moondogs carried these giant soup bones, and during our bouts they would use them as weapons. Stan and I didn't carry weapons, and we certainly couldn't do much damage with our top hats or bowties. We always had to be on high alert not to get seriously hurt by the Moondogs when things got nuts inside the ring.

Larry Booker hit me so hard with a soup bone once that it ripped a big chunk of hair and scalp out of my head.

"You asshole!" I yelled when I realized what had just happened. "I'm gonna *kill* you!"

Larry *immediately* tagged out. He knew he'd gone one step over the line. I was already on edge just from being in there with him, and I knew what Larry was trying to do. I didn't take it out on Randy Colley, though. He was just working, and I knew it wasn't the team that was after me; it was a lone actor.

In the aftermath, there was a lot of heat between the two of us where I didn't want to sell for Larry, and he didn't want to sell for me, either. I'd have to force him to sell by doing things like smashing him against the announcers' desk or cracking him with chairs. I literally hit him with anything at ringside that I could get my hands on, and that's when things became increasingly more hardcore.

The action in the ring would always deteriorate into a semi-shoot, and there were *plenty* of times when I got really pissed off at Larry in particular. More often than not, I re-entered the dressing room after the matches thinking that we were about to exchange harsh words, if not real punches. Instead, Larry and Randy would catch us completely off guard with praise.

"Oh, man! What a great match!" Larry would say.

"Yeah that was awesome!" Randy would add.

I would be thinking, "*What?!* You just tried to *kill* us out there! We were fighting for our lives!"

I hadn't fought like that in any in-ring situation aside from the peak of the Bob Roop angle in Florida, but Bob Roop was always on the defensive during those exchanges, and backing away from me. Larry Booker was always coming *straight* for me, and always trying to stop me, slow me down, and cut me off. In the business, guys know that if they can outshine the wrestlers who are supposed to be featured, it's possible that they can convince the bosses that the wrong guys are being pushed. I was mature enough in the business and enough of a veteran not to take any shit.

Larry and I had words with one another in the ring a couple times, but I'm convinced he considered it all to be part of the match. I meant every word, and I F-bombed him at least 100 times.

They'd categorized me as a shooter out of Florida, so Larry Booker didn't know anything about my history, and he thought I might come unglued and actually light him up during a match. I was *always* really snug with him. When I hit him, I never pulled my punches, and I also never took any of the steam off of it when I blasted him with boards and bells. Anything that wasn't attached to the ground around the wrestling ring, I can guarantee you that I hit Larry with it one time or another during a match.

I'd always been told that it was impossible to get over Lawler and Dundee, yet the Fabulous Ones had finally been the ones who had accomplished the impossible. We soon learned that there were consequences for toppling the King from his throne. Dundee liked me well enough, but Lawler wasn't happy having his throne stolen from him by a bleach-blond tag team. No one had ever matched his popularity level in that region, including Austin Idol.

If you saw what the card was and saw who was booked, you would notice that the Fabulous Ones and the Moondogs would be booked in the semi-main-event position despite having the hottest angle in the territory. Lawler always tried to reserve the main-event slot for himself, along with Jimmy Valiant, Austin Idol, Ron Bass, or someone else along those lines, and then put that bout on last. The Fabulous Ones were receiving the most attention, but Lawler could put himself in the main event and claim that the main event had drawn the crowd.

The Fabulous Wrestling Life of Steve Keirn

The resulting tension created a very goofy and imminently pointless political war that sometimes played out during live wrestling events. The Fabulous Ones would ride out to the ring in a limousine, which no one had ever done before. No one had ever had entrance music like ours before either. Then one night they put us in an eight-man tag match with Lawler and Dundee, and Stan and I rode to the ring in our customary limo. Out of the blue, we saw Lawler riding to the ring on a white horse, and then Bill Dundee rode to the ring on a dirtbike. It was an obvious instance of them attempting to upstage us.

"Bill, whatever you do, don't lose control of this motorcycle," Jarrett said to Dundee.

Ironically, when the spotlight hit Bill, the song playing over the arena speakers was "Wipeout." The song included a long drum solo, and that's when Bill opened up the throttle on the dirt bike and came roaring down to the ring while Stan and I were standing there watching everything unfold. As Bill's noisy dirtbike approached the ring, he slammed on the brakes, but one of the bike's wheels struck a Coke can or something, and that became trapped beneath the tire. The bike slid, turned sideways, skidded toward the ring, and *wiped out* two or three rows of people seated in the ringside area. They looked like jack-in-the-boxes flying up in the air as Bill was clipping them with the bike.

When the lights came on and we were able to adequately survey the carnage, Bill's eyes were the size of cantaloupes because he was so terrified and trying to extract himself from the accident scene that his actions had created. The motorcycle was wheeled out of there, and a young girl had to be carried out behind the motorcycle because her ankle had been broken.

Jerry Jarrett could plainly see that the egos were all clashing, and he decided that nothing like that should ever happen again. However, he truly loved the fact that his wrestlers were so competitive, and if anything, he continued to instigate it. For a pair of young guys to be getting his veterans so fired up that they were working hard to stay on top of the heap, it was like a dream come true for Jerry. No one had ever gone the extra mile to challenge Lawler and Dundee before.

Still, there was nothing we could do about the booking arrangements. Those duties would rotate, with Lawler booking the territory for six months, and then when he got burnt-out in that role, the responsibility would swing over to Dundee. You would notice how the cards would shift depending upon who was in charge. For six months it would be the Fabs on top along with Lawler, and then for the following six months, the Fabs would be sharing the spotlight with Dundee. They would take turns boosting themselves over the Fabs. I'd already dealt with that in several territories, so I knew that it was inevitable.

I was so cocky and arrogant at the time that when Stan and I would blow the roof off of the building, I'd walk into the dressing room and yell, "Follow that!" and just keep walking. I knew there was no way Lawler, Dundee, or anyone else in that dressing room could follow the shows that Stan and I were presenting each night.

One of the areas where Stan and I were the most dominant was in the area of concession sales. In Tennessee you could sell your own merchandise, so Stan and I started selling photos that were taken by our photographer, Jim Cornette, who was just breaking into the wrestling business himself. In addition to photos, we sold t-shirts, hats, bandanas, and anything else we could think of.

As time wore on, Stan and I began to wear less and less clothing in our promotional photos, and that really began to kick the merchandise competition into high gear. I would take our paystub from the guy who would sell our merchandise in the Memphis area, and I'd lay it on the floor of Lawler's dressing room while he was changing just to irritate him.

Things were far better for us financially than they'd ever been before, but it wasn't the result of the payoffs from the towns; it was from the extra money we were making from selling merchandise at live events. There was a very popular photo circulating of the Fabulous Ones wearing towels, and

Stan and I made $60,000 apiece from that photo in just one year. That was a downright *absurd* amount of money to be making from the sale of a photo back then. Stan and I each bought a mid-1960s-model Corvette with our concession money. *All* of the extra money I had in hand was owed to how well we were doing with sales in the concession area.

Stan left it up to me to be in charge of the business side, and he deferred to me when it came time to decide what we should sell. When we started off with t-shirts, it was a bulky item. You had to figure out the colors and sizes, which was a royal pain. That's when I decided that bandanas were the perfect item to sell.

The Fabulous Ones show off their classic Corvettes

Bandanas were just square pieces of cloth of only one size, and they were far easier than t-shirts to stock, sign and sell. We were *really* raking it in, and we were staying two steps ahead of everyone else because they were all stuck with the belief that they only needed to be selling very small photos that weren't even as large as 8x10s. At one point in time, there were photos of the Fabulous Ones on the walls of practically every home in Tennessee.

An even more bizarre competition amongst the talent ensued when Stan and I started getting racier with the content of our photos. Dundee showed up to the concession area one day with the latest photo that he was offering for sale: He was lying naked on a bearskin rug with a cowboy hat over his groin. Lawler followed that with a similar photo where he was lying naked with a crown over his privates. Unsurprisingly, the photos of Stan and I sold a *whole* lot better, since two chiseled guys in towels is just generally more appealing than a tubby, naked man with his genitals stuffed in a crown.

I knew I couldn't do this forever, so I was really grabbing for whatever money I could make. Stan was just enjoying the ride, and he wasn't nearly as concerned about the future as I was because he didn't have a family of his own yet.

Before too long, Stan and I became popular enough that other territories began to make inquiries about acquiring our services. Jerry Jarrett eventually loaned us to Bill Watts for one of Mid-South's Superdome shows in New Orleans. The Fabs were booked as heels against "Dr. Death" Steve Williams and "Hacksaw" Jim Duggan, who were two of the biggest babyfaces in that territory.

When the Fabs arrived at the Dome, Bill Watts gathered the four of us together in the dressing room and encouraged us to talk through the match since we had never worked together before. When we got down to the business of discussing what we wanted to accomplish during the bout, Stan and I made it clear that we were just visiting, and we were there to get the two of them even more over with the fans in their home territory.

Frankly, Dr. Death and Hacksaw weren't exactly two guys that I would have been tempted to force anything upon or play games with. They were both huge, badass guys. At the same time, I could also tell that Hacksaw was just a big, pleasant, goofy guy like me who just wanted to have as much fun as possible.

"When the time is right, I'll take the tag, and whoever wants to make the comeback, feel free to make the comeback on me," I said. "But listen, I really don't mind takin' any move you got, but there's one that I really *can't* take, and it's a backdrop."

A lot of times during comebacks, babyfaces liked to shoot heels off the ropes and give them a sky-high backdrop.

"Please do *not* call a backdrop," I repeated.

"Got it," nodded Steve Williams. "No backdrops."

"Anything else you want to do is fine," I added. "Hip toss, power slam, press slam... anything! I just can't take a backdrop. I'll *kill* myself. I've tried and tried, and it just doesn't make any sense to me. I *can't* do it."

Satisfied that we were all in agreement as to the sort of match we intended to have, we each retreated to our respective dressing rooms. Soon we were out in front of the huge Superdome crowd, and the match was going fine. Everyone blended well, and Stan and I went out of our way to make Duggan and Williams look exceptional, not that it was hard. I worked diligently to get heat as a heel, which wasn't something I was accustomed to doing, but I thoroughly enjoyed the change of pace. I relished the opportunity to mess with the audience.

Eventually, the time came for the big comeback. Steve Williams gave Hacksaw the tag, and then Duggan came in and bounced me around like a basketball with a few slams and other moves. Finally, Duggan backed me into the ropes to fire me over to the other side, and as I was running by him, he very clearly said, "Backdrop!"

I couldn't believe what I'd heard. A feeling of sheer terror shot through me as Duggan had called for the *only* move I had specifically requested that I not be asked to take. Cold chills ran down my back as I sat on the throne of indecision. I didn't know if Duggan was testing me, playing a rib on me, or if he had simply decided he was going to backdrop me no matter what, come hell or high water.

I had a full six steps – three toward the rope and three back to the center of the ring – to make a decision. Instead of feeding Duggan for the backdrop, I came off the ropes, slammed on the brakes, and *punted* Hacksaw hard in the center of his head with my right foot. Honest to God, I'd meant to hit him in the shoulder. I'm not saying that Jim moved, but somehow between the time my foot left the ground and when it made impact, his head got in the way. The instep of my foot caught Duggan right between the eyes.

After that, both of us wound up down on that mat and incapacitated. Duggan was sitting down on the mat in a state of dizzy bewilderment because he'd been booted in the head, and *I* was down because I actually thought I'd broken my foot from kicking him so hard. As Duggan sat there rubbing his forehead, he turned and looked over at me with a bit of a smirk on his face.

"Oh, that's right; *no* backdrops!" mumbled Duggan.

I looked over at him and couldn't help but return his smile because of how funny he sounded. I was certainly glad Duggan found some humor in it, because he was such a big, tough guy that I would have preferred that it be someone else that I'd kicked in the head if that situation absolutely had to unfold that way.

Afterwards, I always told people that Duggan's eyes used to be okay until I kicked him in the head, and that it was my fault that one of his eyes always seemed to wander off. That wasn't true of course, but I'd *certainly* kicked him as hard as I could.

Watts brought the Fabs back to work against the Guerrero brothers in Texas. Watts was a lot like Eddie Graham inasmuch as he was a major stickler for kayfabe. He kept the talent in separate dressing rooms, and we never got to speak to the Guerreros ahead of our matches together. Like Eddie, Bill would also stand there and watch every move you made during the shows.

"Chavo Guerrero is kind of a moody guy," Bill warned us. "He's a babyface and we're close to Mexico, and he thinks he has this Guerrero family legend to live up to. You've got to go out there and make him look good, and try to make Hector look good, too. Okay, kid! Go out there and *light* 'em up! Chavo is really lazy. He's a grumpy old guy, but *light* 'em up!"

"Yeah, no problem," I said.

Stan and I went out to watch the matches that were on before us so that we could get a handle on what sort of action the people liked. Each place you wrestle is a little bit different, and crowds in different parts of the country had all received different educations in wrestling. It's something that was always wise to take into consideration. Then we went out to the ring and worked, and the major purpose of the match was to establish an angle that would lead to Chavo and I having a one-on-one return bout later on.

Once we'd successfully accomplished our mission in the first match, Watts booked me against Chavo in a loser-gets-painted-yellow match on the border in Brownsville, Texas. The first thing I did was strut to the ring, stand on the ring apron, and grab the microphone.

"I've got a joke for ya!" I said to the audience. "As a matter of fact, I've got two jokes! What do you call four Mexicans standing in quicksand? Quatro *sink*-o!"

The audience booed me vociferously, but I still had one more joke remaining.

"What is the most popular thing at a Mexican picnic?" I asked. "A set of *jumper* cables!"

I cheated to defeat Chavo in the match. Then it came time to paint Chavo, and Bill had laid out a plan for me to double-cross Chavo ahead of time.

"Don't just dab the paint on him!" instructed Watts. "*Paste* him with that paint! I want you to paint him good so that he's embarrassed and mad and the people get it!"

Everything was fine until I disrespectfully slapped paint onto Chavo's face with the paintbrush. Once that happened, he angrily sprang to life, grabbed the can of paint, and tried to douse me with it. I dove out of the way as he made his rage-fueled heave with the paint can, and instead of coating me with it, the yellow paint splashed upon every fan occupying the front row on one side of the ring. All of the fans who had been cheering for Chavo to take his revenge on me were now decorated with yellow paint and *extremely* angry with him.

Chavo never liked that story very much.

Choking Jonathan Boyd of the Sheepherders during a cage match

After concluding our run with the Moondogs, Stan and I were pretty high-spirited. As the Fabulous Ones got molten hot and then somehow kept growing even hotter as an attraction, Jerry Jarrett was smart enough to feed different tag teams to us.

The version of the Sheepherders that Stan and I worked against consisted of Jonathan Boyd and Luke Williams.

Luke was always a little bit slower than Jonathan. Luke wasn't a race car; he was more like a Cadillac. Meanwhile, Jonathan had a little-man complex. When you worked with him, he was trying to get over constantly. It was very similar to the situation with Larry Booker. It wasn't at the level where things might have devolved into a shoot, but I still had to be very stiff with Jonathan, or he would've eaten me up.

Between Stan and I, Stan was more inclined to cruise during matches, whereas I was the aggressive one. If you watch the matches, you'll see that we really had to take it to the Sheepherders. They drew from their own experiences in their wrestling careers and brought those ideas to the feud. When we incorporated some of those ideas into our bouts, things just became increasingly more violent. The fans of the Tennessee territory responded to it and loved it, and it really helped to maintain the territory's momentum.

Jon and Luke would walk out to the ring carrying a flag pole bearing the flag of New Zealand. I'd gone from dealing with a guy with a small-man's complex who carried a soup bone to another guy with a small-man's complex who carried a flag pole. To make things worse, the Sheepherders didn't carry a "working" flagpole either.

"Can't you carry a PVC pipe, or get some aluminum thing to put that flag on?" I asked them.

"No," laughed Boyd. "It needs to be sturdy!"

The pair of them absolutely insisted on tying their flag to a *steel* water pipe. When Boyd hit you with that damn thing, he *hurt* you. We sold it, but we had no choice but to sell it. That thing lit me up. It was a good thing we had separate dressing rooms most of the time, because I'd constantly come back from the ring bitching to Stan.

"Did Boyd hit you with that damn flagpole?" I'd ask.

"No," Stan would say. "Not *this* time."

"I'm gonna kill him some day!" I'd continue.

Those bouts with the Sheepherders had a lot of color. We were cutting our heads six or seven nights a week. Sometimes we could reopen the incisions we'd made in previous bouts, but if we couldn't do that, we'd have to make fresh cuts in our heads. At least five nights out of seven, I was bleeding, because we had to sell the fact that we were getting cracked with that flagpole each night. Despite all of the bleeding and scarring, it was worth it to go through that for the sake of how much those performances separated us from all of the other talent on the Memphis roster.

Some of those matches were the epitome of hardcore wrestling in that era, where we tore up all kinds of tables and desks, used chairs and bells as weapons, and the only person in the ring who wasn't bleeding at the conclusion of the match was the referee. It just got to the point where everything we were doing in the ring was quickly becoming increasingly more dangerous to top. At the same time, Jarrett somehow kept coming up with fresh ideas for us, which was crucial to holding the fans' attention.

Terri came to very few matches while we wrestled in Tennessee, and I certainly didn't want her seeing our matches with the Sheepherders. Those weren't exactly fun matches for a wife to watch her husband endure. However, I was very open about the fact that I had a family on the Memphis broadcasts. In fact, I'd get on TV twice a year and say, "It's my daughter Heidi's birthday!"

Fans would respond by sending Heidi all kinds of presents. They'd bring Cabbage Patch Dolls to every town we would go to. She still has a lot of them to this day.

Seeing how well that worked for Heidi, I shamelessly did the same thing for myself. I unabashedly claimed *two* different birthdays for myself. I got on the interview segments and said, "This match is on my birthday, and I ain't about to lose on my birthday!"

We left the interview desk, and Stan said, "I thought your birthday was in September."

"It is, but you never know: I might get a present out of this!" I joked.

I *did* get presents out of it. Fans brought plenty of stuff to the matches for me. Most of it was junk that you'd end up tossing out the window on the way home from the show, but some of it was kind of cool, like candy or food.

The Fabs with Heidi and one of her Cabbage Patch dolls

No matter how popular the Fabulous Ones became, even when we were at our most colorful, and even after I'd matured as a performer and gained a measure of confidence, I would still walk away from my interviews thinking that I'd said nothing of any real substance.

"What were you talking about?" Stan asked me once after we'd just wrapped up an interview segment.

"Beats me," I shrugged. "I was just talkin'!"

I often left my interviews having no earthly idea what I'd just said. On one unforgettable occasion in Nashville, I left one of my matches with no earthly idea whether or not I would even survive the night.

SIXTEEN

One of the trademarks of the Tennessee territory was that so many of the buildings were dilapidated and awful to work in. Jonesboro, Tupelo and Blytheville all had dreadful buildings, and so did the entire state of Kentucky except for Rupp Arena in Lexington and the Louisville Gardens. All of the other buildings were dumpy.

We were working one night against the Sheepherders at the Nashville Fairgrounds, which was a crappy little building just like the rest of them. It was a flea market on the weekends, and the dressing room was probably the size of an ordinary bedroom. All the chairs had to be set against the walls to maximize space, and there was a single stall shower and one exposed toilet that afforded its user no privacy. If you had to take a crap, you'd have to do it out in the open while staring *deep* into the eyes of everyone else in the dressing room.

The Fairgrounds had bleachers and folded chairs at ringside. There usually wasn't a huge audience, and the reception for the television channels in that town was atrocious. I once tried to record one of my matches off the television there so that I could evaluate the bout and see what it looked like on TV, and the channel quality was so poor that I could barely make out anything on the screen. I attributed our poor attendance figures in the region to that, because we were selling out the large venues like the Mid-South Coliseum, Rupp Arena, and the Louisville Gardens, but we couldn't even sell out the tiny little Fairgrounds facility.

This was one of the many matches where Stan and I had been asked to get color. The more our profiles increased, the more blade jobs were requested of us. I had learned the art of blading while working in Florida. Dusty had a bad habit of not pushing the blade down into the mat and breaking it off after he'd used it. This meant he would often slice his opponents' shoulders by locking up with them after he was done blading himself.

That wasn't a responsibility I wanted; I didn't ever want to accidentally cut someone else. That's one of the other reasons I always carried the blade in my mouth.

When I would get around to cutting myself, I would roll over on all fours, hold my breath, and then watch for the blood to start dropping onto the mat cover. If it wasn't dropping quickly enough, I would cut myself a second time and check the blood flow again. There were plenty of guys who would cut themselves who weren't very good at it. They would cut themselves, only draw tiny trickles of blood out of their foreheads, and then 10 minutes later all of the bleeding would have ceased.

I was accustomed to watching Eddie Graham work, and when he got color, his head remained red until the end of the match. The saying that made the rounds was, "Go to the bone for the business." That meant that you were supposed to cut deep and get the blood flowing; don't just *scratch* your forehead like a kitten.

I didn't have any special formulas for bleeding like some other guys in the business. I didn't drink any special alcohol mixtures or take any pills. I was a pretty good bleeder without any chemical assistance. I simply cut very deep, but very short. I always measured off my Gilette double-edged blade, broke it in half, and then I would break that remaining piece in half once again. That left me with a corner of a double-edged blade. I'd cut a long point on the sharp end and then I'd tape the other end of it.

When guys would watch me make a blade, they reacted like I was crafting a prison shank.

"Oh my God!" they'd say. "What are you gonna do with *that*?!"

"I'm gonna cut my head!" I'd answer matter-of-factly.

Then they'd show me their blades, and I'd say, "Well what are you gonna do with *that*? You're not gonna want to follow *my* match!"

If you look at a razor blade, there's only one sharp side. Once you spit it out of your mouth and get ready to slice, you need to see which way the sharp side is facing. If you pull the blade in the direction where the steel was cut by the scissors, it doesn't work well, and it hurts *a lot*. On the flipside, if you pull in the direction that the sharp end is facing, it opens you up quickly and didn't hurt all that much.

Battering Jon Boyd to get him off of Stan Lane

You also needed to make sure the guy you were working with knew you were getting color so that he wouldn't kick you or jostle you while you were trying to cut yourself. If someone had kicked me in the back of the head, I might have cut my *entire* forehead off.

As usual, I was carrying my blade in my mouth when I went to the ring that night in Nashville. A lot of guys carried it taped to their fingers, but I didn't usually tape my fingers in my regular matches, and I didn't want the tape on my fingers to be a dead giveaway to the audience that I was carrying a blade, and that I was going to be bleeding that night.

About two moves ahead of time, I'd take a bump, spit the blade out into my hand, and then when I had to get color, I would try to cut my head during a natural fall instead of lying down and cutting it in a way that let everyone in the audience know what I was doing.

When I first started in the business, I looked at the foreheads of guys like Jos Leduc, Dusty Rhodes, King Curtis Iaukea, and Abdullah the Butcher. They all had *huge* gig marks in their heads. I decided early in my career that I shouldn't be cutting up and down. Vertical cuts were obvious; I cut side-to-side because the cuts would run in the same direction as my worry lines or other natural lines.

After I got my blade out to cut myself in anticipation of being struck with Jonathan Boyd's flagpole, somebody blasted me in the back, and I got completely disoriented. I had been expecting someone to strike me, but not in my back, and not *that* hard. Right after that, they rammed my head into the turnbuckle, which I also wasn't prepared for. I'd had the blade gripped firmly in my hand, but when my head bounced off of the turnbuckle pad, the blade popped clean out of my hand and flew into the audience.

I knew I still needed to get color, and I started freaking out and flashed back to my match in Florida with Bob Orton Jr. when I needed to get color and had lost my blade. Back then, asking someone to bust me open hardway hadn't worked, so I figured the best thing to do would be to ask one of the Sheepherders to borrow their blade. That's when I made the critical mistake of talking to Jonathan Boyd and saying, "Do you have your blade?"

"Yeah," Boyd replied.

"I lost my blade! I've got to get color!" I told him. "*Give* it to me!"

History would show that I would have been *infinitely* better off if I had asked Boyd to just bust my head open in a hardway fashion. Boyd indeed pulled his blade out, but instead of handing it to me, he quickly sliced it into my temple. Blood spurted forth in rhythm with the beating of my heart, and it became immediately apparent to anyone watching us that Boyd had nicked an artery. I didn't notice it at first, but I was soon rolled out to the floor, and there was a lady in the front row with a light-colored dress on. When I turned my head to look in her direction, the blood from my forehead *sprayed* her dress.

"Holy crap," I thought to myself. "I've never seen that before. *That's* not good."

I raised my hand to the level of my temple a few inches away from my head, and I could feel the steady squirting of the blood splashing against the inside of my hand.

I clasped my head and looked down at my tights, and that's when I noticed that the eruption of blood had caused an impromptu change in my clothing's color scheme: My black-and-white zebra-print tights were now black-and-red, and I was now wearing red boots instead of white.

I immediately panicked and made a beeline for the babyface dressing room. Meanwhile, Jonathan Boyd was so excited by the blood that he began to chase me with the hopes of battering me some more. That quantity of blood made it easy to tell a wrestling story, and I found myself literally fighting to get Boyd away from me so that I could seek needed medical attention. I knew that level of uncontrolled blood flow was well beyond the rational range of what would be expected from a standard blade job, and something awful was bound to happen if I didn't get it under control very quickly. Almost on cue, I could feel myself starting to grow groggy and weak.

Somehow, I got free from Boyd long enough to successfully escape through the dressing room door, and I sat down on one of the folding chairs with my hand pressed against my temple. Tojo Yamamoto walked over to me and began to assess the situation with my bloody head and reddened ring attire.

"No good! No good!" declared Tojo.

"I *know* it's no good!" I concurred. "What do I *do*?!"

"Ambulance!" answered Tojo frantically. "No good!"

I looked down to the area of the metal folding chair near my crotch, and a crimson puddle of blood had pooled there in the few moments since I'd sat down.

Stan arrived in the dressing room and stood next to me, and I looked up at him and wearily said, "Call an ambulance."

"Oh shit!" yelled Stan once he got a good look at my head.

Stan freaked out, sprinted into the arena and yelled for someone in the crowd to call an ambulance from the building's payphone.

When the ambulance finally arrived at the building, I'd already lost a great deal of strength. I'd been bleeding for a full 20 minutes by that time, and had been applying pressure to the wound as best I could. At the sight of the paramedics, I began to relax, and breathed a deep sigh of relief knowing that the experts had arrived. The blood on my head was all coagulated, and my long, blond hair was now thoroughly red and matted down. The EMTs could also tell that I'd been trying to stop the blood from coming out.

"What happened?" one of them asked me.

"A guy cut me with a razor blade," I answered. "He got me right here, on my temple."

"Take your hand away so we can see it," he ordered.

The instant I removed my hand from my temple, the blood began to gush again, albeit not with the same velocity that had enabled me to coat the dress of the lady in the front row from several feet away.

"Okay! Gotcha!" the paramedic said. They immediately began to wrap several layers of gauze around my head to the point where I looked like I was wearing a turban.

I knew that wasn't going to completely stop the bleeding, and I was wondering why they weren't doing anything else to inhibit the flow of my blood. Next they carried me to the ambulance, loaded me onto a gurney, and slid me into the back of the vehicle. Stan ran to his car so that he could follow the ambulance to the hospital, and then we took off with the siren blaring.

The paramedic riding next to me said, "Which hospital do you want to go to?"

"I live in Hendersonville," I said. "Can you take me to one by there?"

"That's 10 miles north of here," the paramedic said.

"Well is there one around the corner from here?" I asked.

They decided upon a hospital closer to where we were, and then they started to check my blood pressure. The first time they checked my blood pressure, it was around 90/40. After a few minutes, it dipped to 50/20.

"Call the hospital!" the paramedic shouted to his associate. "Call the hospital *now*! Let them know we're coming in with a bleeder, and we're losing him!"

"What?!" I said, and I shot upright in the gurney. "What do you mean you're *losin'* him?!"

"Stop that!" the paramedic pleaded. "Lie down!"

I never suspected that one day I'd be flirting with death as the result of a blade job.

We got to the hospital, and Stan dashed right up to the rear of the ambulance at the very moment when the EMTs were yanking me out of the back. They wheeled me into the surgical center, and the surgeon on duty rushed over and began to unwrap the gauze from my head.

"Oh man! Oh man!" he repeated as he unraveled the gauze from around my head. "His blood pressure is so low! He's almost gone! He's almost *gone*!"

That wasn't a very reassuring thing to be hearing. Meanwhile, Stan was standing right next to me the entire time, and began to completely freak out once again.

"What do you mean he's almost *gone*?!" yelled Stan. "You can't lose him! Get on it!"

A couple of members of the hospital staff grabbed ahold of Stan and ushered him away from where I was being treated.

"What did this to you?" the surgeon asked me. "What do you have?"

"I've got a razor-blade cut," I told him. "It's here on my temple."

The doctor knew immediately which artery had been sliced open. He filled a bucket with water and doused it over my head. The coagulated blood was washed away, and I could barely see through the blood in my eyes. I could just make out that the doctor was trying to pull as much of the superficial blood away from my head as he could so that he could get to the actual wound and treat it.

"I got it! I got it!" the surgeon repeated, before adding, "I've got you!"

"Okay, he's got me," I thought to myself, and then I allowed myself to relax.

The surgeon sewed up the artery inside of my temple, and then he got to work on the superficial part of the wound. Finally, after I'd been lying there for an hour and a half, the doctor came back to explain the next stage of my treatment.

"We need to give you a blood transfusion," he told me. "You've lost so much blood that your blood pressure is incredibly low."

"No way!" I told him. "Don't give me *any* blood!"

I didn't want *anything* to do with a blood transfusion. AIDS had been all over the news during that time, and one of the few things we knew about it – other than the fact that it was a certain death sentence – was the fact that you could get it through a blood transfusion. I wouldn't even let them give me an IV treatment.

"What's my alternative?" I asked.

"This is how replenishing blood works," said the doctor. "I can't allow you to go home tonight because you've lost so much. Your blood replenishes 50 percent of what you lose in the first 24 hours after you've lost it. Every 24 hours after that, the amount you've lost is reduced by 50 percent. So the next day you'll regain 25 percent, and the following day you'll regain about 12 percent. Your blood level will be back to normal in four days."

So that's what I did. I went home the next day, and I took a few days off while I recuperated, but once my blood had returned to its normal volume, I went right back to work in the ring. I hated to miss any time at all. When you know you've built enough of a reputation for being a performer who worked hard, never missed towns, never stopped due to injuries, never argued about putting someone over, never complained about having to lose cleanly to the world champion (except once) and overcame all obstacles to show up and give the best performance possible, you have *a lot* of credibility riding on it.

Even though I'd nearly died and had to miss a few shows, I didn't hold any serious grudges against Jonathan Boyd. I knew it had simply been an accident.

"I guess you didn't understand what I meant when I said 'Give it to me' after I asked if you had your blade," I joked with him. "I meant to *hand* it to me, not *cut* me!"

One of the valuable lessons I learned that night was to never let anyone else cut you under any circumstances. They're not the one feeling the insertion of the blade, and they don't know the extent of the damage they're doing. That used to happen all the time back then; quite often it was the referee who was carrying the blade and then cutting the wrestlers' foreheads at the appropriate times during the matches.

I'd been told early on by Jos Leduc to never let anyone cut your forehead for you, but it's not like I had explicitly asked Boyd to cut me. My most dangerous night in the wrestling business had been the result of simple miscommunication.

The first time I ever laid eyes on the Road Warriors was when I was watching them on TBS. I must admit that I absolutely loved their gimmick from the moment I saw it. With their facepaint, shaved heads, colossal muscles, and metal spikes, I thought they looked inescapably cool and compelling. They were *very* intense.

When Stan and I clashed with Hawk and Animal for the first time, there was a capacity crowd present. Many of the fans in Memphis also watched the wrestling on TBS, so they were already quite familiar with the Road Warriors. The match was a major draw, because it was a dream match for the fans of the Tennessee territory to see their local favorites compete against the latest tag team sensation to achieve national notoriety through the reach of cable television.

Despite the presentation of the Road Warriors as an unstoppable force, the crowd was educated enough about the Fabulous Ones to know that we weren't pushovers. We weren't presented like the Rock 'n' Roll Express; we were 30-year-old men who would fight toe-to-toe with you as opposed to boyish-looking young guys who would always try to outmaneuver their much larger adversaries.

In Memphis, they had dressing rooms that connected, so we went in and met with the Road Warriors ahead of time, and we spoke about mutual friends and anything else that would help us to establish a rapport with them. We also decided on the finish for our first match together, and I'm pretty sure we agreed to a disqualification.

The Warriors had no plans to return to Memphis, and we were staying in the territory, so there was no reason to let them smash us and downgrade us if they were just going to depart afterwards. We were the talent that needed to be protected, because we needed to remain a draw to our fans long after Hawk and Animal were safely back in Georgia.

Once we were all in the ring, the match quickly commenced. Almost immediately, I took Hawk's arm and tried to give him an arm wringer, but he just stuck his tongue out at me and refused to budge.

"Okay, he doesn't seem to feel like selling *that* tonight," I laughed.

Then I tried to give Hawk a snapmare, which is a very basic move where you grab a guy by the head and pull him over your shoulder. Hawk completely blocked me. I was trying to get Hawk off of his feet, but he just pulled his head completely out of the move and walked away. This was far and away the most resistance that I'd ever gotten from another wrestler so early in a match.

In response to this, Stan and I got very aggressive and stiff with the Road Warriors to try to force the issue somewhat. At the same time, we also had to control our own selling of moves so that we didn't oversell any of their stuff. To me it was a really good match by the end, and it was kind of what people expected, but it wasn't close to being one of our best matches overall. It was more of a fight for our lives that we ultimately survived. Stan and I held our own, and when it was over, we were still standing. The audience liked it, but I don't think they had a sense of what a legitimate struggle it had been for us to work through.

Getting pressed into the air by Hawk during our first match

There was really only one logical way to work with a tag team like the Road Warriors, and it was also the only reasonable way to design a match where you're taking on a much larger opponent. You shouldn't work a headlock or an arm; you have to take them off their feet and work the legs. That's a far more logical story for the audience to understand. Once the larger person is down, they have to fight to get back up so that they can be in a position of dominance once again. If you do enough damage, they'll limp around and sell the damage you've done to their legs.

If you take them down, get them off their feet, work the leg, tag in and out and stay fresh, it's like you're keeping a turtle on its back. You can gain a lot of respect from an audience while wearing down a big man simply by working over his leg. They'll understand and appreciate the use of strategy, along with the logic of what you're doing.

Besides, wrestlers like the Road Warriors weren't going to sell their arms for too long no matter what you did to them. All of their powerful offensive maneuvers were reliant upon repeated use of their arms, and they weren't going to omit their big moves from their matches just because it would have enhanced the logic of the storytelling; they were hellbent on getting all of their big moves in and basking in the pops from the crowd… despite the fact that they were *supposed* to be heels.

On one Monday when I got home from Memphis, my very pregnant wife Terri was waiting for me when I got through the door.

"I've been feeling contractions for a while now, and I didn't want to go to the hospital like I did the last time to wait for 10 hours, but I think it's time," she said.

I rushed Terri to the hospital, and I did the same thing I did to the guys at the Peachtree Hospital in Atlanta: I lied to them and concocted a way to oversee the birth of my second child.

"The guys down in Atlanta let me deliver my daughter," I said. "I did the full delivery while the doctor just stood over my shoulder."

The doctor in Nashville said, "Well, we can't be outdone by guys in *Atlanta!*"

We rushed from the emergency room to the hospital area, and the doctor was summoned to meet us in the delivery room. The only problem was that Terri had waited too long; the crown of our inbound son's head was already showing.

"Oh my gosh! He's ready! He's ready!" screamed the nurse. "He's comin'!"

I dropped down there and authoritatively said, "Hey, I got this!"

The nurses looked at me with great confusion and said, "What?!"

"I'm tellin' you, I *got* this!" I repeated.

I delivered Cory all by myself, and around the time I was completing Cory's delivery, the doctor finally strolled in.

"I knew he was going to do the delivery," the doctor said. "I was just going to stand over his shoulder anyway. So how did he do?"

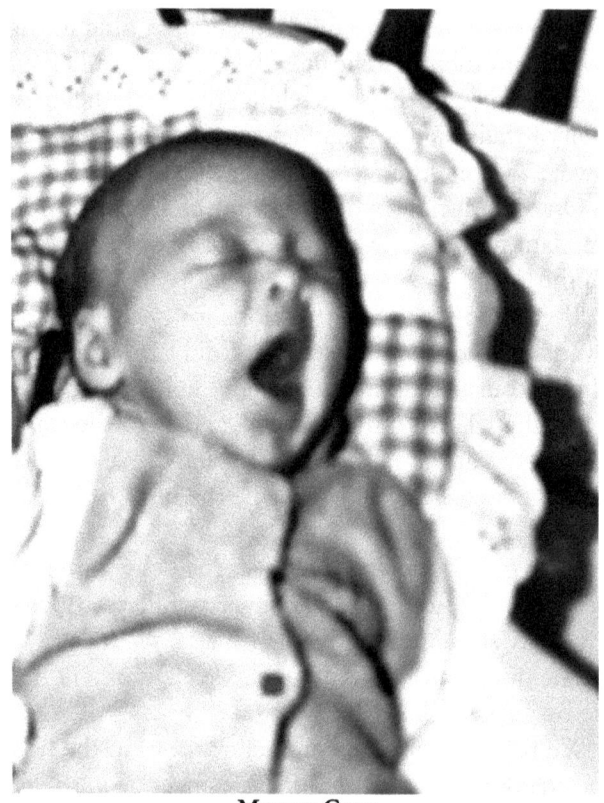

My son Cory

"Well the baby and the *wife* did all the work!" the nurse said, as if to reroute the credit for the successful delivery. "*He* just pulled the baby out!"

And she was absolutely right. I claimed credit for delivering my second child, but Terri did 100 percent of the work. She was *quite* a woman.

Cory's birth happened on a Monday night, and the very next day was Tuesday. When Stan and I arrived at the Louisville Gardens, Lawler charged straight up to us and said, "Hey, you guys need to stay over and go to Evansville tonight! We want you guys to do an AM radio station interview to support the show there tomorrow night."

"What?!" I said. "First of all, nobody listens to AM radio. Second of all, my son was just born. I'm *not* stayin' over!"

"I'm telling you, you've gotta go do this!" said Lawler. "We've already lined it up!"

I looked over at Stan and said, "Okay... That's it. That's *it*!"

They'd just pushed me too far. I walked back into the dressing room and began to remove my boots.

"What are you doin'?" Stan asked upon reaching my side.

"I'm quittin'," I replied.

"You're what?!" he asked.

"I'm *quittin'*!" I repeated. "That's it! I'm walkin' out!"

"It's a sellout!" said Stan. "We're on top!"

"Yeah... well... I'm sorry, Stan!" I said. "You don't understand havin' a son. You don't get it, but someday I hope you do."

Stan looked at me for a moment and then said, "Well, I've been your partner this long, and I suppose I'm *still* your partner... so let's go!"

I can't overstate how gracious this move of loyalty was on Stan's part. He backed me up in a moment when he wasn't required to do so by any means. On that night, I gained even more respect for Stan Lane, and I'd already had a staggering amount of it.

Both Stan and I got our clothes on, and instead of walking out the back door of the building to our cars, I tapped Stan on the back, gestured toward the arena entrance, and said, "Come on!"

So the two of us boldly strolled out right in front of a sold-out crowd at the Louisville Gardens. We walked all the way to ringside, traced a path completely around the ring, and waved to everyone in attendance while yelling, "Goodbye! Goodbye!"

Once we'd completed our lap around the ring, we walked out through the main entrance of the building and drove home.

To the surprise of no one, Lawler *buried* us to Jerry Jarrett when he reported the incident to him, and that stunt didn't go over well with Jarrett when he found out.

The next day, Jarrett met with the two of us and said, "I can't take you guys back! You just walked out on a *huge* house! What kind of example would I be setting if I took you back?!"

"I don't care what kind of an example it would be," I said. "Lawler and I just don't get along. That was the straw that broke the camel's back. I'm not dealin' with him anymore."

Jarrett paused for a moment and then asked, "So where are you guys gonna go?"

"I haven't thought about that, yet," I admitted. "I'll figure out somethin'. Maybe New York!"

At that time, Vince McMahon Jr. had been in the early stages of getting the World Wrestling Federation going nationally. My high school friend Hulk Hogan had just won the WWF Heavyweight Championship, so it seemed like that would be a very easy call to make.

I was sitting around at home and thinking about contacting Vince, but Jarrett called me out of the blue and said, "Listen, I just talked to Verne. He'd love to have you guys. Get out of here for a while and go work for him up in Minneapolis."

"Cool!" I said.

I called Stan to let him know what the plan was, and then I went and got the U-Haul and started packing immediately. The size of the family traveling with me kept getting larger. By the time I made the shift to Minneapolis in

March of 1984, I was making the move with a wife, a three-year-old daughter, a brand new baby, and a Weimaraner dog.

    I flew Terri and the kids up to Minneapolis first, and I followed behind them driving a packed U-Haul with my dog sitting beside me in the passenger seat, and hauling a little Toyota car behind us.

    The travel plan called for me to drive through Chicago to get to Minneapolis. I had to wait to call Terri in the hotel, but once I arrived there, I had to contend with a problem that required my immediate attention.

    "Hey, where are the credit cards?" I asked Terri. "I can't find them."

    "Uh oh," said Terri. "They're in the safe box."

    The safe box was dead in the center of the U-Haul on the floor. Very late at night, with no money in my wallet and with the U-Haul running on fumes, I had to pull into a rest area on the other side of Chicago and begin unloading my stuff from the U-Haul right in the middle of the parking area.

    Once I'd tied Elton to the trailer to make sure he was secure. I climbed into the U-Haul while holding a flashlight, and I crawled around until I finally reached the safe box. I jostled some of my possessions as I was digging through the U-Haul trying to reach the safe box, and they all shifted and began to settle around me, potentially trapping me in there.

    I fought my way free and jammed as much of my stuff back into the U-Haul as I could, but I damaged plenty of it in the process. Still, I was relieved to have access to my credit cards once again. I went to the nearest gas station, filled up the gas tank, and ordered a large cup of coffee. Then I drove back onto the interstate while holding the coffee cup between my legs.

    Unfortunately, I hit a bump, and the coffee spilled all over my lap. I still made it onto the interstate, and I was certain that I was going to make it to Minneapolis unscathed. When I regained my bearings after clearing up the coffee, I looked up and saw a sign that said, "Chicago: 15 miles." I felt *so* stupid. I had gotten so worked up that I'd gone the wrong way on the interstate, and was headed back the way I'd originally come from. Truly, I was having a terrible day *and* night.

Silly navigational errors aside, I safely reached Minneapolis to begin wrestling for Verne Gagne's American Wrestling Association.

The first time I met Verne face-to-face was when he traveled down to Florida while my big push there had been in progress. He traveled to Florida for the same reason everyone else did: Florida is a tropical paradise. Everyone came there once in a while if they could, and it certainly wasn't because Eddie Graham was a great payoff guy. Eddie had deep pockets and short fingers just like most wrestling promoters. If you worked in Florida, you had access to the beach, fishing, and just the general heat, so some guys considered it a working vacation… and *especially* if they'd been stuck working in Minneapolis for an entire winter like Verne usually was.

The fact that everyone came down to Florida presented me with golden opportunities to interact with plenty of people that would be instrumental to my career later on.

It was a natural move for Jerry Jarrett to have called Verne Gagne on behalf of the Fabs; the two of them regularly traded out talent. When Nick Bockwinkel was the world champion of the AWA, they would fly him in to work against Lawler. Lawler would also head up to Verne as an occasional attraction, but neither Stan nor I had ever been up there to work for Verne, at least not while we were members of the Memphis roster.

There might have been a far more extensive business relationship between Jarrett and Verne, but if there was, I wasn't aware of it. There are always things going on that you aren't aware of, and that you don't have to care about, especially if you're simply one of the talent. All I wanted to do was make money and remain an attraction.

When Stan and I first arrived in the AWA, the babyfaces on their roster were all old guys. The Crusher, Baron Von Raschke, Billy Robinson and Larry Hennig were all at least in their 40s, if not their 50s. Even what we wore in the ring was way over the top compared with what they were accustomed to. There was a clear generational difference. Stan and I went out in bowties and suspenders, Japanese t-shirts, headbands, chaps and vests. We were *way* overdressed by the standards of their usual performers who simply walked to the ring in plain wrestling tights.

Verne's son Greg Gagne rented a house to me in Eden Prairie just southwest of Minneapolis, and my family stayed there. It was a very nice home. I didn't like living in Minneapolis because I was uncomfortable with the weather. If I didn't see a palm tree during my daily drives, I wouldn't be happy, and most people in the wrestling business knew that about me. Minneapolis was the polar opposite of Florida; there wasn't a palm tree in sight, and there was a reasonable expectation that it might *still* be snowing there in May.

When I first moved to Minneapolis, I had a Corvette, and that wasn't going to work in that climate. I also had a small Toyota Tercel that Terri drove, and I ended up trading the Corvette in for a Bronco. I wanted a four-wheel-drive vehicle in case I got stuck. The thing is, they're so prepared for snow up there that the instant a snowflake touches the ground, they lay salt on the ground, and the snowplows are out to clear everything away.

The first month we were in the AWA, Stan and I were testing out a new move where I would tag Stan, and then I would take right off to the ropes while our opponent was down on his back. Stan would catch me coming off the ropes in a press slam type of move, and then he would step away and I would drop straight down onto our opponent in a pancake type of maneuver. One of the very first times we attempted the move, things went *very* badly for me, and I broke my big toe when I landed on the mat. We purged that move from our arsenal immediately following that accident, but I had to take a couple weeks off until my toe healed up enough for me to keep working.

Sadly, that injury stalled our momentum early on, but it wasn't anything we couldn't overcome. I'd heard several nightmarish anecdotes about how long the car trips between towns were in the AWA, but it wasn't nearly as bad as people made it out to be. For any of the shows that were long distances away, like our events in San Francisco, Las Vegas, or Salt Lake City, we'd be flown out there. When you weren't flying, you usually weren't driving more than 150 miles, which was great for me. The thing I disliked the most about wrestling in territories was always the long car trips. The insanely long car trips had been the primary reason why I never worked for Bill Watts in Mid-South. The drives between town from one night to the next could extend as far as 600 miles, which was completely ridiculous.

Injuries aside, things were somewhat rocky for Stan and I in the AWA in the early stages. Verne had been a tyrant in his heyday, but now he was beginning to slip. One of the ways he remained dominant over the wrestlers was because he was a fantastic shooter, and he could have physically dominated almost everyone, even when he was on the precipice of old age. Well, Verne had gotten into it with Hulk Hogan and tried to shoot in on him, and Hogan ended up putting Verne in a front facelock and nearly choked him unconscious.

That incident embarrassed Verne and broke his spirit in the aftermath, and the guy who'd had a reputation for being such a skilled shooter no longer appeared to be quite so tough. The fact that I was from Tampa simply added to Verne's misery; he knew I was friends with Hogan from way back when we were teenagers, and Verne also knew that I'd heard the story of his embarrassment already.

Stan and I dealt with other hurdles when we first arrived, in the form of resistance to our style. In particular, guys like Nick Bockwinkel considered Stan and I to be highly erratic in our in-ring mannerisms. To be perfectly honest, I didn't particularly like our style *either*, but it was a style that made us money in Memphis, so I wasn't going to stop doing it as long as it remained a profitable gimmick. We just continued to do our thing despite how much it irritated some of the AWA's established veterans.

    No matter how much internal resistance we faced in the AWA, Stan and I would prove that we could get over even if we were a warm-weather act that had been transplanted to a frigid climate. We knew that our abilities would have us headed for the top. What we didn't know was that some of our comrades would eventually be headed off to *prison*.

SEVENTEEN

In early April of 1984, Verne Gagne rented a plane to fly Stan and I into Waukesha, Wisconsin, along with Blackjack Mulligan, Ken Patera, and Masa Saito. When we arrived, we had to travel about 30 miles to a small town, and then 30 miles back to the hotel before we flew out the next morning.

After the show, we were driven right back to our hotel. By that time, it was 11:00 p.m., none of us had eaten dinner, and we were all *starving*. We noticed a McDonald's behind the hotel, and Stan and I agreed that we shouldn't waste any time at all by carrying our bags to our rooms. Instead, we left all of our belongings at the front desk and ran down the hill to the McDonald's.

When Stan and I walked in, the crew working the evening shift had already begun making preparations for shutting down the restaurant. We were the very last customers they were going to take. The two of us ordered our food quickly and got out of the restaurant. As we were climbing up the hill, we noticed the unmistakable, hulking frame of Ken Patera walking down the hill in our direction.

"Hey, they're closed," I said to Ken.

"Oh, I'll get somethin'!" laughed Ken. "I'll get in there. They'll open for *me*."

Stan and I continued into the hotel, got our bags, walked to our rooms on the second floor, ate our food, and went to bed. We always stayed in separate rooms, so we agreed on a time to meet up in the morning and then turned in for the night. The next day, we went through our customary morning routine, met up, and then headed over to the front desk to turn in our room keys.

Awaiting us at the lobby was a startling scene. There were cops everywhere, and Blackjack Mulligan was chatting to them in an animated fashion. When Blackjack saw Stan and I, he came straight to us.

"Boys, you ain't gonna *believe* what happened!" said Blackjack frantically.

"Yeah, what's all this about?" asked Stan.

"Ken went to McDonald's last night, and they wouldn't open the door for him!" said Blackjack. "He ended up throwin' a big rock right through the glass door! Then he walked straight back up to the hotel!"

"So the police are here lookin' for him?" I asked.

"Oh, they *found* him!" laughed Mulligan.

What I found out from all the sources involved – and *primarily* from Masa Saito – is that the police were told by the employees of the McDonald's that Patera was staying at the hotel, so they came to the hotel and asked for him. Those of us who were wrestlers stood out like sore thumbs; Ken had a head full of bleach-blond hair, along with his massive powerlifting frame. When a male and a female police officer arrived at the hotel's front desk and provided that description of a suspect, the hotel manager knew precisely who they were looking for and told them that Ken had just gone to his room.

The thing is, Ken wasn't alone. Saito and Patera had been sharing rooms together on the road to cut down on travel expenses.

"Answer the door!" Patera told Saito when the officers knocked. "If they're lookin' for me, tell them I'm not here!"

Saito's English comprehension was below average at best, but he did what was requested of him and opened the door in his underwear.

"Is there a big, blond guy in here with you?" asked the male cop.

"No. He not here," answered Saito, before abruptly shutting the door.

The cops returned to the front desk to talk to the manager, who assured them that he had just seen Patera walk to his hotel room moments before they'd arrived. Sensing that they might have to forcibly enter and extract Patera from his hotel room, the two officers on the scene now called for backup in the form of the highway patrol and the Sheriff's department. Before long, at least 10 law enforcement officers were on the scene.

The same two officers approached the door of the room shared by Patera and Saito once again, while the remaining officers remained positioned in the narrow hotel hallway. This time, the lady cop knocked on the door, and Saito answered once again and told them to go away. When Saito went to shut the door, the female officer stuck her foot in the room to prevent the door from shutting, and she also reached for some mace. At that point, the male officer in the hallway began to shove against the door to try to force his way into the room.

"Hey, hey, hey, I'm *here*!" said Patera. "There's no need to get into a big fight over this!"

When Patera approached her, the lady cop raised the mace toward Saito's face and sprayed him, which is a perilous move to make against a man who's already blind in one eye. Now that Saito had been *totally* blinded by mace, he freaked out and shoved the lady back into the hallway, and she struck the wall. Saito was now fully in the hallway, rubbing his eyes to try to remove the chemicals from them.

"Hey! *Stop* this!" yelled Patera, as he walked out into the hallway and attempted to settle everyone down.

It was to no avail. The female cop's partner grabbed Saito, which was their second critical mistake. Saito was a superpowered shooter with excellent combat skills, and now that he was totally sightless, he was perceiving everything to be a threat. To defend himself, Saito hooked the officer who had grabbed him and flung him straight through the wall, leaving a massive hole in it. Now the remaining officers tried to jump on both Saito and Patera, and the two of them shoved the overmatched officers in all directions, leaving holes and impressions in the walls all along the hotel's hallway.

Several of the officers sustained broken arms, dislocated shoulders, and other injuries from trying to subdue the two monstrous wrestlers. The thing is, the police *never* fully subdued the pair. Patera had been trying to surrender the entire time, but cops kept jumping on him because Saito was blinded and continuing to toss them around.

Once Saito's vision cleared enough that he could recognize that everyone piling onto him had been a police officer, he relented and gave himself up to be arrested. Both Saito and Patera were handcuffed, driven to the Waukesha Police Department, and booked. Verne eventually managed to get them bailed out of jail.

As the rest of us were sitting in the lobby and Blackjack was telling us what he knew about the incident, I looked out of the window and observed as five police cars pulled up to the hotel. When they came to a stop, an officer opened up the rear door to one of the cars, and a handcuffed Masa Saito climbed out. They'd given him a police t-shirt and sweatpants to cover himself up, but Saito's body was so thick that the clothes barely fit him. He honestly looked pretty humorous stuffed into an outfit like that, but he failed to see the humor in that moment.

The police escorted Saito into the hotel, removed the cuffs from his wrists, and released him to get his bags and catch his flight with the rest of us. Saito sat next to me on the plane and gave me a detailed account of the events, although it wasn't much different from what Blackjack had said, except he obviously provided more firsthand details.

"If this would have been New Orleans or Miami Beach, they would have *shot* you!" I told Saito on the plane.

In essence, the whole thing was Ken Patera's fault. Ken was a pretty arrogant guy, but that seemed to be a trait shared by a lot of the guys who had broken into the business in the Northern territories, or who had been raised in the North to begin with. Nick Bockwinkel, Jesse Ventura and Freddie Blassie were all like that. They just had ruder dispositions, and an elevated sense of entitlement.

Even when I was in Florida, the guys who came from the North like Paul Ellering, Dennis Stamp and Steve Olsonoski all seemed to suffer from that affliction as well. Their personalities, egos, or views of the wrestling business simply made them harder to blend with.

I'll never forget when Dennis Stamp made the cocky remark to Mike Graham, "You're awfully short for a wrestler. You're lucky your dad's the owner!"

Mike snapped back on him so quickly.

"When I stand on my wallet, I can look right at the top of *your* head!" remarked Mike.

Dennis seemed to appreciate that answer, and maybe that was the key to getting along with the guys up North; if you replied to them by also sounding like a jerk, they were more likely to respect you. Nine months out of the year, these guys are cooped up indoors due to snow and cold weather. When you spend all that time inside, there's no telling how miserable of an attitude you're likely to develop.

Some guys from the North were far milder and very easy to get along with, like Barry Darsow and Curt Hennig, but they were the exceptions. The majority were clearly ego-inflated, and seemed to be living off of the reputations they'd established from things they didn't really do. Many of them would want you to believe they'd actually won every championship belt they ever wore inside of a wrestling ring.

Stan and I were long gone by the time Saito and Patera were ultimately handed multi-year prison sentences for the hotel incident. I was always very sympathetic to Saito, who had really just been a guy with a poor understanding of English, and had gotten trapped in a situation that Patera had caused by being an arrogant jerk.

Aside from Patera and Saito, Stan, Blackjack and I were the only wrestlers with any first-hand involvement with the events that transpired that night. Going forward, it became a running joke between Stan and I that whenever we happened upon a restaurant that was closed, one of us would mockingly say, "Oh, that's okay; they'll open it for *me*!"

It became readily apparent to us that Verne had been willing to accept Stan and I onto the AWA roster on the strength of our industry reputation and Jerry Jarrett's recommendation, but Verne hadn't conducted much firsthand research for himself. He had barely even seen any footage of us in the ring; at most, it had been a one-minute video montage.

Seeing so little footage, and out of context, the Fabulous Ones' gimmick wouldn't have made much sense to him. With so little information to base any booking decisions on, Verne didn't even seem to know what to make of us.

"What are you guys: babyfaces or heels?" he asked.

"Well, we're babyfaces down in Memphis, but we worked for Watts as heels against the Guerreros and guys like that," I said. "We can do either one. I think you should book us as babyfaces, though. We're going to stand out in a territory like *this* one."

The AWA had some pretty good heels, but the babyfaces at the time were a bit lame and played out. Most of the AWA's recognizable babyfaces had been in the area for at least a solid decade at that point. They were like antique cars. They were slow-moving, and because they knew they were over, they also knew they didn't have to do much to get a reaction from the audience. They were like a band that could get a pass by playing its greatest hits every night, and the Fabs tried to give the crowds something new and exciting to cheer for.

As far as I was concerned, the AWA was a perfect-timing scenario for the Fabs. When Verne also brought in the Road Warriors from TBS, I knew there was an opportunity to pair a popular heel attraction with a babyface team that had achieved equivalent levels of popularity, albeit in a smaller territory. We had a bit of a head start on the Road Warriors for a week or two, and that set the stage for our two teams to feud.

The Road Warriors vs. The Fabulous Ones was a natural pairing of babyfaces and heels. They fed us some other heel teams in between, and the Warriors also worked with some other people, but the main focus of the tag team scene was on the four of us. The other teams had been there for so long that they were stale. Most of the tag team combinations that had been active before us were made up of guys that were old enough to be my dad. They were established, but the fans had been seeing some of those guys for 20 straight years at that point, and many of the fans were dying for them to retire and disappear.

The advantage of the AWA for the older guys was that they didn't run weekly towns the same way we did in Tennessee, Georgia, the Carolinas and Florida. We'd appear in the same places every week when we were in those territories, with the possibility of a special or irregular location thrown in on a Saturday or a Sunday. The Minneapolis territory was so spread out. It stretched from the Upper Peninsula of Michigan sometimes, all the way to as far west as San Francisco, Salt Lake and Las Vegas, and through major cities in the Midwest like Chicago and Duluth, and Canadian cities like Winnipeg. They also had some miserable towns where it was always snowing, and where we always wound up *freezing* our asses off.

When you're ice fishing and you can drive your vehicle right out onto the ice, that was mind-blowing to a Florida boy like me. In fact, the entire concept of ice fishing was insane to me.

Curt Hennig was the first person to introduce me to ice fishing, and we drove out in my Ford Bronco looking for a place to cut a hole in the ice.

"Hey, drive right out there!" yelled Curt, pointing to a spot out on the lake.

"Nah. I'm good," I told him. "I'm not doing that."

"I'm *serious*!" he answered. "You can drive right out there, and we'll cut a hole in the ice!"

"No," I shook my head. "It's *not* happening."

It *did* happen, and it was a miserable experience. As far as I was concerned, you weren't living a normal life if you were sheltering yourself from the cold for nine months out of the year, fishing inside of a cabin sitting on top of a frozen lake, and dropping your line into the water through a hole that you'd cut in the ice.

"I can't even fit the *bait* I want to use through that hole!" I complained.

I wasn't even kidding. In many cases, the fish you would catch in Minnesota would be smaller than the bait you would use to catch fish in Florida. I think the whole objective of ice fishing is far more about getting drunk and playing cards than it is about catching fish to eat.

The whole experience was made even worse by Curt's fondness for country music. I thought I'd left it behind in Florida and Tennessee, but Curt listened to it just as much as any wrestler in the South.

"Brother… I can't listen to this shit anymore!" I whined. "Everything is about a guy with a pickup truck whose wife runs off and shoots his dog. It's always somethin' like that. Give me a break!"

The farthest north I had ever regularly worked prior to appearing in Minnesota had been Tennessee. I'd grown accustomed to riding around all year in a t-shirt and jeans with the windows of the car rolled down. All of a sudden, I'm driving through the frozen tundra wearing a snowsuit. Stan and I would laugh all the way to some of those towns while saying, "This has got to be the *dumbest* place in the world to choose to live!"

Before you left your house to go to the car, you had to put on your snowsuit, your gloves, your scarf, your boots, and your winter hat. In Tennessee, I needed to immediately roll the car's windows down as soon as I got behind the wheel, because the car would be even warmer than the open air. In Minnesota, you would discover that your car was freezing cold, you would be able to see your breath inside of it, and your first prayer was that it would even *start* for you.

I saw people who owned those devices where you would plug your car in to keep it warm, but I never got desperate enough to buy one of those.

Once you're inside the car and it completely warms up, that's when you would begin to slowly strip off every layer of clothing in order to get comfortable again for your long car rides. Before you knew it, you'd be totally undressed again because the car is toasty. Then you'd get to the town, and you'd have to put all of that shit back on and bundle up so that you could walk from the car to the entrance of the building, and then you'd remove it all again once you reached the dressing room. When you left, you had to go through the exact same ordeal just to get home at night.

It was like grocery shopping, where you take it off the rack, put it all in the cart, then take it off the cart to check out of the store, pile it all back in to take it to the car, then unload it all from the cart again to stick it in the car. Getting ready to go to a show in Minnesota required the *same* pattern, except it involved your clothes.

Inevitably, I would lose a glove or misplace a scarf, and then a part of my body would end up freezing until I could find or replace the missing article of clothing. It was a *nightmare*. On top of all the changing in and out of clothes, you'd get the snow and ice all over your feet, you'd carry it into the car with you, and once it started melting, you'd end up with a mud puddle under your brake pedal.

Driving in all of that snow caught me off guard. I knew it was there, but I didn't know how annoying it would truly be. The only serious issue I ever had was in the driveway at Greg Gagne's house. I attempted to back out of the garage one time, only to be blocked by the four-foot wall of snow sitting in our driveway. I couldn't get out, and the snow was also resting against the exterior walls of the house.

I made it next door and asked my neighbor if I could borrow a snow blower. The only issue was that I'd never run a snowblower before; I'd only ever run lawnmowers during my life. My neighbor let me borrow his snowblower, and I took it out to the end of the driveway, started it up, and began to use it exactly like I would have used a lawnmower. I walked around the edges of the driveway, and the snow was flying off to the side and being blown even further into the middle of the driveway.

I got all the way around about two or three times before I realized that I'd made things even harder for myself since now I had a 10-foot pile of snow in the middle of the driveway. I looked over toward the home of the neighbors who I'd borrowed the snowblower from, and everyone in the family was standing in the living room with their faces pressed against the glass, pointing toward me, and laughing their asses off at me and the predicament I'd created for myself.

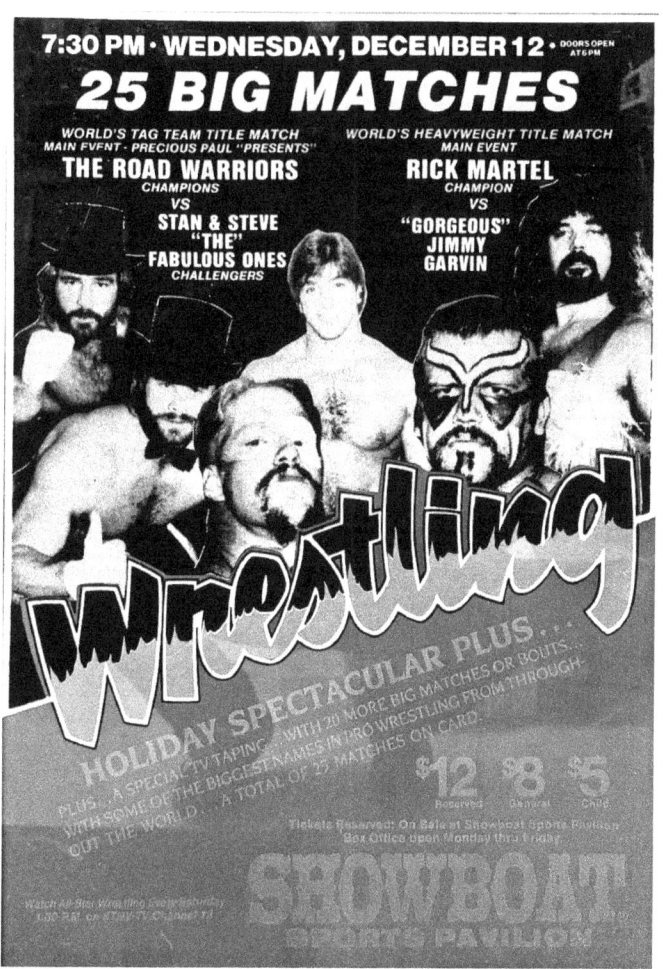

An AWA show headlined by the Warriors and the Fabs in Las Vegas

When you run a snowblower, you start in the middle and work your way out so that the snow flies outward rather than inward. When you run a lawnmower, you start with the edges and work your way in because it doesn't pile up. I learned *that* particular lesson the hard way.

The Road Warriors were from the Minneapolis area, so for them, wrestling in the AWA was a homecoming. Hawk and Animal were heels in theory and also based on the way they were slotted on the cards, but they were really babyfaces in the grand scheme of things, and especially in the way their entry into the AWA was handled.

They were billed as being street fighters from Chicago even though they were actually hometown boys from Minneapolis, and they were frequently going to be wrestling in Chicago against two bleach-blond pretty boys from the South who were adorned in sequin tuxedos and bow ties.

It shouldn't have taken much brain power to deduce which team Chicagoans and most other fans in the Midwest were going to cheer for.

The first time we wrestled Mike "Hawk" Hegstrand and Joe "Animal" Laurinaitis in the AWA was in their authentic hometown of Minneapolis. They'd both been bouncers there, and they worked out at the same gym that was frequented by several other wrestlers. Barry Darsow, John Nord, Rick Rude, Curt Hennig and several other guys all trained at the same place alongside Hawk and Animal. Most of them had known each other since they were kids.

Verne came into the dressing room in Minneapolis and said, "Listen… Do you guys have some kind of tricky way you could slide over the Road Warriors and not hurt them by overpowering them or something?"

"Yeah, we've got a finish in mind," I said.

"What are you gonna do?" inquired Verne.

"You get the heat up on Stan. You beat him up and beat him up, and then he keeps trying to tag me but can never quite do it," I explained. "Then Stan and whoever he's in there with will crash into each other, and they both go down. Stan's close to the apron, and closer to me, but not quite close enough to where I can touch him. As the referee comes to check on Stan to see if he's okay, I'll come in like I'm going to help Stan, then Mike will come in to help Joe."

"Okay, okay…" said Verne as he followed along.

"When the referee sees that, he'll go to put Mike out, and I'll drop off the apron, pull Stan out to the floor, and then I'll roll back into his exact spot like I'm him, and I'm unconscious," I continued. "Then when Mike gets the tag, he'll come to me to pick me up for something, and I'll just cradle him real quick and get a one-two-three. He'll explode out, and then I'll roll to the floor with Stan and we'll haul ass out of there and get the win. So we'll surprise them and beat them with the illegal man."

Verne listened to me come up with that finish so intently, like I was the second coming of Eddie Graham.

"That's *great*!" said Verne. "I'll tell the Warriors that's what we're going with for the finish."

Stan and I got to the ring, and I was looking into the stands excitedly because we'd drawn such a huge house in Minneapolis. I started bouncing around the ring so that the people could tell I was worked up and prepared for a major fight. Meanwhile, Stan was in the center of the ring chatting with the Road Warriors while he was getting his hands checked.

I could overhear Hawk saying, "Verne Gagne can kiss our asses; we're *not* doin' the finish."

I knew what I'd heard, but I couldn't believe it. In my entire career, I'd never heard anyone outright refuse to use the promoter's finish like that before, and certainly not after the match was already in the ring. Any problems with the finish would usually be discussed and worked through before the participants of the match had already reached the ring.

I bounced straight over there and said, "What?!" I felt the need to directly ask Hawk if I'd heard him correctly.

"Do it *our* way and nobody gets hurt," answered Hawk.

Clearly, the Road Warriors could have beaten us up for real if Stan and I tried to physically force ourselves upon them, but that's not how you're supposed to do business. In scenarios like that, I was taught that the wiser move was to outsmart people.

The match commenced, and unsurprisingly, I was the only one in the ring doing any selling. The Road Warriors were *constantly* slamming me.

"I'm getting enough time above your guys' heads to get a pilot's license!" I said to Hawk.

Getting fed up and hitting Hawk with a chair

Hawk just chuckled and then slammed me *again*, so I bounced right back up and tagged Stan. Stan came into the ring and started fighting, and he was doing okay for a little while, but then the Warriors dragged him down and started pounding on him as well.

That's when I brainstormed the idea to show the Road Warriors how to truly get over once you've been backed into a corner. I rolled out and grabbed a chair, and I decided it was time for hardcore. I knew if I turned the chair loose and it somehow got away from me, Hawk was going to kill me. With that in mind, I started beating Hawk as hard as I could with the chair while gripping it as tightly as I could. The referee signaled for the bell to ring to mark the conclusion of the match. Hawk tried to snatch the chair and take it away from me, but I just kept right on whacking him.

Meanwhile, Paul Ellering was standing there hollering at both Hawk and Animal, yelling, "Get out! Get out!"

The Fabs got disqualified for using a chair, but that stunt appeared to get us over with the fans more effectively than if we'd actually beaten the Road Warriors. We looked like two guys who'd taken all we could stand, and we weren't going to take anymore. Yet again, poor Stan was an innocent bystander in the whole thing, just as he was for most things. I had improvised the chair stunt all on my own.

When we got back to the dressing room, there were plenty of shooters awaiting our return on the babyface side, like Baron Von Raschke, Brad Rheingans, Billy Robinson, and Larry "The Axe" Hennig. All of them were famously tough guys. When Stan and I came walking through the door, they all stood up and gave us a standing ovation.

"That didn't look like it worked out the way Verne wanted it to!" Larry remarked.

Everyone started laughing.

I told them everything Hawk said to us in the ring, and how we needed to do it his way or no one would get hurt.

"I decided to do it *my* way instead," I laughed.

They were all patting me on the back and congratulating me for sticking up for the business. In the midst of that scene, Verne stormed into the room with his entire bald head flushed red with anger.

"What the hell was that?!" Verne screamed. "What happened to the finish?!"

"Stop! Stop!" I replied, trying to get him to calm down. "First of all, that wasn't *my* fault, and it's not *Stan's* fault."

From there I explained directly to Verne how Hawk had invoked his name so disrespectfully, and subsequently threatened us with violence if we didn't go along with his preferred way of finishing the match.

"I wasn't taught like that, and I don't have to shoot when I work," I told Verne. "If I did, I wouldn't win any matches. But that's not the point; I have to take care of myself and my character and my partner."

Verne turned abruptly and burst back out the door. I presumed he was headed off to have a little chat with Hawk.

The concluding event to the show was a battle royal involving all the talent that was present in the building. Different guys kept coming up to me to ask me what I was going to do in the bout.

"I ain't goin'!" I told them. "I'm *not* goin' out to the battle royal!"

Larry Hennig came up to me. We had a great relationship because I had been close friends with his son Curt ever since Curt had first gotten into the wrestling business.

Larry grabbed me tightly by the arm and said, "Kid... we're going to the battle royal, and I'm going with you."

Larry was a monster; his *wrist* was the size of my thigh.

I started to answer Larry, but then Billy Robinson walked up.

Don't worry, kid," he said. "Nobody is gonna touch you."

Then Brad Rheingans strolled over. He was an Olympic wrestler who had won a gold medal in the Pan American Games.

"They're not so tough," Brad assured me. "Come on. Let's *all* go to the battle royal."

The implication was clear; Stan and I would be well protected if we decided to return to the ring that evening. As we were being swept up by the shooters and ushered over to the entrance, I looked at Stan and said, "Well... I guess we're headed off to *die* now!"

Stan and I were the last two wrestlers to make it into the ring. As soon as the battle royal began, Larry and Brad each grabbed a Road Warrior, dragged them down, and began cross-facing them and working them over on the mat. As the Road

Warriors were getting stretched by Brad and Larry, they were being repeatedly told, "Leave the Fabs *alone*!"

Apparently, Saito had also heard about what happened and wasn't thrilled by it. Even though he was a heel, he still took a turn manhandling the Road Warriors.

Hawk wasn't nearly as comfortable acting tough when it was these renowned shooters who were threatening him. He listened intently to their admonishment not to attack us and didn't fight back at all. When the Road Warriors were permitted to rise to their feet, they backed away from us completely. Not only did they not attempt to take a shot at us that night, but they never brought up the incident ever again. I got the sense that they knew what they had done was wrong, they knew our response to it was appropriate, and they weren't prepared to escalate the situation if it would stoke the ire of all of the most deadly shooters on the AWA's roster.

I liked Joe "Animal" Laurinaitis at least 10 times more than I liked Michael "Hawk" Hegstrand. My admiration and respect for Joe was infinitely greater than my feelings for Mike. At least Joe seemed like he was rational enough to be reasoned with. Hawk was dangerous, crazy, wild and sporadic, and he got far too excited far too easily. He was always concerned that people would take advantage of him, and as a result, he sold as little in the ring as he possibly could. That often worked out well to protect his character, but it usually hurt the effectiveness and excitement of the matches he was in.

I wish I could say that the match in Minneapolis marked the end of the contentiousness in our relationship with the Road Warriors. Unfortunately, it was only the tip of the iceberg.

EIGHTEEN

When the Fabs faced the Road Warriors in Chicago, Verne put the Crusher with us as our manager since he was supposedly from Chicago, even though he was really from Milwaukee. They figured we would get the rub from him since he was like the Jackie Fargo of the territory.

We put a bow tie on the Crusher and brought him out with us in the Rosemont Horizon. When the lights in the arena dimmed, we emerged from the tunnel, and even though we were somewhat blinded once the spotlight hit us, Stan and I could faintly make out some guys jumping over the railing not too far away from us. It was a set of four brothers who had hopped the fence on a quest to kick our asses. The lights went out completely when that happened, and we heard a bunch of whacking and grunting taking place in our general vicinity. We could hardly make anything out in the dark, but neither Stan nor I were touched, nor did we have to lay a finger on anyone at all.

When the lights suddenly came back on, Stan and I were standing there, and all four of the brothers were lying prostrate on the ground with the cops handcuffing their ankles and preparing them to be dragged up the runway. To most people in the building, it looked like Stan and I had just beaten up four fans from out of the audience. It was the *furthest* thing from the truth, but that's what the audience thought.

So let that sink in for a moment: Even though Stan and I were booked as babyfaces who were accompanied by a certified babyface legend from the area, we still got attacked by the audience when wrestling against the Road Warriors. It was the polar opposite of getting the Jackie Fargo rub in Memphis.

At that very instant, some members of the audience actually went from booing us to cheering us because we looked like a couple of genuine badasses. It was never a small feat to get liked in the first place; being insanely over with the fans in Memphis had nothing to do with getting over in the AWA. You weren't just automatically liked no matter where you migrated to, and fans weren't going to automatically cheer for us just because the AWA's announcers advised them that they should. We had to start from the bottom and build a fanbase for ourselves all over again.

I went to Hawk and Animal and said, "Listen… no offense… I like you guys. If I was a fan, I'd *definitely* like you guys. But you guys aren't exactly being heels. Could you guys maybe do something where Stan and I make a double comeback on you, and then you guys take a powder to the floor and then run around and hug each other like two gay guys?"

Hawk and Animal looked at one another, and then Hawk said, "No way!"

"Well, it would probably get some actual heat on you," I offered. "You'd still be big and strong. I'm just sayin'…"

The Warriors weren't about to heed any suggestions like that. In their minds, they were convinced they were supposed to be the good guys. They would come away from every encounter saying, "We're *really* over!"

"You're *not* getting it!" I said. "When you're bigger than everyone, you don't sell anything, and then you smash everyone in sight, of *course* you get really over!"

That's what I tried to explain to them. Hawk was always the more defiant of the two Road Warriors. Animal was much easier to get along with, but Hawk was a crazy man. He always had the impression that I was trying to make them look like they weren't tougher than us; I was trying to make the *matches* more interesting, and to make it look like the bad guys actually needed to cheat to win. That clearly wasn't happening. The Road Warriors never gave the fans anything to actually dislike about them.

I was trying to explain to them what their role was supposed to be as heels. On top of the fact that, they had a manager, too. The *whole* point of managers in most cases was to have someone on the outside to interfere for you. Well the Road Warriors brutalized all of their opponents so convincingly that Paul Ellering never needed to interfere on their behalf. At a minimum, the heel has to be a chickenshit or back down from a babyface at least once. The Warriors *never* did.

I had to really get jacked up when we worked against the Road Warriors. I went so far as to start taking veterinarian steroids. I got so strong and powerful as a result of them. If you were going to get any respect from Hawk and Animal while working against them, a lot of it was going to come from the way you looked. Even if they hated you, they were so into bodies that they would compliment you once they got in the ring with you.

"Look at your shoulders; your delts are really poppin'!" said Animal.

Doing push-ups in the dressing room before a match

I did lots of close-grip bench presses; it helped that I'd been a powerlifter in college. I could load up 315 pounds on the bench and do it for 15 reps with a slightly narrow grip. When Hawk saw that in the gym in Winnipeg when I was training with Stan, he said, "Holy shit! Fifteen reps with 315?! How much can you do with a *single*?!"

"Why would I do a single?" I asked him.

"What do you mean?!" he said.

"What is that going to do for me?" I replied.

I didn't want to show anybody how much I could do; I was trying to get as many reps in as I could with a reasonably heavy weight.

That was typical of Hawk, though. He was very into publicly demonstrating that he was the biggest and strongest person there was, even in the fake sport of pro wrestling.

"What's your win-loss record?" Hawk asked me in the dressing room one night.

"What do you mean?" I asked him.

"Your win-loss record," repeated Hawk. "How many matches have you *won*?"

"I don't have a clue, but I'm pretty sure I've lost a whole lot more than I've won," I told him.

"Well, we've *never* lost!" said Hawk, haughtily.

"And you ain't gonna lose tonight, either, and it don't matter to me because *none* of this is real!" I laughed.

That response blew Hawk's mind. He looked at me in amazement at the thought that I truly didn't care if I lost. For a little while after that, it almost seemed like he felt weird for being the only wrestler in the dressing room who was so obsessed with winning all of the time.

I legitimately didn't care if I lost every night; I just wanted to get *paid*. That's what I'd gotten into the business for. I didn't get in the business to win a lot of titles. Thankfully, Stan and I *were* getting paid. When Stan and I saw our payoffs for working in main events in the AWA, we were looking at one another saying, "Why haven't we been here all along?"

I started to sense that Greg Gagne was jealous of Stan and I because he and Jim Brunzell had been the AWA's flagship babyface tag team as the High Flyers for a long time, and Stan and I were now dominating the babyface side of the tag team scene. They weren't booking the High Flyers against the Road Warriors; they went straight to the *meat*. They knew the Fabs against the Road Warriors would be a much better draw. The resentment from Greg felt similar to the attitude I felt from Mike Graham.

Their situations were also quite similar. Both were the sons of the owners and felt like they'd been pushed aside, but they'd been in the same territories for their entire lives and never had to make major improvements or adjustments in order to guarantee themselves acceptable spots on the roster. While Mike's biggest physical problem had been that he was too short to be taken seriously as a main eventer, Greg had been *far* too skinny to be pushed into main events. He looked more like an elementary school gym teacher than a believable pro wrestler.

Many of the other AWA veterans seemed surprised by what they saw from us in the ring when we wrestled against the Road Warriors. When we got back from our matches, some of the older wrestlers in the dressing room said things like, "You guys do a lot of stuff out there!"

"Yeah," said Hawk. "Of course we do. So what? You guys don't do *anything*! We like to stay busy when we're out there!"

The Crusher, Baron Von Raschke and other wrestlers from the AWA's older generation did a whole lot of punching, kicking and stomping. There were usually more unique moves in a single match between the Road Warriors and the Fabs than in all of their matches combined. It was a culture shock for me to be in the AWA, but it had also been a culture shock to be in Tennessee. Being in the Gagnes' territory also demonstrated to people that the Fabulous Ones could slow things down and work in the methodical, plodding style of the AWA as well as the flamboyant, up-tempo style of Tennessee.

The feud between the Road Warriors and the Fabulous Ones wasn't isolated to the mainland United States. Luke of the Sheepherders was acting as the booker for U.S. talent down in Puerto Rico for Carlos Colon's World Wrestling Council, and he got the Fabs booked to wrestle the Road Warriors at Roberto Clemente Stadium. Over the course of the evening, as we were sitting in the babyface dressing room, Luke kept sending over different finishes to our match. All of the finishes involved us beating the Road Warriors since we were scheduled to return to wrestle in Puerto Rico once again, and there were no imminent plans for Hawk and Animal to return.

"I can already guess how *this* is gonna end," I told Stan.

Sure enough, we received the word that the Warriors kept saying, "No, we don't do jobs," whenever Luke presented them with a finish that involved the two of them losing to us. Luke's conduit for relaying this information to us was one of the Puerto Rican referees who spoke very little English. His way of informing us of the Road Warriors' insistence upon being uncooperative consisted of shaking his head and saying, "They don't wanna do nothin'! They don't wanna do nothin'!"

Finally, I just got fed up.

Okay, so what *do* they wanna do?!" I said. "Just tell us what they *want* to do!"

The referee scurried off to the heel dressing room to make the inquiry for us, and returned with the Road Warriors' desired finish. They wanted to do a finish where they got the heat on Stan, he would give me a hot tag, and then I would come in and start bouncing them around the ring. When both of the Road Warriors were down, the Sheepherders would approach the ring. Stan would drop off of the ring apron to square off with them, and then I would approach the ropes to point an accusatory finger in the Sheepherders direction. From there, I would turn around and get double teamed, clotheslined, and beaten cleanly via pinfall at the hands of the Road Warriors.

Once again, the Road Warriors would get to emerge victorious and appear dominant, and then they would leave Puerto Rico forever while the Fabs returned as losers.

Our bout didn't begin until after midnight because there were so many matches on the card. The fans in Puerto Rico were always insane, and usually drunk. By midnight, the crowd was usually still raucous, and most assuredly drunk.

The wrestling ring sat atop the pitcher's mound in the middle of the stadium, which usually granted the police adequate time to chase down any rioters who hopped out of the bleachers and attempted to storm the ring. *Usually.*

Stan and I stepped up and out of the dugout and then marched toward the ring, and I never betrayed the fact that we had absolutely zero intention of performing the Road Warriors' proposed finish.

Working over Animal's leg in Puerto Rico

Hawk repeated that finish to us in the ring before the match got underway, and then asked, "Ya got it?"

"Yeah, we got it," I said.

When we walked back to our corner, I looked at Stan, smirked, and asked him, "Was your bag packed?"

"What?" he asked.

"When you left to come to the ring, was your bag pretty packed?" I elaborated.

"Oh, yeah," said Stan. "I don't leave nothin' sittin' out in the locker room in Puerto Rico."

"Good, because we're not goin' through the dressing room," I warned him. "We're goin' straight to the car, then either to the hotel or the airport."

"Oh no!" said Stan. "What are you gonna do?"

"I don't know yet," I shrugged. "I'll figure it out as we go."

When it was time for the Sheepherders to come down to ringside, Stan and I had worked the match exactly the way the Road Warriors had wanted us to. Sure enough, Stan dropped off of the apron just as Hawk had scripted it.

Hawk and Animal had both taken bumps for me, and they were lying motionless on the mat. I looked at the two of them lying there, smiled at them, and yelled, "See ya!"

With that, I ran toward the ropes and dove in between them and out onto the Sheepherders.

"What was *that*?!" Stan asked me as we both began fighting the Sheepherders. "*That* was your big plan?!"

"Screw those guys!" I said.

"No, mate!" said Luke. "You're supposed to finish the match!"

Despite his protests, I dragged Luke with me, and Stan and I began to fight the Sheepherders all through the audience, and the crowd followed us all the way over toward the heel dugout. The Sheepherders eventually escaped into the dressing room, and I looked back toward the ring to see the Road Warriors getting their arms raised in victory because we'd been counted out. They may have won the bout, but the last thing the crowd saw in the ring was the Road Warriors getting beaten up by me before I pounced onto the Sheepherders and Stan and I began brawling with them. At the end of the show, *all* of the attention was on the Fabulous Ones.

Hawk's head was so crimson red with anger, you could practically see the steam emanating from it. Even from way in the back of the baseball stadium, I could tell that he was visibly upset. Stan and I dashed into the dressing room, grabbed our bags, and dashed out to the cab. However, we didn't leave the island; we still had three more shows in Puerto Rico we were booked to wrestle in, and against the Road Warriors of all teams.

"You know, Stan, if you want to, we'll stay and deal with it," I said from the security of our hotel room. "I really don't want to get beaten up. I know they can beat me up, but it's not about that. I don't want to deal with this kind of work."

"Yeah, you're right," said Stan. "Let's get out of here. I'm *sick* of dealing with those guys."

Stan and I went to sleep, but we were awakened a couple hours later by a thunderous pounding on our hotel room door.

"Open up! I'm gonna kill ya!" bellowed the unmistakable voice of Hawk. "Open up! I'm gonna kick your ass!"

I went to the door and asked, "What was that?"

"Open up!" repeated Hawk. "I'm gonna kill ya! I'm gonna kick your ass!"

"Well which one is it?" I asked through the door. "Are you gonna *kill* me, or are you gonna *kick* my ass? Before I open the door, I *really* need to know this."

"I'm gonna *kill* ya!" Hawk answered.

"Well *that's* good to know!" I replied. "I'm calling security!"

I grabbed the phone, called the front desk and said, "There's a guy trying to beat my door down!"

About a minute later, someone arrived at our door and told Hawk that he would be arrested if he didn't go back to his room.

The next morning, Stan and I drove straight to the airport and left Puerto Rico without finishing our scheduled dates. The Road Warriors were so upset by the way things unfolded that it took a couple of months before they would even talk to us again. However, a few months after that, they were actually able to laugh about it.

"As much as I hate you sometimes, I've gotta say that I kind of love you," conceded Hawk.

Hawk saw the situation a little differently after he'd cooled off. For the life of me, I don't know why he saw every match as a life-or-death scenario to preserve his reputation and mystique.

When the Fabs weren't sticking and moving against the Road Warriors in and out of the ring, we were often competing against Nick Bockwinkel and a rotating cast of his partners, and they were always managed by Bobby Heenan.

Nick Bockwinkel was a Larry Zbyszko type of worker. Neither was really aggressive, or got too excited. The thing is, when I went to the AWA and worked with Nick Bockwinkel, he had been advertised as being an elite worker on the level of Harley Race. There was *no* comparison. To me, working with Bockwinkel was like working with Jerry Lawler, which is to say that Bockwinkel benefitted from being positioned as a star and from being isolated from many of the NWA's great workers for so long.

Bockwinkel was all show to me. It's possible that he was better when he was younger, before I arrived in the AWA, but when I was there, he'd apparently lost a gear. He gave great interviews, but I would have called him an imitation of Buddy Rogers in the ring, and not really in a good way. Similarly, Dick the Bruiser, the Crusher, and all of those guys were big showmen in the AWA, but from my perspective, they were Midwestern versions of Bruno Sammartino. They were just brawlers who gave good interviews, but even those interviews were usually repetitive stories about throwing guys out of bars when they were teenagers.

On the few occasions where Stan and I got to communicate with Bobby Heenan, Bobby would always explain to us how much Nick Bockwinkel disliked us, and that Bobby never understood what Nick's problem was.

"What the hell *are* these guys?! Nick would ask. "Are they heels or babyfaces?! We're the heels, but we look more like babyfaces than *they* do!"

The Fabs were so different from what they were used to, and Bobby made Nick sound like he was being a real dick towards us. That just made me want to mess around with Nick and annoy him even more once I got him in the ring. Nick was slow, methodical, and boring. I would get him in holds where I would position him onto his back where he couldn't see me, and then I would start strumming my fingers like I was waiting for something to happen. It was the *exact* same thing I did sometimes with Dory Funk Jr.

Headbutting King Kong Bundy

I would also get Nick down on the mat and make it look like I was outwrestling him by spinning around on top of him, and making him look slow and weak. In essence, I made it look like I wasn't respecting him in the ring, but he'd brought it on himself. He was very cocky and arrogant, and reminded me of Freddie Blassie in that respect. He had a little bit too much of an inflated ego, and that always rubbed me the wrong way.

Whenever you worked with Frank "Bruiser Brody" Goodish, he was an aggressive monster. His demeanor, character, and personality were all built around him being a big, relentless brawler that came after you and just didn't stop. His structure and size were intimidating also. It's not like he did a whole bunch of different moves. It's easy to work with a big guy that does a lot of moves because that makes them more versatile.

When you get involved with guys that won't go off their feet very easily, it's actually a smart way to work a match because it adds to the believability. Frank liked to stay up and moving, and he was also a fantastic athlete. You'd have to really take it to him since he could quickly spring to his feet and chase you down no matter where you went or what you did.

Nine times out of 10, a match with Frank wouldn't involve anything that was so dramatic that the audience would freak out thinking that you were going to somehow defeat Bruiser Brody, let alone beat him up. Usually, it was like a fight for your life, but Brody would work with you to make it exciting most of the time.

During one evening in Salt Lake City, Stan and I were strutting to the ring to wrestle against Bruiser Brody and Masa Saito, who probably had a grand time laughing in response to what happened to me that night. Stan and I were making our entrance to the ring first, and entered through the audience, high fiving people like we usually did as our theme music played. The two of us had condensed our outfits down to travel more lightly and easily, meaning that we were only wearing bowties and suspenders instead of sequin tuxedos and top hats.

Out of nowhere, I got absolutely *blasted* in the back. I thought someone in the crowd might have clubbed me with a baseball bat or a chair. I got hit *so* hard, and I couldn't identify what hit me, but I did spot my bowtie flying through the air as

I stumbled forward. Whatever had struck me, the force of the impact had blown my bowtie *clean* off, and also popped my suspenders.

It was a miracle that my head hadn't also been knocked off, or that I hadn't fallen to the ground as well. What had actually happened was that Bruiser Brody had come running up from behind me and booted me dead in the center of my back without any forewarning. It was a good thing that he had pulled the force of his kick somewhat, or I undeniably would have sailed through the air and landed flat on my face.

Brody was merely trying to get the match started in a way that would fill the building with excitement, but it wasn't like I could just roll into the ring, fire up like a babyface, make a big comeback, and then bounce Bruiser Body all over the ring. First of all, it's hard to settle things back down from that level of excitement so early in the match and then develop the action with the audience so that it would reach the desired crescendo once again. Second, Brody simply wasn't going to bounce around for me like that. It was *never* going to happen.

At this point, Frank was a big main-event monster in Japan, and he was working in the U.S. the way he was used to working overseas, which usually involved trampling guys and running right through them. I went from trying to fight back against Frank straight back to selling, because he just hammered me again, and he would shut me down or cut me off with a forearm or a knee whenever I tried to come back against him. It was a classic example of Frank being overpowering and not allowing the two guys wearing bowties and suspenders to interfere with his plans for the match.

Frank really took it to me, although he never hurt me in any way that did permanent damage. In my career, no one ever went out there and hurt me purposefully. People would get stiff with me, and occasionally did things that came across as aggressive, but that was often simply a matter of personal style.

Some guys were so big, but they wouldn't come to life at all when they locked up, and they probably should have been more dominating. When Frank worked, he worked aggressively, pressed the action, and took it to you.

There was never any resulting animosity, and I never felt like I had to try to outsmart him in any way like I did with the Road Warriors. I never felt threatened, or like I was putting my health on the line when I was in there against him. Also, Frank never felt the need to get in there and say, "Do it my way and nobody gets hurt," like Hawk did. If Frank had said that, I'm sure I would have been more than happy to accommodate him. I was going to get paid the same no matter what, so there was no sense in getting injured over it.

I was never in danger that night, but I absolutely got manhandled. Frank threw me around really well.

"Man, Frank got you good with that kick!" Stan said once we got to the dressing room.

"Yeah, and he owes me a new pair of suspenders!" I joked.

One night, some of the AWA staff approached us and asked us to sign a document to get an action figure deal. They were going to make action figures that had two figures in each package, so it would be natural to include tag teams. They would be the first action figures of wrestlers ever produced in the United States.

"Are you guys interested?" they asked.

"Of *course* we're interested!" we replied.

When the figures finally came out, the Toys "R" Us in Minneapolis was the first place to have the figures for sale in our area. I walked straight to the back of the Toys "R" Us, and they had a whole section full of these action figures made by Remco toys. I could see the Road Warriors, the Fabulous Ones, and a few others, but those were the two I paid attention to because it was us and our most frequent opponents in the territory. I stuck a shopping cart underneath the rack and pulled *all* of the Fabulous Ones figures off the rack and into my cart. Pleased with my haul, I pushed my cart containing about 15 sets of figures right up to the sales register.

I set all of the figures up on the counter, and the guy at the register surveyed my purchases and then looked back at me, and he said, "Oh wow. *Big* wrestling fan, huh?"

"No, man!" I said. "That's me right here! That's *me*!"

The guy looked at me carefully, then he looked back at the action figure. Then he repeated the process before he finally said, "Man, *that* ain't you!"

The Fabulous Ones action figures

This was one of those times where it was actually useful to have been working as a wrestler under my real name. I reached into my wallet, pulled out my driver's license and presented it to the man.

"There's my name," I said, as I pointed to the figure with white suspenders. "You see that? Here's my name on this package. That's *me*."

The man's eyes got wide, and then he smiled and said, "Well, I'll be darned! That *is* you! No wonder you're buying them all!"

Most of the sets of figures were saved and put away, but Stan and I would also play with them in our cars on the way to the shows. It may sound childish, but can you blame us? It was the only time we could ever beat the Road Warriors, and we beat them to *death* in the car. I even took one of my bootlaces, tied it around the neck of a Hawk action figure, and threw him out of the window to bounce him around the interstate as we were speeding at around 70 miles per hour. Then I pulled him back into the car, and had my Steve Keirn action figure cover him for the pinfall while the Stan Lane figure counted to three.

That was the *easiest* pinfall anyone ever scored on Hawk in their career, and also the only way I could ever get him to put me over. After all, the two times that I manipulated the Road Warriors into using different finishes than the ones they wanted to go with originally, we *still* didn't win those matches. They did.

I don't think Stan and I ever saw a dime of the action figure money. It really didn't matter, though. We were just thrilled to have action figures out with our likeness on them. It was like being a kid again with an action figure, except *we* were the superheroes.

Receiving our own action figures was just further evidence to us that the Fabs had made the correct move by joining the AWA. Verne was turning us into national stars, but with that enhanced notoriety came an increased number of invitations from people who were hellbent on using their media platforms to discredit the wrestling business. There was *no way* we were about to let that happen on our watch.

NINETEEN

Working for Verne Gagne in the AWA was an opening to a much bigger door for the Fabulous Ones. In Tennessee, the wrestlers were really boxed into that territory. We may have gotten a lot of magazine coverage because of our record-sized crowds, but it wasn't just us; the entire territory was on fire. The Rock 'n' Roll Express were also coming alive, and there were plenty of young teams that were following in our pattern of doing more creative things to get over with the crowds.

Despite their efforts to emulate us, these teams didn't resemble athletes at all, and hid their underdeveloped bodies in t-shirts. They looked far more like little kids as opposed to grown men.

The AWA's reach was far closer to national, and even international in some respects with its regular stops in Canada. When we started doing speaking engagements for Verne, like being on talk shows, those appearances were held in places like San Francisco, Las Vegas, Chicago and Salt Lake City, and they were often viewable from coast to coast. Verne was a pretty creative guy in that respect, and the people working for him were always coming up with ideas.

The AWA was definitely a step up in the amount of air travel we were obligated to do. We never traveled by air in Tennessee unless we were flying out to work in some other territory, and the most we ever flew while I was in Florida was still within the state of Florida, or just outside of Florida to the Bahamas.

Sally Jessy Raphael hosted a very popular talk show for women. It wasn't like I watched it, but *Terri* certainly did. Sally was known for her look, which included red hair and red glasses. Stan and I were flown to St. Louis just to appear on her show. It just so happened to have been one of her special anniversary shows as well.

Stan and I walked out onto the stage wearing our sequin tuxedos and bow ties. Even if the viewers weren't familiar with wrestling, the two of us looked like two Chippendale dancers, and plenty of people were familiar with that look by then. We figured the viewing audience would be composed almost entirely of women. We took off our jackets, almost like Chippendale dancers, and played to the crowd. It was easy work based on how the two of us looked at the time, and it just fit. They played a few of our music videos to get the crowd revved up, and then we took our clothes off a little bit, and then each of us kissed one of the ladies there. I think I actually kissed Sally Jessy Raphael.

That was one of the Fabs first huge talk show appearances where the two of us appeared nationwide. Now people that didn't know us from Tennessee were seeing us around the country from everywhere.

Stan and I were very used to speaking on television because giving interviews was an essential component of the wrestling business. To us, going on a talk show was a piece of cake, and our personalities really got over with the audience during that appearance. Also, we were paying attention. Plenty of guys in our industry drank or did drugs before they made major appearances like that just to loosen up, but a lot of times they sacrificed a bit of their ability to focus when they were saying and doing.

Stan and I didn't drink before appearances, so we focused on getting ourselves over with the crowd that was present in the studio. Stan was *always* levelheaded. I *never* saw him even close to being drunk.

We often walked into appearances like that cold, and then once we arrived we asked the producers what they wanted us to get into, or if they just wanted us to organically kick around topics.

When producers said things like, "We'll just go live and whatever happens is what will make air," that always made me nervous, like we were somehow being set up.

There was a local daily show in the San Francisco Bay area called San Francisco AM on the KTSF television station. Stan and I were scheduled to make an appearance at the Cow

Palace that night, along with the rest of the AWA stars. Verne instructed us to head down to do the show, and then someone drove us down there.

Stan and I were standing in the back, and the host of the show approached us and began priming us for what he was hoping we would do during our segment of the show.

"I was a wrestling fan when I was a kid, but then I grew up," said the host. "I know Verne Gagne used a sleeper hold. So I'm going to ask if either one of you guys knows the sleeper hold."

"I used the sleeper hold earlier in my career," I told him.

"Perfect!" the guy said. "So when I ask if anyone knows the move, you can say, 'I do!'"

"Okay, so then what?" I asked.

"Well, we all know that wrestling is fake, so let's do this…" he grinned. "I'll tell the audience that I know wrestling is all fake, and that I'll ask to have the sleeper hold put on me to show them how fake it is."

"So you want *me* to put the sleeper hold on you, and then you want to use that to show the audience that wrestling isn't real?" I asked him.

"Yeah. I'm going to pretend to go to sleep," he answered. "Once I go down, I'll pretend I'm out cold, and then when you let go of the hold, I'll jump up and say, 'See? I told you!'"

Anyone who knows me at all knows that I would *never* let a situation unfold the way this guy had described it, but I also wasn't going to ruin my opportunity to appear on the show and teach him a lesson either. Working with the Road Warriors had taught me a lot about situations like this, when I knew I couldn't talk the person out of what they wanted to do, but I also knew I could work out a better arrangement for myself once the show was already in progress.

Half the time, Stan could accurately predict whenever I was planning to do something outlandish or off-script, and *this* was one of those times. Here was a case where a guy was asking me to apply a hold to him on live television that I had already put so many marks to sleep with during my career. *This script was writing itself.*

"This is going to be unbelievable," I thought to myself. "Verne is gonna *love* this."

I knew Verne liked to protect his territory, and he also wouldn't want this guy disrespecting his own classic finishing maneuver on live television as part of the ploy.

Stan and I got out there and went through the entire show with the host. When he asked me if I knew the sleeper hold, I asked him to get comfortable so that I could apply the hold to him properly.

Stan and I took off our jackets, which got some of the folks in the audience a bit worked up, and especially the women.

"I didn't know you were going to take your clothes off," the guy said.

"Well, it helps to be comfortable," I told him.

He was a tall guy, and I asked him to bend his knees a little bit so that I could apply the hold to him.

"Also, you should loosen your tie," I told him.

"Loosen my *tie*?" he asked.

"Well, you're goin' to sleep," I reminded him. "You might want to loosen your tie."

The guy laughed it off, but we were on a live show, and he didn't understand live TV like I did. There would be no editing or removing what was about to happen to him during this broadcast. I slowly wrapped my left arm around his neck, grabbed ahold of my right bicep with my left hand, and placed my right hand on the back of his head. Stan began to jokingly sing the song "Goodnight Sweetheart," because he knew this guy would soon be taking a nap.

I began to squeeze, and sure enough, the man began to crumble to the ground in two seconds. Then he started gurgling, and by the sixth second, he was convulsing on the floor. Stan carefully removed the microphone from the man's hand so that it wouldn't be in the way once we began to revive him, which we started to do immediately after we were certain he was out cold.

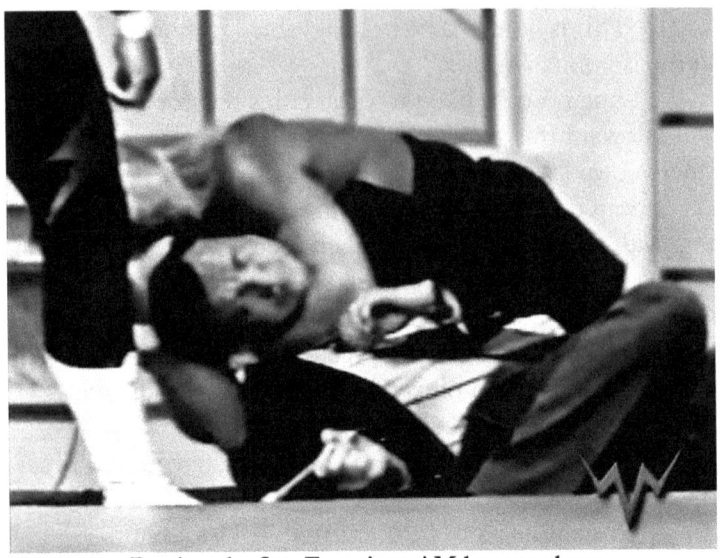
Putting the San Francisco AM host to sleep

The lady host of the show was freaking out, because she knew I'd put her co-host to sleep legitimately. Stan and I were already doing whatever we could to quickly revive him so that the show could progress. One of the reasons we woke him up was also for the sake of kayfabing the audience. Gordon Solie used to tell the audience members that if you didn't wake up the person you'd squeezed into unconsciousness with the sleeper, you'd give him permanent brain damage. I was decent and respectful to him, because I *knew* we were on live TV.

"Come on," I encouraged him. "Come on back."

His eyes slowly opened, and then gradually the recognition of what was happening returned to his face. He also remembered that he was on live TV.

Once he got his wits about him, the host called for a commercial break. As soon as the red light to the studio camera clicked off, he turned toward me and he said, "You son of a bitch! You *double-crossed* me!"

"Easy, big boy," I told him. "You tried to make a fool out of me and my partner and my business! I ain't lettin' you do that! I wasn't about to argue with you. I just had to show you that you shouldn't be tryin' to do things like that! Did you learn a lesson?"

"What do you mean, 'Did I learn a lesson?!'" he snorted.

"Did you learn not to ask people to do stupid shit like that and to insult their line of work?" I prodded.

The man whirled around and stormed off, and Stan and I immediately left the studio and drove back to our hotel. Little did we know that we had just participated in a television segment that people would still be watching on the internet several decades later.

That whole incident got over *huge* with the boys. When the Fabs reached the Cow Palace dressing room that night, everyone there who had seen the show was going crazy. They were even imitating the quivering of the host's legs as he slid to the ground.

In the middle of our celebration, Verne burst into the room.

"What the hell was *that*?!" Verne asked in an accusatory tone. "I put you guys on a talk show, and you put the son of a bitch to sleep right on live TV?! What was *that* all about?!"

"The guy that brought me into this business taught me to protect it!" I fired back. "He taught me that people like that needed to have an example made out of them. *That's* what that was!"

That response calmed Verne down a bit, which was good. Despite his age, Verne still had the knowledge of an Olympic-caliber wrestler, and he would easily have kicked my ass if things had escalated into physicality between us. That would still have been true if he'd been 100 years old and I'd only been 20.

"Well, did you think about what would've happened if you'd *killed* the son of a bitch on live TV?" Verne asked.

"I guess I'd have missed the Cow Palace tonight then!" I joked.

During another of our trips to San Francisco, Stan and I thought we were such a big deal that we ventured onto a street that was known to be a meeting place for gay men, and we decided to test to see if we would get hit on. We walked up and down the street, but to our surprise no one would even *talk* to us. It was actually a little bit ego-deflating.

"I don't get it," I said to Stan later. "We're handsome and muscular. What's the deal?"

"I think *I* know what the problem might be," said Stan.

"What?" I asked.

"Everyone probably thinks we're *a couple* and they want to be respectful of our relationship!" said Stan.

"Oh man! You're *right!*" I laughed. "I need to quit hangin' out with you in public!"

The things was, whether I was present or not, Stan could usually pick up anyone he wanted to. Stan's reputation for being a ladies' man was every bit what it was portrayed to have been on television. He was definitely "The Gangster of Love."

Stan was an only child who had been well protected by his parents while he was growing up. He was a good-looking guy with a great body. Despite the fact that he was naturally attractive to women, I always said that Stan's real secret was that he could dance extremely well. He could walk into any bar, and fearlessly walk up to any girl with a smile on his face and say, "Would you like to dance?"

All girls want to dance, and they especially want to dance with tall, handsome, muscular guys like Stan Lane. Stan would get out there with the girl and dance exquisitely well, and then all of the other ladies there would see this guy moving gracefully and effortlessly on the dance floor, and then they'd *also* want to dance with him. Within moments, every woman in the building would be *dying* to capture Stan's attention, and he always had his pick as to which lady he decided to leave the bar with later that night.

The people in most of the AWA territory stayed locked indoors during the winter months. It snowed there nine months out of the year in some of those places, and so going to bars and clubs was the only place where members of the opposite sex could reliably congregate and mingle. Stan *loved* the AWA territory for that specific reason, because for Stan, having access to pretty women in that sort of enclosed environment with music playing was as easy as shooting fish in a barrel. Stan could cruise a bar like nobody's business. He had a gift of gab to go with all of his other talents.

If I went to a bar or a club with Stan, I'd stand against the bar drinking a beer, and I'd just watch him do his thing. I was married, and even if I wasn't, I still would have been the same terrible dancer that I am. Whenever someone asked me to dance, I dismissed them by quickly saying, "I *can't* dance."

"I don't *ever* want to get married," Stan told me.

"How come?" I asked him. "Why don't you wanna get married?"

"All the guys I see in the business get married, and then they have a kid or two and end up divorced," said Stan. "Then they're paying child support and having to split everything they make. That ain't for me."

Stan's life was very different from mine. Whenever we got home from wherever it was that we'd been, I was heading straight home, and he was headed right to the nearest bar or nightclub, whether it was in Nashville or Minneapolis.

In the middle of all of this, Stan was actually dating Verne Gagne's daughter, Kathy. I viewed that as Stan going the extra mile to maintain our job security. Of course, I still had to poke fun at him for that.

"So this means that after the first lousy night she has with you, we're gettin' our notice, right?" I asked with a grin.

Stan looked dead at me and said, "She won't *ever* have a lousy night with *me*."

Being Stan's partner was the epitome of a great time. I was older and had more overall ring experience, so he often let me have the last word on a lot of decisions. At the same time, we always talked things over. It's not like I was acting as the team's dictator without making sure he was okay with what was happening. During my wrestling career, Stan was the best friend and partner I ever had. Inside the ring, he was an excellent worker. Outside of the ring, he was a lot of fun to be on the road with, and we never fought or argued at all.

The fact that we got along so well was essential, because I was about to test the bonds of our partnership yet again. Living in Minneapolis was an experience, but it was an experience that I wasn't fully enjoying. I was miserable, my wife was miserable, Heidi was miserable from being stuck inside all the time, and even though Cory was a brand-new baby, I'm pretty sure *he* was miserable, too. Both of my kids had to be so bundled up every time they walked outside that they could barely breathe, let alone walk.

Whenever I came home to Minneapolis from the road, it was inevitable that there would be a pile of snow for me to contend with, and Terri would have cabin fever from being cooped up with the babies all week. I felt like I was torturing my family simply by forcing them to continue dwelling in one of the coldest places in the country.

The weather affected my comfort in every conceivable way. I remember going to Milwaukee one night wearing my customary cowboy boots. The Fabulous Ones gimmick had been indelibly influenced by Tennessee, and even though we weren't cowboys, we wore the boots. I stepped out of the car once in Milwaukee while I was parked on a little bit of a ramp. I planted my foot on the ground, slipped immediately and busted my butt. Then when I tried to get up, I slipped again and slid all the way down the ramp. Even after falling over twice, I still had a hard time standing up, because cowboy boots are slick on the bottom.

The only way I could get around in cowboy boots was to walk as gingerly as a 100-year-old man, taking baby steps. I didn't want to take any bumps on the ice – which was as hard as concrete – but I was adamant about not switching up my attire and wearing rubber boots. In my mind, rubber boots were something that someone's grandmother would wear. Stan and I defied all logic and stuck with the cowboy boots against all odds, but it remained impossible to confidently stroll around in them. You were taking your life into your own hands by wearing them.

I got so sick of the snow in the Minneapolis territory by the start of 1985 that I totally snapped. I told Stan, "I can't take it here anymore. I've *got* to move."

This was no small request on my part to suggest that Stan should endeavor to follow me out of a territory once again. Stan and I were making the best money we'd ever been paid in our lives while working in the AWA. The cities were much bigger than any that we'd ever worked in prior, and we were working at the tops of the cards in a lot of places – including a massive market like Chicago – while being featured all over the central and western parts of the country. Also, while the lifestyle in Minneapolis may have been a nightmare to everyone in my household, Stan was loving his life as a single guy with money, who was free to cruise all the bars of the territory with impunity.

"Really?!" Stan said. "You wanna *leave*?!"

"I can't take it, Stan!" I told him. "I really can't take it!"

"Okay!" said Stan. "Well, I guess I'm *still* your partner!"

"We're gone," I said with a smile, cementing our pact to move away from the frigid Minneapolis weather and keep the Fabulous Ones intact.

Stan and I had an excellent run in the AWA, and we were still being used in an excellent position on the cards, but sometimes it's better to give your notice to the promoter than to have your notice given to you. I was always the one who liked to say goodbye and head off to work somewhere else the instant I felt like I was no longer being used properly. There were so many options in those days that you could usually drive just 200 miles away and be in another promoter's territory and commence making money there.

When Stan and I left Minneapolis, we were still marketable. We hadn't been jobbed out, because we didn't give

The Fabulous Wrestling Life of Steve Keirn

Verne enough notice for him to have the opportunity to job us out. Guys were bailing on Verne left and right to go to work for Vince McMahon Jr. in the WWF, and that's a trend that started before we arrived and continued while we were present.

Vince was outright stealing guys out from under Verne's nose. He had already snatched up Hogan before we even got there, and then he snagged everyone from wrestlers Jesse Ventura and Ken Patera to manager Bobby Heenan and announcer "Mean" Gene Okerlund.

I knew it was only a matter of time before the Road Warriors were going to take off and leave Verne as well, and then we'd have a hard time finding a high-profile tag team to draw money with.

"This is kind of an old, established-guy territory," I told Stan. "Maybe it's better if we just slide out when we're on top instead of giving them too long of a notice."

It was customary to give the promoter a two-week notice. The old-timers always warned me, "Don't burn a bridge with a promoter, kid. You never know when you'll have to go back there."

The way I figured it, if you left while you were on top and making money, it really didn't matter if you left early, because their last memory was that they'd made money with you, and they'd want you back regardless, and wouldn't hold it against you if you didn't give them a full two-week notice. If you lingered too long and fans lost interest, the promoter's final thought about you might have been that your drawing prowess had declined. Outstaying your ability to draw money was the last thought a wrestler ever wanted to be linked with.

After talking things over with Stan in the car that day, I made the decision to talk to Verne. Stan was very leery about the way I was going to handle things with Verne.

"You're not going to ruin it for me, right?" he asked me. "You know I'm *still* dating Kathy!"

It's not like I had a bad reputation for burning bridges, but I was also very straightforward and never minced words. I didn't hesitate to drop the bomb on people when I was ready to do so, and they knew that. They knew I wouldn't stick around if I was unhappy, and that I would be lightning quick to move on.

My skepticism was due to a lot of factors. Pro wrestling was a business of nepotism and cronyism, and I didn't have *anybody*. I couldn't count on anyone to look out for me in this business. I always felt like I could secure a more favorable deal if I left a place when I was hot, as opposed to when I was struggling. It's hard enough working your way up the cards when you're in a new territory, but when you're in the process of dropping back down the cards, it becomes very easy to develop a judgmental attitude. That's when you start getting jealous and aggravated about the people that are getting pushed instead of you.

A lot of old guys would accept getting de-pushed until their entrance music was once again the national anthem, their career was almost dead, and they had no clue what else to do with their lives.

If I felt like I was being used as a tool to get someone else over, as opposed to being featured as an attraction in my own right, I wouldn't hesitate to make a call to U-Haul to request the largest truck they had. In this case, my own family wasn't aware that we were leaving until the U-Haul truck rolled up.

"So I guess we're leaving?" asked Terri.

"Yep. Start packin'!" I said.

Even though I didn't have a place for us to go yet, I figured I should start the packing process and figure the rest out later.

I dropped the bomb on Verne when I saw him at the next television taping.

"How are you doing?" asked Verne with a smile when he saw me walking in.

"I'm doin' alright, but we're leavin'," I told him.

Verne's smile dropped into a scowl, as if he was wondering how personally he should take what I'd just told him.

"What's the matter?" Verne finally asked.

"I'm *miserable*!" I told him. "I'm really not happy here. The money is great, the travel is okay, but here's the deal: I'm freezin'! I don't want to be miserable even if I'm makin' money."

It was true. One of the reasons why I'd hated the idea of going to the WWF even though that door had been opened for us is because I dreaded the idea of living in the Northeast. The main WWF cities of New York, Boston, Philadelphia, and Pittsburgh were all in very cold areas, and Minneapolis, Chicago and Milwaukee were no better. I had zero interest in permanently settling anywhere in that territory.

I wanted to stay in the South. *Everything* was nicer in the South. People were also nicer in the South. If you drove to a Southern town for the very first time and had trouble finding the location you were supposed to be wrestling in, you could pull off and go to a 7-Eleven or any gas station. If you asked someone, "Hey, do you know where the Coliseum is?" someone would say, "Sure!" At a minimum, someone would write down the directions to the venue for you, and many people would go so far as to say, "Hey, do you want to follow me there? I can show you where it is!"

If I pulled off somewhere in New York and asked for directions to Madison Square Garden, there was a good chance the person would say, "What do I look like, pal? A road map? Find it *yourself*!"

I wasn't used to that sort of rudeness coming from the average citizens on the street. From Florida up to the Carolinas and Tennessee, everyone was very nice, but people in the North were always angry, and the further you drifted toward the Northeast, the angrier the people became.

It wasn't always about the kindness of strangers, either. Every time you changed territories, you had to think about getting a new doctor, a new auto mechanic, a new dentist, a new grocery store, a new gym, a new family restaurant to eat at, and new friends. In several situations, you had to figure some of those things out for every town you were working in. More importantly, you also had to learn about the places in the towns where you shouldn't go.

Once I had a family, that just added to the complications of decision-making. As a dad, I had to think about pediatricians, school districts, and those sorts of things. The people in the North and Northeast simply weren't as accommodating, and I simply wanted to interact with more pleasant people in my everyday life.

Everyone has to make choices in life, and this was one of those times when I allowed myself to be influenced by factors other than money.

I didn't tell Verne where we were going. Quite frankly, I didn't think it was really any of his business. Realistically, I didn't think there was any chance that I would ever be back in Minneapolis to work for him ever again, and I figured that I'd at least left him with the impression that Stan and I weren't leaving over anything that he could really control, or anything that he would take personally.

No promoter is ever happy when a talent is leaving, or at least not when that wrestler is making the decision to leave on their own. If the wrestler is giving their notice, then it means the promoter didn't get a chance to plan for it, and has to work around it.

During the period of time when Stan and I were making our transition from the AWA back to Memphis, Eddie Graham committed suicide by shooting himself *twice*. He'd shot himself a first time and blew his mouth out, then he had to cock the gun again and shoot himself in the temple. The thing is, he *still* didn't immediately die from his injuries.

Eddie tried to kill himself while Mike was away at the Super Bowl in San Francisco. Apparently, Eddie had tried to time his death so that his only son wouldn't be home when it happened. Unfortunately for everyone involved, Eddie remained on life support, and Mike had to be summoned while he was away at the Super Bowl so that he could quickly fly home, assess the situation, and pull the plug on his own dad. According to what I'd been told, Eddie's wife had caught him in bed with the lady that cleaned their house. He was also dealing with a lot of financial issues, several of which stemmed from the decline of his wrestling territory in Florida.

When it comes to Eddie Graham and my feelings toward him, people need to come to grips with the fact that your idols and your mentors will often let you down, and that's a scenario that played out in my life. With Eddie's drinking and his general conduct during my final tour of Florida, I was finished with Eddie Graham in my mind. I was also through with the entire notion that I owed him some sort of *eternal* debt for getting me started in the wrestling business.

Reciprocity and loyalty are nice sentiments, but they can't guide your actions forever. At some point, you have to recognize when a debt has been more than repaid, and if you find yourself sticking around to be mistreated, then your loyalty has ventured into the realm of stupidity.

I had paid my dues in Eddie Graham's company, and I'd made plenty of money for him. I had the impression that Eddie had broken me into the business exclusively to be a jobber, and I had managed to surpass every expectation he'd set for me.

I'd originally compared Eddie to my dad and ranked him above my own dad at one point, as a star, as a man, and for the significance he held in my life. When Eddie died, I felt neither let down nor saddened, but I did lose every bit of remaining respect I had for Eddie when he committed suicide. Following that, I took my dad and pedestalized him far above Eddie.

Understanding what my father had done for his country, having been a POW twice, and the *years* of torture that he had endured during the process, it truly made what Eddie had done seem like he'd taken the coward's way out by comparison. I'd overlooked my father and not given him his due, and I'd placed my faith and my respect in Eddie thinking that he could be an adequate substitute. That had been a *grave* mistake.

At the time of his death, Eddie no longer held any meaning for me. I didn't want to grow up to be Eddie Graham. I was *done* with that. I had no desire to emulate a man who had absolutely every physical possession that a person could ever want in his life, only to commit suicide when things got difficult and destroy his family in the process.

Life is tough. There are trials and tribulations in life that everyone has to go through. I can't walk in everybody's shoes, but I can honestly say that people who end their lives and leave behind devastated children and grandchildren to grieve over them have no feelings, thoughts or love for the ones they're leaving behind. I have *zero* respect for that.

I had my own family, and I'd been blessed with a choice my father never received, which was to remain with them, care for them and watch them develop. I wanted to be an honorable man like my father, and I wanted to dedicate my life to being there for my family.

The person I definitely did *not* want to be like was Eddie Graham. No matter what else happened in my life, I didn't want to grow up to be *that* guy.

TWENTY

While Stan and I were off in the AWA, Jerry Jarrett had tried to replicate our success by creating a knockoff edition of the Fabs called "The New Fabulous Ones," comprising Eddie Gilbert and Tommy Rich. It was like Kentucky Fried Chicken; if Stan and I had been the original recipe, Eddie and Tommy were Jarrett's attempt at producing an extra-crispy version.

Tommy Rich absolutely *hated* being tossed into a Fabulous Ones revival group. He had already established a name for himself on a national level during his run in Georgia and through his appearances on the TBS cable network. Conversely, Eddie Gilbert was a great worker who was capable of doing anything, but he had far less name recognition than Tommy, and was infinitely happier simply to have a job.

They were a shameless carbon copy of the original Fabs in a lot of ways. They appeared in the same style of music videos, while wearing the exact same outfits, and then they came out and worked matches like us while executing moves similar to ours. Eddie Gilbert had a decent body, but Tommy Rich always had a bit of chubbiness to his physique. He simply didn't train and diet with the same discipline that Stan and I did. He was excellent at being Tommy "Wildfire" Rich, but he was a very poor substitution for Stan Lane.

I honestly don't know what Jarrett had been thinking. If Dusty Rhodes left Florida, you couldn't just trot out another fat guy with a birthmark on his belly, ask him to talk with a lisp, and call him "The *New* Dusty Rhodes." At best, it still would have been a piss-poor impersonation of Dusty.

We knew Jarrett wanted us back, and so did everyone else who was working in Tennessee. I received updates from plenty of people who remained in Memphis or started wrestling there after we left, including Tracy Smothers. Their territory had caved in without us. It didn't matter who was there attempting to replace us; no one could even come *close* to replicating what Stan and I had been able to accomplish in that territory. No matter how they tried to bury us and replace us, the Fabulous Ones were irreplaceable.

It's like Jackie Fargo said: "Often imitated, but *never* duplicated, Daddy!"

Striking a defensive stance against Eddie Gilbert

Even if we'd burned a bridge by walking out on a sold-out crowd in Louisville, I knew Jarrett would still want us back if we could help draw an audience. Some of the guys in this business who have pulled the dirtiest double-crosses on promoters would end up coming back later, getting put over, and making even more money. There is a long list of guys in this business who walked out on territories or refused to put other wrestlers over only to return to the same place a year or two later and benefit financially from it.

I had been the driving force behind our team's departure from Memphis in the first place, so it made logical sense that Stan would be the one to talk to Jarrett just in case Jarrett had been harboring any lingering embers of resentment towards me.

We'd been making such good money that the idea of taking a steep cut in pay just to return to Memphis when we didn't really need to leave the AWA in the first place was a painful one. We were going from a big-city territory with huge attendances to small Southern towns with only two relatively large cities – Louisville and Memphis – with Lexington thrown into the mix once a month. We were both concerned that we would be taking a massive reduction in pay by returning to wrestle for Jerry Jarrett.

"Let me talk to him," said Stan. "I'll see if I can get some kind of a guarantee from him."

Stan actually handled the business of our return to Memphis, and arranged for each of us to receive a downside guarantee from Jerry Jarrett. That was great in theory, but when you have that sort of a guarantee, it attracts a lot of heat from the other wrestlers. When someone in the territorial era had a deal like that, everyone was going to find out pretty quickly. The second that the wrestlers in the Memphis dressing room found out that we had a downside guarantee that ensured us a minimum dollar figure each night that most of them weren't even close to making, they were all pretty upset.

Upon our return, I felt the heat from Lawler, Dundee and others due to our guarantee. However, they didn't say anything to us directly; if the territory is collectively attracting fans, everyone involved with it is making more money no matter where they are on the card.

The company put together a video set to "The Boys Are Back In Town," which was well-suited to the idea that we were returning to revitalize the territory, and all of the fans should get amped up to see the Fabulous Ones once again. They also did a video for us to the song "Born In The USA" and a few other videos set to newer hits to try to promote us. However, it soon became painfully obvious that we simply didn't have the star power that we'd once had.

Unfortunately for everyone involved in the Tennessee territory, the fans did *not* treat us the same when we returned as they had before we left. Thanks to the spin that Jarrett had placed on the Fabs' departure from Memphis, it had been inferred by the fans that Stan and I had shit on them.

In the words of the commentary team, we had supposedly grown too big for our britches and felt like we had outgrown the Memphis territory. We had turned our backs on the fans and left for larger territories to chase bigger paychecks. They had buried us in our absence, and it was difficult to rekindle the spark that had once been there, especially after Jarrett had attempted to replace us with such a pale imitation.

Gaining an advantage of Rip Morgan of the Kiwi Sheepherders

The fans had this impression that the Fabulous Ones were sellouts who were constantly looking for bigger and better mountains to climb, and it would only be a matter of time before we bailed out on Tennessee once again and sought the limelight in a larger territory. We weren't receiving the effortless babyface reactions that had once rained down upon us. Instead, we were met with such mixed reactions from the audiences that casual observers might have thought we were borderline heels. Many of the fans resented us, and plenty of people in the audience outright *booed* us. Very few fans accepted our explanation that we had to go off somewhere and accomplish something for ourselves before returning to them.

There were also fans who wouldn't commit to us because they assumed that if we weren't happy, we would abruptly leave them hanging once again, and there *was* some truth to that. Everyone was aware that neither Stan nor I was from Tennessee. We hadn't grown up there like many of their heroes. The fans knew I was from Florida, and a lot of them suspected Stan was also from Florida. They assumed both of us would be headed for Florida before too long, and there was *some* truth to that as well.

For all of those reasons and more, the Memphis territory simply wasn't the same friendly place it had once been for the Fabulous Ones.

Although the return of the Fabs hadn't lit the territory on fire as expected, we were *still* sitting on a guarantee that assured us that we were going to make our money. I wasn't counting the houses anymore with the head counter like I used to. There had been a time when I would go to Jarrett and let him know what the real figure was, and let him know if I felt he was being ripped off. With our payoff guarantee in place, I no longer cared.

No one ever spoke to Stan and I directly about our guaranteed deal, but it was certainly the talk of the dressing room at times, and difficult to avoid.

"If the Fabs are such a big deal, why aren't the houses sold out?" some people would chime in. "I thought the *boys* were supposed to be back in town!"

There were plenty of snide comments, but the majority of the guys wanted us to draw, because it would guarantee that their money would also come up.

We wanted our guarantee because it meant we didn't have to blindly accept whatever the promoters wanted to hand us at the end of the week. No matter how many nights we worked in a week, we were guaranteed to get paid a set amount.

"I don't want to go to these little towns to waste time and nickel-and-dime," I told Jarrett. "If you don't want us to go to a little town, just let us sit at home."

In some respects, our guarantee backfired. Smaller promoters – like Buddy Wayne who ran small towns in Mississippi – didn't want to use us. Buddy knew the first chunk of guaranteed money had to go to the Fabulous Ones, and then everyone else would have to split the remainder of the money. So there was heat between us and some of the promoters who ran small towns, and there was also heat between us and Jerry Jarrett's mom, Teeny.

"She's like this one school teacher that I had once," Stan used to say.

Teeny would pull Stan aside and ask him things because she knew I would have lied straight to her face. She could *always* tell. If she asked me a question and I didn't want to tell her the truth, I would just casually lie while looking her dead in the eyes. She wasn't *my* mom, so I didn't feel any obligation to tell her the truth.

Now that we were back in Tennessee, Stan and I were no longer selling t-shirts and hats at the concession area. We only sold photos and bandanas, because the bandanas were just a square piece of one-size-fits-all material. They cost us 10 cents each to have them made, and we sold them for $2.00 apiece. You could carry a stack of 1,000 of them to your town without them taking up all of the space in the trunk of your car.

When Teeny Jarrett would come up to me because she had run out of Fabulous Ones' pictures in her town, she'd say, "Steve, do you have any extra pictures with you?"

"No, we don't," I'd tell her.

That was a bold-faced lie of course. We usually carried *thousands* of photos at a time, including four or five different poses of us in 8x10s to tiny 3x5s.

The thing is, it was bad business for us to give our photos to Teeny. She would take what we had in our inventory, pay us back the 10 cents per photo that we had invested in their creation, and then pay us another 10 percent of the sale price. When we sold them ourselves in the southernmost parts of the territory, Mr. and Mrs. Coffee would sell the photos at their concession stand, giving Stan and I the full payoff from the merchandise that was sold, and then we would give them the 10 percent. So we were making far more money from concession sold in the southern region, but in the north we weren't making *nearly* as much.

Early on when we were buying the photos from Jimmy Cornette in Louisville, Teeny could ask around and would know straight away that Jim had just sold us 2,000 pictures because she was also from Louisville.

"Steve, we need some pictures," Teeny asked me. "We've run out of them completely. Do you have any pictures?"

"No. Sorry. We don't have any," I lied.

"Okay..." said Teeny.

Then Teeny would run right off to find Stan.

"Stan... don't you lie to me," she would begin. "Steve just lied to me. Don't be like Steve. Steve is a *liar*."

Then Stan would tell her the truth. He'd be so nervous like he had to answer to his mom. He'd have to look around in every place but Teeny's eyes and shuffle his feet. He just wasn't a very gifted liar.

Stan had a guilt complex; I had a *business* complex.

Once we were in the car, Stan said, "Oh my God! It's like my *principal* had me!"

"Stan, *relax*!" I told him. "Jerry isn't going to give us our notice because we're not givin' his *mom* pictures. If he wants to say somethin' to me, I'll just come right out and tell him."

Bashing my opponent with a board

I could pretty much tell Jerry Jarrett anything. Even if Jarrett didn't like what we were doing, he would never let on that it bothered him. He was very much a businessman and promoter. He could recognize that his mom wasn't loved by everyone in the business, and he didn't make it an obligation that everyone needed to adore his mom in order to work for him.

Due to the time Stan and I spent tussling with the Road Warriors in the AWA, apparently a lot of the pre-Memphis stiffness returned to my wrestling, and I brought it back there with me. In particular, Dennis Condrey complained about me a lot during our first few bouts together.

"You're too stiff!" he would say. "You're actin' like this is all real! You know it's a work, right?"

All Dennis did was bitch about my work. He would work so loose whenever we'd lock up, like he didn't even want to touch his opponents at all. I'd been trained that lockups are the most important part of the match, and that's how you establish the believability of the match straight out of the gate. You have to lock up aggressively to show that you're into it.

Dennis didn't feel the same way. When we'd lock up, he'd be struggling against me and repeatedly saying, "Oh man! Oh man!" in his Southern accent. Then he'd throw in the occasional, "Loosen up!"

If anything, I *stiffened* up. When people would work with me too loosely, I would make it a point to go overboard because it was entertaining for me to make the loose wrestlers uncomfortable, and to force them to react to my intensity. That was *fun* to me, and when you're working about 360 days a year, and usually seven days a week, you need to enjoy what you're doing. Otherwise, you're just going through the paces and collecting a check.

When we got back to the dressing room, Stan would laugh and say, "I could hear Dennis sayin' 'Oh man' all the way around the ring!"

Curt Hennig was flying into Memphis, Tennessee to wrestle there for the first time. Along with a few other guys, I came up with a plan to rib Curt from the moment he arrived at Memphis International Airport.

Back then, airports didn't have the same level of security as they do today. In Memphis, this meant that I was able to go right out onto the tarmac and watch Curt get out of the plane.

I arranged for this humongous cop – a true redneck who stood 6'4" and weighed 400 lbs – to be waiting at the airport in uniform with an *authentic* arrest warrant to serve to Curt.

I remained hidden behind a huge, round pillar, and I could hear everything that was being said as Curt descended from the steps leading from the plane to the tarmac, and the burly cop approached him.

"Are you Curt Hennig?" the cop asked.

Curt thought the cop was a wrestling fan and extended a hand to shake hands with him.

Staying perfectly in character, the cop followed up by saying, "I don't wanna shake your hand, *boy*! You're under arrest!"

Curt was caught completely off guard and scanned the cop's face for signs that he was joking.

"*What?!*" Curt replied.

"Here you go; *read* it!" the cop said, as he shoved the warrant right under Curt's nose.

Curt studied the arrest warrant for "Kurt Hennig," and read all of the details. It explained that Curt was being arrested for statutory rape, and that a father had sworn out the warrant because he had overheard his daughter elaborating about her sexual escapades with Curt Hennig to one of her friends over the telephone. The father then confronted his daughter, and she reluctantly confessed that she'd had sex with Curt.

Curt's face gradually grew more contorted as panic seeped into his features. His face flushed a deep shade of red; I couldn't tell if the color change was due to embarrassment or worry.

"I've never even *been* to Memphis!" protested Curt.

"I can beat *that*!" replied the cop, sarcastically. "I've never arrested anyone who was actually *guilty* either!"

"What do we do?!" asked the nervous Curt.

"Well, you've got *two* ways to leave the airport," began the cop. "I can handcuff ya, and we can walk up there and get your bags, and you can go out and get in the back of my patrol car. We can take the drive. Or, if you *don't* want me to handcuff ya, I'll handcuff ya by force and drag your phony wrestlin' ass all the way through this airport. How 'bout *that*, boy?"

Once again, Curt studied that cop's face for any hint that the whole thing might be some sort of prank, but the cop didn't crack in the slightest bit. He sold it unbelievably well.

"I'll come with you, officer," said the defeated Curt. "But I *promise* you I've never been to Memphis!"

"Like I said, and I've *never* arrested anybody who's guilty," repeated the cop.

The officer handcuffed Curt's wrists in front of his body, and then he marched him right past the pillar where I remained obscured from Curt's view. The officer proceeded to walk the handcuffed wrestler through the airport and over to baggage claim to collect his bag. In the meantime, I ran out and got in my car, and then pulled it up and parked it behind the police car and waited.

Eventually, the officer emerged from the airport with the handcuffed and dejected-looking Curt Hennig still in front of him. He opened up the door to the backseat of the squad car and helped Curt get situated inside of it, and then he walked around to the other side, started up the car, and pulled off.

I followed closely behind them, and I could see Curt gesticulating wildly in the officer's direction. He was clearly in full freak-out mode, pleading his case to the massive officer. Meanwhile, in my own car, I was laughing so hard that my sides were aching.

It was a long drive to downtown Memphis, but we didn't quite make it all the way there. I found out later that Curt stammered when he told the officer, "I have a wife and four kids... *No*! I have a wife and *five* kids!"

The officer responded with, "See? You don't even know how many *kids* you've got!"

"I *do*!" Curt pleaded. "Isn't there *anything* I can do?"

"We can pull over, and you can call the dad's phone number and explain to him that it must be a case of mistaken identity cuz you've never been here," the cop answered. "His number is right on the warrant."

"Oh, man!" said Curt. "Let's do that! That's great!"

They pulled off the road and into the parking lot of a 7-Eleven that had a Shoney's Big Boy restaurant attached to it. I did the same, and pulled my car in alongside the squad car.

As I remained hidden behind the blacked-out windows of my vehicle, the officer opened Curt's door, and when Curt stood up, I heard him say to the officer, "I don't have any change."

"So now you want me to lend ya a quarter, *too*?" asked the annoyed officer.

"Could you?" pleaded Curt. "I have some dollars in my bag…"

The cop reached into his pocket, extracted a quarter and handed it to Curt, whose arms were still handcuffed in front of his body.

At that moment, I rolled down my window.

"Hey… where are *you* goin'?!" I asked Curt.

Curt looked at me with startled eyes, hesitated for a second, and then appeared to be simultaneously relieved and excited when he recognized the face of a friend.

"Oh, man!" exclaimed Curt. "The *shit's* on! The *shit's* on!"

Curt must have thought I was there by pure coincidence. I emerged from my car as if I had no clue how it was that Curt had found himself detained in the back of a Memphis police officer's patrol car. The two of us stood face to face between the two cars, while the officer stood on the walkway adjacent to the 7-Eleven.

"What's the matter?" I asked innocently.

"I've been arrested," answered Curt.

"You got arrested at the airport?" I chuckled.

"Yes!" said Curt.

"Well what did you get arrested for?" I pressed him.
"*Statutory rape!*" he yelled.
"You know… Curt…" I began. "I've been tellin' you for *years* that you need to leave those young girls alone."

My statement seemed to confirm the cop's initial suspicions that the charges against Curt were true. Curt glowered at me as if he wished death upon me.

The infamous warrant for Curt Hennig's arrest

"I'm just kiddin' officer," I said, in the hopes that it would lessen Curt's hatred for me somewhat.

"Here… read the warrant!" Curt said, and he shoved the warrant toward me.

I scanned the warrant line by line and said, "Yeah… okay… Curt Hennig… yeah… this is *your* phone number… yeah… Ooooo, *that* doesn't sound good…"

Curt looked altogether exasperated by the time my eyes reached the bottom of the page. Finally, I held the warrant in front of his face and said, "And see? Here's where *I* signed it! The *judge*!"

Curt stared at me as the revelation took a moment to sink in. I had signed the warrant as Judge "Stevens." Then Curt looked at the cop. As if to signal the end of an acting performance that had been worthy of an Academy Award, the officer *finally* burst into laughter. Then I started laughing, too.

"Son of a *bitch*!" screamed Curt.

Still handcuffed, Curt began to chase me, and I took off running completely around the Shoney's Big Boy restaurant. Curt was hot on my tail the entire time. I completed a full lap around the Shoney's and 7-Eleven, and Curt was *still* right at my heels, so I took a *second* lap.

By the time we'd completed the second lap, Curt was laughing uncontrollably.

"Stop! Stop!" laughed Curt. "I'm blown up! Just forget about it!"

This is one of the reasons it paid off that I always made friends with the cops who watched our matches. Because of the great relationships I formed with those cops, I was able to regularly rib guys by having them arrested during my career. It always works tremendously well. After all, who's going to argue with a *cop*?

It was great that I'd managed to indulge myself and rib absolutely everyone when opportunities presented themselves. However, none of that could distract me from two unavoidable realities: The return of the Fabs had been a bust, and I was getting older. Another change of scenery was required, and with any luck, it would be the final move of my career.

EPILOGUE

Financially, the Memphis territory was on its ass, and it wasn't going to get any better. There were no great teams on the horizon for Stan and I to work with that were really going to help us to bring the territory back to life. There were plenty of adequate workers around, but there were no standouts like the Road Warriors, the original Sheepherders, or even the Moondogs. There were no looming matchups that the fans were chafing at the bit to see.

Despite Memphis not being in great financial shape, what ultimately caused Stan and I to leave Memphis the second time around was the fact that I was already contemplating quitting the wrestling business. I had vowed as a young guy when I entered the business that I would never be an old wrestler. I didn't have a whole lot of respect for guys that I'd worked with who were really old and who were clearly trying to hang on for dear life.

Physically, I was still in the best shape of my life. I could have wrestled for an hour without a problem with any NWA world champion – from Harley Race or Terry Funk to Ric Flair – and I could have done it in any building in the world, and without any air conditioning system on the premises. However, I knew that it all had to end at some point, and I needed to prepare myself to walk away from pro wrestling.

I was already starting to see the end of my career coming. I didn't know what I was going to do going forward, but I had some ideas in my head.

When the Fabs finally pulled the plug on Tennessee at the conclusion of 1985, it was because I was homesick and wanted to return to Florida. The only issue was that Florida had now been taken over by the Crocketts, who were based out of Charlotte. Hiro Matsuda kept the Florida territory clinging to life somehow or another, but the Crocketts were moving in, and the territory was deteriorating.

It was clear to see what was happening. Cable television had made it so easy to draw the eyes of fans from all over the country and to market to them. If you had money and access to cable television, you could showcase all of your wrestlers in major venues with high production values supporting your broadcasts. You could also clearly trot out all of the departed superstars from the raided local territories and present them before the fans who had supported them, rubbing their noses in the fact that the wrestlers they *really* wanted to see could no longer be found in their favorite local venues because those wrestlers were playing in a bigger, better sandbox

Vince McMahon Jr. had capitalized on the access he'd had to the USA Network and MTV. He was now getting to showcase his *Saturday Night's Main Event* specials on NBC, and he was able to bring the WWF almost anywhere he wanted and outclass and outdraw whichever incumbents were there. This included Florida.

My buddy Terry "Hulk Hogan" Bollea – the guy I'd advised to steer clear of wrestling because there was no money in it – was the most popular wrestler on *earth*. He was earning more money in a single year than I'd made in my entire career, and plenty of stars were drawn to the WWF simply hoping to land within hailing distance of wrestling against Hogan, or on the undercards of his shows.

It was difficult to fathom. With Hogan leading the charge, Vince was laying waste to the territories. None of my mentors, from Eddie Graham to Jack Brisco, had predicted an event like this. As I was witnessing this, I knew I needed to find another viable career that I could transition to as quickly as possible. I also needed to make that move while I was still young enough that I could get into another profession without being considered too old to get into it. That was the main reason we returned to Florida: It was my *home*.

With that being said, it wasn't an abrupt decision. Rather it was a consequence of the conversations Stan and I were having while riding together in the car every night, when we had nothing else to do but to talk about the state of the wrestling business. We both knew the Tennessee territory was underperforming, and we didn't see any signs of improvement on the horizon.

Driving a knee into Rip Morgan's skull

"I'm pretty tired of all this," I said to Stan.

"Tired of what?" he asked.

"*Everything.* I kinda just want to go back to Florida and figure out something else to do," I said.

"You want to quit wrestling?" asked Stan.

"Not yet, but I need to do it soon," I said. "I can't be movin' my kids all over the place every year or two. I just need to make the move back home and figure it out from there."

The objective in my mind was to move to Tampa and make it the final move of my life, at least as far as the city I lived in was concerned. I had no desire to relocate my family ever again. I wasn't planning to pursue the wrestling world anymore, and especially if it would require me to uproot my family and drag them to a place where I didn't truly wish to live. If a wrestling career couldn't pan out for me while I was living in Florida, then I would no longer be a wrestler.

Terri was receptive to the idea of moving back to Florida even though there was so much uncertainty as to what the next step in my career's progression would be. Thankfully, I was blessed with a wife who was willing to accept whatever I wanted to do, because she was with me 100 percent.

I contacted Hiro Matsuda to get Stan and I booked, and then we said our goodbyes in Memphis and hit the road. Whatever happened in Championship Wrestling from Florida, I was determined to make that my last stand in the wrestling business. I felt like I had already been in every wrestling territory that I ever needed to be in, and checked every item off of my essential wrestling bucket list. Besides, I didn't have the political connections necessary to be a major success in a wrestling business where true money-making opportunities were shrinking. I was going to plant my feet in Florida and figure out the rest of my life from there.

Stan and I arrived to discover that the Florida territory was in a state of pure chaos. Nobody knew what they were doing. Nobody knew how to run the territory properly. Hiro Matsuda had been a successful trainer, but he wasn't a true promoter, and he was doing everything he could just to hang on while the business was in a state of pure turmoil.

Mike Graham still wielded some control in the office with respect to Hiro Matsuda, and he managed to manipulate his way into a few things. Mike and I had been spread apart for years at that point, and he wanted to know why I didn't call him or contact him in the aftermath of his father's suicide. The thing was, I no longer had any lingering respect or admiration remaining in me for Mike's father. Don't get me wrong: It was tragic, but I wasn't sad about it.

I was also no longer inextricably tied to Championship Wrestling from Florida. I'd worked in several other territories since the last time I'd left Florida, including major runs in Memphis and the AWA. I wasn't the same kid who'd left years ago; I was a mature guy that had been through Jim Barnett, Ole Anderson, Antonio Inoki, Jerry Jarrett, and Verne Gagne.

I also hadn't forgotten what had driven me out of Florida in the first place. At one time, I'd thought of Eddie as being the equivalent to a father, and Mike as being like my brother. However, both of them had made it crystal clear through their actions that I wasn't as irreplaceable to them as I'd once thought I was, and from Mike's perspective, I was a situational sibling *at best*.

The Fabulous Ones stand victorious in the steel cage

Now that I was back, it was easy to see the differences between our personalities. I departed and matured out of necessity. I'd been successful elsewhere, and I'd accomplished it without the protection of a high-ranking family member. Mike was still in the same place he had always been in.

I'm not saying Mike openly envied me, but it wasn't the same relationship it had been before. I was the kind of guy who would stand up to promoters and question things, and I had also been a bigger fish in an even bigger pond. I now had significantly less respect for people who played it safe, lived off the reputations of their family members, and never tried to forge their own paths in life.

Through no fault of his own, everything around Hiro Matsuda was deteriorating and only adding to the complications. The towns were weak, the territory was weak, and the payoffs were weak. It was a constant struggle, and it was plain to see that we were probably going to be eyewitnesses the death of true territorial wrestling in the United States.

That's not to say that the in-ring product in Florida was that bad. Stan and I wrestled quite a bit against Kendo Nagasaki and the young White Ninja, who was Keiji Muto of Japan. Muto would eventually become a star in the U.S. as The Great Muta, and an even *bigger* star back in his home country. This is representative of the fact that the Florida shows still had several excellent workers performing on them during that time, but that didn't do much to improve the overall quality of the promotion.

You could walk out to the ring and work with the greatest wrestlers in the world, but if a promoter is lacking in the knowledge, the money, or the resources to support a territory and keep it running, it will eventually fall apart no matter how talented the wrestlers are. *Period.*

Still, we did the best we could. We tried angle after angle to try to attract interest. We did one angle where I didn't show up for a tag match at the Tampa Spartan Sport Center – the renamed Fort Homer Hesterly Armory – because I'd been beaten up in the parking lot. In reality, I simply went outside, rolled around in the dirt, and then walked into the building wearing dirty jeans and a filthy t-shirt, and then limped inside looking like I'd just been mugged.

It was well received, and it was a good angle. The people we worked with tried hard, but it was like the handwriting was figuratively on the wall already. I knew that it was all coming to an end.

Things had come full-circle for me. When I'd started out in Florida, I accepted everything. I was strictly a job guy for five years, and never made more than $350 a week. I accepted whatever came my way because I had such a burning passion for the business. *That* was over.

When I came back to Florida, I had an independent mindset and my own set of goals. That's why I bonded with Barry Windham. He was a second-generation wrestler, and I knew his father Blackjack Mulligan was one of those guys who would stand up to the same way I aspired to do.

Mike wasn't receptive to my choice of friends at all. We didn't ride together often or hang out at all during this time. We no longer went fishing together or did anything requiring the use of his boats or his other aquatic toys. I already had a family and was trying to pattern my life a different way. It was time for the fun and games to be over with. I could sense that the wrestling business was changing, and I wasn't certain that I still wanted to be a part of it.

My loss of interest in wrestling was a slow burn. Returning to wrestling in Florida made me feel like I was back in Robinson High School with all of my peers, and wondering what I was going to be when I had finally grown up. The thing is, I was *supposed* to be a grown-up now, and the business that I had dedicated my life to appeared to be dying.

Stan and I still had some notable matches during that period. We faced the updated version of the Sheepherders, consisting of Luke Williams and Butch Miller. At that point, we were the heels and the Sheepherders were the babyfaces. The most significant event from those matches occurred when Luke gave me improper information during a bout.

"Butch is gonna duck; throw a punch," said Luke.

Following Luke's instructions, I wound up and swung at Butch as hard as I could, except Butch didn't duck. Instead, the blow connected, and Butch crumpled to the mat, unconscious. I stared at Butch's limp form, and then turned my head to look at Luke.

"Well, I guess maybe he's *not* gonna duck," Luke shrugged.

Stan and I also ventured up from Florida to work with Barry Windham and Mike Rotunda at the AWA's WrestleRock event. It was a colossal stadium show that seemed to be Verne Gagne's attempt to get something going on the level of the WWF's Wrestlemania event. Stan and I were just there to get Barry and Mike over, and then neither one of us ever went back. Vince was tearing things down in the territories so quickly that the AWA was never in a strong enough position to host a stadium show ever again.

Slapping a front facelock on Mike Rotunda at WrestleRock

Back in Florida, guys were bailing out on the promotion left and right. They weren't sticking around like past wrestlers who had a goal in mind of living in Florida and spending their entire careers there if possible. Everyone seemed to be biding their time until they could jump ship to work for the WWF, to sign a deal with one of the companies in Japan, or to land a spot on the roster of the Crocketts in the Carolinas.

This made things frustrating for both the remaining Florida wrestlers and the fans, because you couldn't depend on a wrestler beginning an angle and then seeing it through to its conclusion. You didn't know if they were going to be there from week to week. You didn't even know if the *territory* was going to be there. We felt like we were gambling with our lives, our money, and our careers just by remaining there. It was difficult to deal with.

It was also time for the Fabulous Ones to die. Stan was a single guy with no intentions of ending his wrestling career, and he needed to go on and progress in the wrestling business as best he could. We eventually stopped riding together, and had began hanging out with different groups of guys. I'd told him up front that this move to Florida would be the final move I would be making. When I started riding more often with Barry Windham, Stan started riding with Lex Luger. Stan knew my interest in the business was fading, and I wasn't shy about letting him know that.

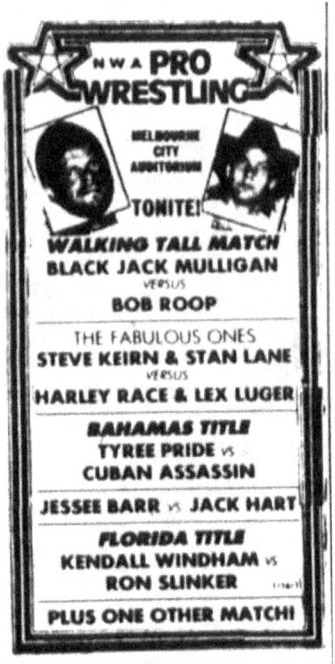

Stan needed to move on, and I didn't want to hold him back by any means. It wouldn't have done his career any good to be lingering in Florida with me while the territory was collapsing around us.

That isn't to say that I allowed my performance level to slip. When I was working against people, I always worked hard, and the people I worked with still gave their best efforts. Also, the Crocketts hadn't completely abandoned Florida quite yet. I *did* wrestle Ric Flair for the world championship in Fort Lauderdale in a solid match that ended in disqualification and enabled me to look strong after Flair left.

I didn't have a college degree or any other sort of expertise to fall back on, and I decided real estate was one of the only professions that I could possibly learn to do well since other wrestling industry people had excelled in it without possessing much of a formal education. My two-year associate of arts degree was absolutely useless in the 1980s workforce. I couldn't quickly become a doctor or a lawyer, but I assumed I could capitalize on being a household name that was recognizable to so many Florida residents, and turn that into a lucrative business where people would feel inclined to come to me for assistance with purchasing real estate.

Taking the fight to world champion Ric Flair

Much like the wrestling industry, the real estate market could also be very hard to predict, but at least it was showing positive trends. I could recall plenty of wrestling promoters who had earned a lot of money in real estate, including Eddie Graham, Mike Graham, the Fullers, Lester Welch and Verne Gagne. They were buying up properties and leveraging them for additional income.

The Fabulous Wrestling Life of Steve Keirn

When I was riding to shows with Barry Windham, I was literally studying for the State of Florida's real estate license exam. I would study the real estate textbook the entire way to whatever venue we were wrestling in. It's 300 miles from Tampa to Miami, so that gave me plenty of time to read through things while Barry drove. Barry drove a Porsche at 100 miles per hour all the time, and he would drive while listening to his headphones. We could leave really late, and Barry would drive so fast that it wouldn't even matter.

Not only did I have the real estate textbook, but I also had the guidebook for taking the realtor's examination. I utilized what was usually just discarded as wasted travel time as an opportunity to study for my test.

Barry provided me with significant assistance while I was studying for my real estate examination. On the way to our shows, I would say to Barry, "I want you to ask me this question out of the blue sometime while we're driving back home tonight."

Barry would nod, and then when we were in the midst of our return trips, he would glance over at me, lower his headphones from his ears, and then ask me a question like, "What kind of relationship do you need to have if you're a real estate guy?"

"Fiduciary relationship!" I would yell.

"I *think* that's right," Barry would nod.

It's not like Barry actually knew, but I appreciated him for making sure I remembered what I was supposed to have been learning.

I managed to pass the exam, and I had that in my back pocket just in case the industry went under.

It would be a lie if I said that all of my time in the car with Barry was spent studying for my real estate exam. I'd also recently bought a nine-millimeter, 15-round pistol, and as we were driving down around West Palm and Fort Lauderdale, we cut through a two-lane backroad, and I said, "Pull the car over. I want to shoot some signs to test out my new gun!"

Barry politely pulled the car over, and when we got out, Barry assumed a position standing just behind me and to the right of me. I opened that nine-millimeter up and began unloading the clip into a road sign, firing off rounds one after the other as they perforated the metal. It was nighttime, it was dark outside, and I couldn't see all that well, but out of the corner of my eye, I could faintly make out the shape of Barry's body rolling down into a nearby ditch. I couldn't *imagine* what he might have been doing.

Not wanting to be distracted, I continued to empty the nine-millimeter's clip into the road sign. Then I decided to turn toward Barry to see what his issue was. My first thought was that a shell casings had ejected from the gun and had burned one of his legs since he was wearing shorts. I was about to laugh at him for vastly overselling it.

I walked over to Barry and looked down upon him as he was writhing in the ditch.

"Barry, what are you doing?!" I asked him.

"You *shot* me!" he screamed.

"There's no way!" I responded. "You were standing behind me and I'm shooting way over there! *How* could I have shot you?!"

"I swear! You shot me!" he continued. "You shot me in the thigh!"

I helped Barry up, and we maneuvered his leg in front of his car's headlights. Sure enough, on the inside of his right leg was a bullet fragment. Luckily, it wasn't deeply embedded in his leg; a portion of it was still protruding from the wound. We squeezed the area around his wound and managed to yank the bullet fragment out. From there, Barry poured a bit of beer on the wound and tied a bandana over the top of it.

I figured out later on that the posts that hold speed-limit signs aren't round; they're horseshoe shaped with holes all along their length. One of those nine-millimeter rounds I fired hit the post, and a fragment ricocheted off of the post and connected with Barry's leg.

For years, I was the guy who was famous for shooting future NWA World Heavyweight Champion Barry Windham in the leg. It's a shame that it could never have been turned into a wrestling angle, as it's hard to get more personal than *actually* shooting a fellow wrestler, accident or no accident.

The legend has it that Barry wrestled Harley Race the next night with a fresh bullet wound, as if a hole had been blown *clean* through his leg. The version of the story that I've heard Barry tell is that I pulled out the gun without it being on safety, and accidentally shot him in the thigh at point-blank range while we were in the car.

It makes for a great story, but it's *far* from the truth. If I'd shot Barry point-blank in the thigh while sitting two feet away from him in a car, we'd have needed to go to the hospital immediately to address the entry and exit wounds in his leg. A tiny splattering of beer and a makeshift bandana tourniquet wouldn't have fixed *that*.

Even as things were looking desperate in Florida, we began to hear word that the Crocketts' operation was also in dire financial straits. Stan was preparing to take off and head for the Crocketts to partner with Bobby Eaton in an updated version of the Midnight Express. It's not like he was asking for my permission to do so, nor was he obligated to do so.

Stan had gotten a ton of experience, and was a *phenomenal* wrestler. If he had stayed in Florida, all I could have advised him to do was go into real estate alongside me, which would have made no sense, and wouldn't have been fair to him. He was younger than I was and didn't have the attachment of a family like I did, so he could afford to take risks that I couldn't.

The imminent death of Championship Wrestling from Florida started to become a topic of everyday conversation. There were rumors circulating through the dressing room that the territory was grinding to a halt. Hiro Matsuda wasn't about to leave Florida because he lived in Tampa, but the Crocketts were rapidly losing their interest in subsidizing the territory and keeping it going, as they had their own financial woes to contend with.

Instead of seven nights a week, we were soon only wrestling five nights a week. If your promotion began to run shows on fewer dates, it was usually a clear sign that something was amiss. We also didn't have any help coming in from the Carolinas, either from people who were coming down to help run the shows, or from wrestlers who could help us strengthen the cards.

The people who remained in charge of CWF still had a conscience when it came to payoffs, so even when the territory was failing, I was still earning a decent salary. If I could have continued making decent money with Championship Wrestling from Florida, I'm sure that I would have stayed on with them since there was nothing physically wrong with me. As long as I was making money, I was happy. But soon there was no longer any money to be made at all.

An announcement was ultimately made in September of 1987 that Championship Wrestling from Florida was in the midst of its final week of live events ever, so everyone started making their plans to leave after that week reached its conclusion. I have a lot of respect for all of the guys who could have bailed out ahead of time but opted to remain in Florida and see things through to the bitter end. For some of the less skilled workers, it was reasonable to think that they were staring down their final opportunities to earn money as professional wrestlers.

In several respects, it was an inauspicious end to what had once been – in my opinion – the very best wrestling territory in the entire National Wrestling Alliance. Despite its heartrending end, no one could ever erase what the Sunshine State had contributed to professional wrestling during the territorial era. So many of the most famous wrestlers in history had either developed into superstars in Florida – like Jack Brisco and Dusty Rhodes – or had gotten their starts in Florida – like Hulk Hogan.

Even if a Florida-based wrestling territory no longer existed, the CWF had left an indelible mark on the professional wrestling industry, and it is impossible to tell the history of professional wrestling without mentioning it *several* times.

As for me, I was honestly hoping that I would never again have to rely on the wrestling business to support my family ever again. Mentally, I had checked out of wrestling, and I was preparing for life as a real estate agent. I didn't want to be a washed-up old wrestler who was begging for work, so I totally walked away from a full-time career in pro wrestling and vowed to *never* seriously pursue it again.

... for about *eight* months. See, stepping away from professional wrestling may have been my plan at the time, but as they say, time makes fools of us all. The rest of the story involves alligators, clowns, failure, recovery, more failure, more recovery, and eventually, *total* redemption. However, that's a story for another time.

Afterword

When I got hired by WWE in January of 2007, my entire life changed. I left my entire life behind in Calgary, Alberta, Canada and I was quickly sent down to the company's developmental program at the time, which was Florida Championship Wrestling. FCW was where Steve Keirn was in charge of the company's developmental talent. Steve became my introduction to WWE, and I didn't realize it at the time, but it was critically important for me to be able to meet someone like Steve right out of the gate.

You meet a lot of different characters in the wrestling business, and not everyone is kind, nurturing, generous and loving. Steve was all of those things - like a father figure to people who didn't have a proper father figure. But Steve was also firm, honest and genuine. Having him as a wrestling coach was like having a teacher that you really wanted to do well for, and whose class you wanted to earn a good grade in because you didn't want to disappoint them. I never wanted to be late, and I never wanted to miss a practice. I always wanted to be there early, and I always wanted to be the last person remaining in class because I loved being around Steve. He just made me feel so accepted. Steve also made me want to be a better person. Not just professionally, but personally.

Inside the ring, Steve was a hand's-on coach. He taught me how to do my first up-and-over, which is like a vault out of the turnbuckle. He would always say, "You can't use the bottom rope. Everybody uses the bottom rope. I want *you* to be a girl that doesn't need to use the bottom rope." To this day, I'm one of the only women that knows how to do an up-and-over without the bottom rope because Steve took the time to teach me that.

However, the value of Steve's advice wasn't limited to in-ring applications. Steve also helped me to keep my head on straight. If your head isn't on straight, and your mental health isn't in check, and you don't feel good about yourself, or you don't feel confident, you're not going to be able to have great matches. This is especially true when you work for a global entertainment juggernaut like WWE. Steve taught me that relationships in this industry are everything and it's so important to cultivate great relationships at every corner. We all need each other to do great work.

Steve Keirn with TJ Wilson and Natalya Neidhart

  Thanks to Steve's guidance, I was able to survive the challenges of the locker room and the road, and also the changes in management as the company evolved. I think the reason we had such an incredible crop of students that came out of FCW and became such huge stars in WWE is because of Steve's careful coaching and his way of handling people from every walk of life.
  It's crazy to think about how long ago my training in the WWE's developmental system took place. As I write this, I'm entering my 16th year with the company as the longest-

tenured female in WWE history, and also as the female with the most overall matches, pay-per-view matches and wins. To me, the foundation that Steve helped to lay down for me in my earliest and most impressionable years in the WWE is what has propelled me to where I am today. Steve believed in me and really took me under his wing. He's a person that changes other people's lives in the best possible way.

    I attribute so much of my longevity in WWE to Steve and the way he was able to blend kindness, love, generosity and acceptance with firmness and honesty. He gave me so many tools for success in the wrestling business and in life, and I'll never be able to repay him for everything he gave me.

Natalya Neidhart

AUTHOR'S ACKNOWLEDGEMENTS

I would like to take this opportunity to thank all of those who contributed so much in my life's story.

First and foremost my God, my Lord and Savior Jesus Christ who carried me the whole way, through the ups and downs. He was always just a prayer away.

To my wife of 43 years Terri, who stayed with me and was my right arm, never tapping out: Your strength and faith picked me up when times got rough. You raised our kids and did an incredible job. To say I love you would be an understatement; you are my Sunshine forever.

To Heidi: I was the first one to lay my hands on you welcoming you to this world. It was love at first sight. You were beautiful then and have been beautiful your entire life, both inside and out. I'm so proud of the woman you have become. Thank you for being the perfect daughter, mother, and pal. I love you, Sweetpea.

To Cory: thank you Son for your love and respect. You are an awesome man and father. You grew up with me gone a lot and never complained. Your mom did the hard work of raising kids in the fast lane of entertainment life.

I also want to include my parents in my thank yous. What a couple of solid rocks to have been blessed to call "Mom" and "Dad." Setting the bar in a military family taught me several of life's crucial lessons: "God, Family, Country, Faith, Love, Respect, Kindness, Patience, Humbleness, and Forgiveness."

They were my Heroes. Dad was the REAL DEAL as a MAN. Mom raised me and led me to Jesus by my witness to her on her knees at night praying. It doesn't get any better.

Thank you, Dad and Mom. I love you, and rest in peace.

While I'm at it, I want to say thank you to all my mentors, tag partners, opponents, and the refs that played a vital role in my career. Also, thank you to all of the promoters, bookers, commentators, friends and fans that I ever interacted with. To have been blessed to share my life with so many AWESOME PEOPLE is truly humbling.

Sincerely, thank you all.

Steve Keirn

Steve Keirn

BIOGRAPHER'S ACKNOWLEDGEMENTS

Thank you to Steve for choosing me to help you narrate the first leg of your life story. It isn't a responsibility that I take lightly.

Also, thank you to anyone who helped with this project in even the smallest of ways. I hope you are able to take pride in the finished product.

On a personal note, I'd like to individually thank Dan Severn, Dylan "Hornswoggle" Postl, Michael "Buggsy McGraw" Davis and B. Brian Blair for permitting me to be involved with the telling of their life stories. Every project challenges me to become a better writer, and elevates my level of experience leading into each successive book. Thank you for providing me with these opportunities.

Thank you to the guys who continuously encourage me to strive to become a better writer through word and deed, like Erik Love, Oliver Lee Bateman, Phil Schneider, Ross Owen Williams and Jonathan Snowden. You're *all* tremendous.

Also, thank you to all of the entities that have ever permitted me to write about professional wrestling outside of these books, including *The Ringer*, *Men's Health Magazine*, *MEL Magazine*, and the International Pro Wrestling Hall of Fame. These have been dream-come-true opportunities for me.

My family continues to be the best in the world. Special thanks is directed to Janet Douglass, James and Pauline Douglass, James Douglass II and his family, and my phenomenal wife Teisha.

Philippians 2:3-4: "Do nothing from selfish ambition or conceit, but in humility count others more significant than yourselves. Let each of you look not only to his own interests, but also to the interests of others."

Ian C. Douglass

CREDITS

Author:
Steve Keirn

Coauthor/Biographer/Editor:
Ian Douglass

Forewords:
Stan Lane
CM Punk

Afterword:
Natalya Neidhart

Cover Art:
Scott Middleton

Behind-the-Scenes Help:
Terri Keirn
Heidi Owen

Photo/Art Contributors:
Pete Lederberg
Howard Baum

Beta Readers:
Oliver Bateman
Dave Meltzer
Mike Johnson
Jonathan Snowden

Executive Producer
Kenny Casanova

www.ingramcontent.com/pod-product-compliance
Lightning Source LLC
Chambersburg PA
CBHW072000150426
43194CB00008B/939